Journal of Biblical Literature
Monograph Series, Volume XIII

THE PROBLEM OF "CURSE" IN THE HEBREW BIBLE

by
Herbert Chanan Brichto

SOCIETY OF BIBLICAL LITERATURE AND EXEGESIS
1010 Arch Street
Philadelphia 7, Pennsylvania
1963

THE PROBLEM OF "CURSE" IN
THE HEBREW BIBLE

ISBN 1-58983-233-7

Printed in the United States of America
on acid-free paper

ACKNOWLEDGMENTS

This study was undertaken at the suggestion of Professor E. A. Speiser and prepared under his supervision. From inception to completion it has benefitted from his unstinting encouragement and criticism.

Grateful acknowledgment is made to Professor Moshe Greenberg for his painstaking criticism and helpful suggestions.

My thanks are freely expressed to the officers of the Society of Biblical Literature and Exegesis and to President Nelson Glueck and Provost Samuel Sandmel of the Hebrew Union College-Jewish Institute of Religion for the subventions which have made possible the publication of this study.

TABLE OF CONTENTS

PAGE

ACKNOWLEDGMENTS iii

TABLE OF CONTENTS iv

NOTE ON THE TRANSLITERATION vii

ABBREVIATIONS viii

CHAPTER

I. INTRODUCTION. 1

I. The Problem 1

II. Previous Treatments of the Problem 2

III. Scope and Organization of the Present Study . . 13

IV. Preliminary Discussion 15

II. THE STEM *ʾlw 22

I. The Noun ʾālā. The Problem and a Hypothesis. . 22

II. The Noun ʾālā -- in Connection with šəbūʿā and bərīt 25

III. ʾālā -- Verb and Noun as Adjuratory Imprecation 40

A. ʾālā in Summons of Witnesses and Malefactors 42

B. *ʾlw -- in Adjuration Designed to Preclude an Action 45

C. Excursus -- hiphʿil šbʿ = hiphʿil *ʾlw . . 48

D. ʾālā -- in Appeal to the Divine/Supernatural to Punish Violations of the Moral Code . 49

E. ʾālā -- Employed, Improperly, as an Accusation 56

F. Excursus on Exodus 20:7 and Psalm 24 . . . 59

CHAPTER PAGE

G. The "flying ʾālā in Zechariah 5:1-4. . . . 68

IV. Summary 70

V. Akkadian māmītu 71

III. THE STEM ʾrr 77

I. Passive Participle ʾārūr, as Rubric in Imprecations 77

II. ʾārūr in its Basic Discernible Sense 82

III. Other Forms of the Verb ʾārar 96

IV. The Noun mᵊʾʾērā 112

V. Summary 114

VI. Akkadian arāru and arratu/erretu 115

IV. THE VERB qillel 118

I. qillel ≠ Imprecation. With Various Subjects and Objects 118

II. qillel ≠ Imprecation. With Parents as Object. 132

III. qillel ≠ Imprecation. With Kings as Object. . 137

IV. qillel ≠ Imprecation. With Deity as Object. . 143

V. An Atnonym to qillel -- with God as Object . . 165

VI. The Term bērek as Euphemism for qillel 170

VII. qillel with the Force of Malediction 172

VIII. Summary 176

IX. Akkadian qullulu, qillatu, qullultu. 177

V. THE NOUN qᵊlālā 180

I. qᵊlālā not in the Sense of "Imprecation" . . . 182

II. qᵊlālā in the Sense of Imprecation 195

III. qᵊlālā in an Ambiguous Sense 197

IV. Summary 199

CHAPTER PAGE

VI. MISCELLANEOUS TERMS 200
I. The Verb qbb 200
II. The Verb zʿm 202
III. The Noun ḥrm 203
VII. CONCLUSIONS OF PREVIOUS STUDIES AND SUMMARY . . 205
VIII. APPENDIX 219
IX. SELECTED BIBLIOGRAPHY 222
X. INDEX TO PASSAGES CITED -- HEBREW SCRIPTURES . 228

A Note on the Transliterations

Hebrew and Aramaic consonants are transliterated according to common convention. The vowels are as follows: *Qameṣ* ā; *Pataḥ* a; *S^əgol* ɛ; *Ḥireq* i ; *Ṣere* e; *Šureq* ū; *Qibbuṣ* u; *Ḥolem* (long) ō; *Ḥolem* (short) and *Qameṣ-ḥatup* o; *Š^əwa* ə ; Complex *Š^əwa* is indicated by the corresponding vowel sign written superlinearly. In Hebrew, the *Š^əwa* is always treated as vocal when immediately followed by a spirantized consonant. The Aramaic from the Targumim on the Pentateuch and Former Prophets, following Sperber's critical edition, indicates no vowel sign for the *Š^əwa*, even when it is vocal.

ABBREVIATIONS

AAJRP - American Academy for Jewish Research, Proceedings

ABRT - Assyrian and Babylonian Religious Texts (Craig)

AfO - Archiv für Orientforschung

ANET - Ancient Near Eastern Texts Relating to the Old Testament (Pritchard)

AOS - American Oriental Series

ARM - Archives Royales de Marie

AT - The Complete Bible, An American Translation (University of Chicago Press, 1944)

ATD - Das Alte Testament Deutsch (Hrsg., V. Herntrich und A. Weiser)

AV - The Holy Bible (King James Version)

BA - Biblical Archaeologist

BASOR - Bulletin of the American Schools of Oriental Research

BDB - A Hebrew & English Lexicon of the Old Testament (Brown, Driver & Briggs)

CD - The Assyrian Dictionary (of the Oriental Institute of the University of Chicago)

CBQ - Catholic Biblical Quarterly

CH - Codex Hammurabi

DM - The Babylonian Laws (Driver & Miles)

HAT - Handkommentar zum Alten Testament (Hrsg., W. Nowack)

HbAT - Handbuch zum Alten Testament (Hrsg., O. Eissfeldt)

HSS - Harvard Semitic Series

JAOS - Journal of the American Oriental Society

JBL - Journal of Biblical Literature

JPOS - Journal of the Palestine Oriental Society

JPS - The Holy Scriptures (Jewish Publication Society, 1917)

KAT - Kommentar zum Alten Testament (Hsrg., Ernst Sellin)

KHAT - Kurzen Hand-Commentar zum Alten Testament (Hsrg., Karl Martl)

King Magic - Babylonian Magic and Sorcery (L. W. King)

MAOG - Mitteilungen der altorientalischen Gesellschaft

RSV - The Holy Bible, Revised Standard Version (Thos. Nelson & Sons, 1952)

SB - La Sainte Bible traduite en français sous la direction de L'École Biblique de Jerusalem (Paris: Les Editions Du Cerf, 1956)

TA - Die El-Amarna Tafeln (Knudtzon)

ZA - Zeitschrift für Assyriologie

ZDMG - Zeitschrift der Deutschen Morgenländischen Gesellschaft

CHAPTER I

INTRODUCTION

I. THE PROBLEM

The subject of this investigation is a complex of biblical terms which are variously, and often indiscriminately, rendered in English (and in other Western languages) by the word "curse" or by its near equivalents.

The noun "curse" is semantically equivocal. The first meaning given by dictionaries is the equivalent of the Latin-derived "imprecation,"[1] i.e., a prayer or invocation that harm or injury come upon some one or something. The other meanings, clearly by metonymy, are: a) the evil itself that comes as if in response to imprecation; b) that which is the object of imprecation; c) great harm or misfortune, in general. Synonyms for curse, in addition to imprecation, are execration, malediction, anathema, ban. The operation of metonymy is so extensive that even "oath," which has its own circumscribed area of meaning, is used as

---

[1]E.g., "An utterance consigning, or supposed or intended to consign, (a person or thing) to spiritual and temporal evil...with implication of the effect: the uttering of a malediction with invocation or adjuration of the deity." --The Oxford English Dictionary, (Oxford: Clarendon Press, 1933). "a calling to a deity to visit evil on one." --Webster's Third New International Dictionary, (Springfield, Mass. G. & C. Merriam Co., 1961).

a synonym for curse. The word "curse" thus has a range of meaning from formal invocation of evil to violent denunciation or condemnation.

Contemporary Western language does not normally discriminate between these terms, because the institutions and conceptual framework that gave rise to them exist no longer. Originally each biblical noun and its verbal counterparts conveyed a distinct meaning. Translation, however, exacts its toll, and the social realities and patterns of thought that are mirrored in the original Hebrew are obscured or distorted in the foreign vehicle.

II. PREVIOUS TREATMENTS OF THE PROBLEM

The curse is not the chief concern of Johs. Pedersen's <u>Der Eid bei den Semiten</u> (Strassburg: Karl J. Trübner, 1914). This study, published in the series "Studien zur Gesichte und Kultur des islamischen Orients," occupies itself mainly with the Arabic literature. Since curses are intrinsic to oaths, Pedersen gives considerable attention to this aspect, and while almost half of his material here is based on Arabic sources he manages to present a comprehensive treatment of related forms and institutions in the Old Testament and cuneiform literature.[2] He examines the following from the point of view of etymology and connotation, common features and limiting contrasts: Akkadian, <u>māmītu</u>, <u>nīšu</u>, <u>adū</u>, <u>arāru</u>; Hebrew, <u>qillel</u>, <u>ʾārūr</u>, <u>ʾālā</u>,

---

[2]Johs. Pedersen, Der Eid bei den Semiten (Strassburg: Karl J. Trübner, 1914), Chap. IV, "Der Fluch," Chap. V, "Die hypothetische Verfluchung," Chap. VI, "Der Eid als Fluch."

zāʿam, and to a lesser extent, šᵉbūʿā, and qāḇaḇ. He notes that the basic oontent of curses (loss of wealth, vigor, power; banishment from society; death) is essentially the same in Israel as among the Arabs, and without going into detailed analysis of the differences in the basic social organization, makes the pregnant observation: "Bei den Assyrern hat der Fluch ein minder soziales Gepräge. Er bezieht sich nicht so sehr auf das Verhältnis zur Gesellschaft als auf die betreffende Person selbst."[3] Thus Pedersen neglects neither the content nor the form of cursing in Israel and among its neighbors. For the present study, however, the latter aspect -- especially the attempt to differentiate the terms -- is of greater importance. In the discussion of the Biblical texts Pedersen's conclusions will be cited and examined in detail.

The first study centering primarily on the biblical phenomena of curse and blessing is Johannes Hempel's, "Die israelitischen Anschauungen von Segen und Fluch im Lichte altorientalischen Parallelen."[4] Perhaps because he published it a decade after Pedersen's work, Hempel makes no attempt at all to distinguish the nuances in the various terms for "cursing." The effect upon his conclusions will appear in the discussion and interpretation of the texts. In general, Hempel adduces the fruits of enormous erudition in support of his conceptions. His analogues are drawn from Mesopotamia, Hellas, Rome, India, the Far East, the

---

[3]Pedersen, op. cit., p. 69.

[4]ZDMG, Neue Folge, (Band 4, 1915), pp. 20-110.

New Testament, and the Babylonian Talmud.

Hempel introduces his study with the observation that Sigmund Mowinckel[5] arrived independently at the conclusion that beneath the Old Testament conceptions of curse and blessing there can be discerned -- despite all the sublimation -- their origin in magical practices. (He feels, however, that Mowinckel builds his cult-theory on too narrow a basis, and that his own more detailed study of primitive phenomena reveals a far greater variety of motive and development than is recognized or acknowledged by Mowinckel.)

1. The Roots in Magic. The ancient Israelite knows of mysterious powers which govern nature as well as his own life and fate. Various phenomena in nature and in history appear to him as the working of blessings or curses pronounced in the dim past by man or deity. Even in later periods characterized by highly developed God-concepts these powers still figure largely and are utilized by Yahweh to execute his will -- whether the blessing or curse is pronounced by himself or a human agent. The origins or roots of blessing and curse in magical practice can be seen in their formulations, which are characterized by the features of incantation ("Zauberspruche"): schematic and rhythmic organization, frequent antithetical parallelism, and repetition to strengthen the force of the utterance.

---

[5]In his "Segen und Fluch in Israels Kult und Psalmendichtung," Kristiania: Videnskapsselskapets Skrifter II, Hist.-Filos. Klasse 1923, 3. Although the conclusions arrived at in the present study bear on Mowinckel's cult-theory and his interpretations of the Psalms, an examination of his much-debated theories is beyond the scope of this investigation.

The utilization in curses of magical devices is to be seen in Joshua's stretching out of the javelin (Josh. 8:18), the pointing of the finger (Isa. 58:9), spitting (Deut. 25:9); all these are devices to effect a kind of contact between subject and object, i.e., the imprecator and his victim. Also rooted in magic is the use of the right hand in blessing (Gen. 48:13).

Blessing and curse share with magic the characteristic of unqualified and irrevocable execution, e.g., the blessing which Jacob extorts by guile remains his nonetheless (Gen. 27:35). Repentance can postpone but not avert the disaster of a curse, as is revealed in Yahweh's word to Josiah through Huldah the prophetess (2 Kings 22:19-20). Hence the importance of preventing the utterance of a curse as in the Balaam story (Num. 22). There is no time limitation on the working out of a curse.

The power of blessing and curse has an adhesive or contagious characteristic: anyone blessed of Yahweh is able to transfer blessing (Gen. 12:1-3), and a cursed person is a danger to the whole land, e.g., Jonathan (1 Sam. 14) and Achan (Josh. 7). Cain must become a wanderer, to be slain by anyone who encounters him (Gen. 14:12, 14). Anyone close to Korah will share his doom (Num. 16:25). The curse adheres to the corpse of a hanged malefactor, so contact with it is fraught with danger (Deut. 21:22-23).

"So oft ein solcher Fluch gesprochen würde, gewänne er ja aufs neue Leben und Wirkungskrafte. Auch tut man gut in der Schwurformel das Unheil nicht ausdrücklich zu nennen, das im Falle des Eidesbruches eintreten soll. Darum verkürzt man die Formel kō yaᶜᵃśē YHWH lī wᵉkō yōsīp ᵓim..."

"Nach zwei Seiten hin ist diese mechanische Übertragung nun gerade bei dem Fluche bedeutsam geworden. Einmal für die Schutz -- und Abwehrriten. Sie vollziehen sich von Haus aus ebenso mechanisch, ebenso ohne Beteiligung der Gottheit oder anderer übernatürlicher Wesen, wie Verbreitung des Unheils. Soweit das Volk, bezw. die Gemeinde als Ganzes in Frage kommt, is die erste Pflicht: 'Du sollst das Böse aus deiner Mitte hinwegräumen!' (Dtn. 13, 6 u.ö...)"

"In allen Fällen aber kommt es darauf an, die Gegenmassenahmen rasch zu treffen, weiss man doch nicht, wie bald ein gesprochener Fluch wirksam werden mag. Darum schützt das Gesetz solche, die durch ein körperliches Gebrechen daran gehindert sind, im besonderem Masse... (Lev. 19, 18)."

The mechanical transferability of the curse can be seen in its employment as a weapon by the slave who is a victim of injustice (Prov. 30:10), by the hungry (Isa. 8:21), against the rich (Prov. 11:25), and against the usurer (Jer. 15:10).

2. The Content. The content of blessing is life, vitality, and everything making for them: victory, fertility of land and livestock, numerous progeny, longevity, heroism. The life-force of one man can be transferred to another, as revealed in the kiss attending Isaac's blessing of his son; and from animal to man, as indicated by Isaac's eating of meat prior to the blessing. The all-embracing expression for the content of blessing is šālōm, which means the absence of danger and disability, the presence of

tranquility, security, good-fortune and well-being in the highest degree; hence its use in greeting. The content of curse, by contrast, is death, illness, childlessness, miscarriage, drought, pest, disturbance of corpses, and peripeteia: man becoming woman(like), the free man becoming a slave, etc.

3. Prayers of intercession and revenge. In both areas, that is, in petitions for blessing and the averting of harm and in petitions for harm to befall an enemy, the realm of magic is left behind and everything is subordinated to the power of God. There is an awareness that only God, the one God of Israel in contrast to the many deities of neighboring societies, is the source of both blessing and curse. Nevertheless, the efficacy of prayers depends in varying measure on the person praying. Particularly potent are the prayers of parents vis-à-vis their children, chieftains and leaders, magicians and priests -- but, above all, those of charismatic seers and prophets. Though Mowinckel is correct in seeing traces of magical practices in the psalms, the outstanding phenomenon in Israel is the battle to suppress sorcery and witchcraft, to subordinate all powers to their source in Yahweh. Mowinckel's emphasis is, therefore, extreme, and his notion that God was thought to be strengthened by human blessing is unlikely. For all that, cursing of the deity was forbidden (Exod. 22:27).

4. Blessing and curse as deeds of Yahweh. The ethical-prophetic movement divorces religion from all elements of magic and magical ceremony. God is the supreme -- indeed, the only -- ultimate power. When He makes a covenant

with Israel, it is not a covenant between equals to both of whom sanctions can be applied, but a covenant whereby the greater power subjects the lesser, and only the latter can incur sanctions.

"The Curse, Blasphemy, the Spell, and the Oath" by Sheldon H. Blank[6] is "an exploration of the curse and related modes of human expression in the Bible...intended as an introduction to a study of the blessing-type of biblical prayer." The author admits the influence of Hempel's work upon his own study, and explains that "its originality lies largely in its emphasis upon the folk-belief in the effectiveness of the spoken word."

Curses have the form of prayer only when God is addressed, directly or obliquely. Curses are analysed according to form as 1) simple curse formula, 2) composite curse, and 3) curses freely composed. The last category is divided into "two subtypes depending on whether the curse (a) is spoken by men or (b) is attributed to God." In the curse formula, the participle <u>ʾārūr</u> is construed as future (rather than present) tense; usually modal in mood, it "expresses a wish and is to be construed as an optative." Yet Pedersen is correct that the participle is not always a wish: in curses "attributed to God in myth narrative... These are not so much wishes as immediately effective decrees." The significance of the passive voice lies in "... The important conclusion that, although usually the expression of a wish, the curse formula is not a prayer." Since

[6] <u>HUCA</u>, Vol. XXIII, Part One, 1950-51, pp. 73-95.

it does not seem likely that either God or demonic agents were assumed as the authors of the effects of the curse, "the spoken curse was itself and alone conceived to be the effective agent. This is the significance of the habitual preference for the passive construction in the curse formula and the consequent absence of any reference to an external agent, demonic or divine. The curse was automatic or self-fulfilling,[7] having the nature of a 'spell,' the very words of which were thought to possess reality and the power to effect the desired results."

"The fear of the effective power of the spoken word best explains the total absence of blasphemy in the Bible ...a fact all the more remarkable because the Bible is by no means lacking in passages referring to the possibility of curse directed against God." This "possibility" is seen in Job's wife's urging her husband "to curse God and die" (Job 2:9); in the resort to such action by a desperate person (Isa. 8:21); in the action of Eli's sons (1 Sam. 3:13) and in Ps. 37:22, if both these passages are rendered according to LXX; in Naboth's conviction on the charge of blasphemy and of lese majesty (1 Kings 21:13); and particularly, in the law of Exod. 22:27. "Lev. 24:16 is an extension and a sharpening of the other laws against cursing God, and it makes it a capital offense even to mention (nqb) the name of God."

"The belief in the effective power of the word is vividly illustrated also by the few examples preserved in

---

[7]The italics are Dr. Blank's.

the Bible of simple spells. These spells do not depend for their effectiveness either upon God or upon any other external agent; the spoken words themselves are assumed to have the power to produce the desired effect." Examples of such spells are to be found in Num. 21:17, Josh. 10:12 and 2 Sam. 16:17.

The oath-formula, which employs the conditional curse, again betrays the belief in, and fear of, the efficacy of the spoken word in the reluctance to define the curse.[8]

Finally, it would seem that the belief was prevalent "that a curse might be neutralized by destroying the words which express it" (Jer. 36:23); that a curse could be voided by destroying its source (2 Sam. 16:9); "that a curse might be eluded by deception," e.g., 2 Kings 22:11 where, "upon hearing the curses contained in the scroll found in the Temple, Josiah tears his garments... Probably by tearing his garments, which is a mourning custom, the one accursed intended to make it appear that he had already suffered the effects of the curse and supposed that he might thus deceive, as it were, and elude the curse itself." But, "a more effective means to neutralize a curse is to administer a blessing as an antidote." Examples of this are to be found in Judg. 17:2, 1 Kings 2:45, 2 Sam. 21:1-3, and Exod. 12:32.

"Thus," the article concludes, "the form of the curse formula, the ban against the blasphemy, the spell, the oath, and the means to neutralize a curse, all point to the

---

[8]See above, pp. 5 f., Hempel's formulation of this notion.

belief that the power of the curse originally derived from the effective power of the words which expressed it. Nevertheless, in Bible times, breaking loose from its profane model, the curse developed into imprecatory prayer, a type of religious expression."

"Curse Motifs in the Old Testament and in the Ancient Near East" by Stanley Gevirtz[9] provides a comprehensive catalogue of curses and curse-motifs found in the Bible, in the literature of Mesopotamia and of the Western Semites (Ugarit, Phoenicia, Aram); included also are citations from Egypt and from the Hittite domain. Curse types from each area are classified as anticipatory and retributive, and according to the targets of the curse: violators of contracts, treaties, inscriptions, tombs; murderers and other malefactors. Curse themes are classified under fertility, human and agricultural; sovereignty; and salubrity, physical and spiritual. Curse formulations fall into two categories: those which invoke divine agency, and those which do not. The author states in his introduction that it is his "hope to illustrate specific uses to which curses were put, to describe the distinctive cultural attitudes toward those powers invoked to effect the consummation of the curse."

Gevirtz's approach to the latter objective is as follows: Taking up Blank's suggestion that the curse formula in the Bible, invoking neither deity nor demons, was re-

---

[9]Stanley Gevirtz, "Curse Motifs in the Old Testament and in the Ancient Near East" (unpublished Doctor's thesis, Graduate Library School: University of Chicago, 1959).

garded as automatic or self-fulfilling, he tabulates and contrasts the curse formulations from Mesopotamia, on the one hand, and from the Bible (and the Western Semites), on the other. The tabulation reveals that the vast majority of imprecations from Mesopotamia explicitly invokes deities, by name, as the agents who are to effectuate the curse. By contrast, the majority of biblical (and West-Semitic) formulations consists of a passive verb and the target of the imprecation, the most common formula being that which features the passive participle ʾārūr. Regarding the latter Gevirtz writes, "The mood of the participle may be understood as operative, and that power through which it is to be effected as residing within the very utterance of the curse itself." The significance of these contrasting formulations he interprets as follows:

> Viewed from the perspective of curse agency and verb construction, a clear distinction between "East" and "West Semitic" curse-formulations emerges. The emphasis in the former is upon divine agency, with the most frequent and characteristic verb form being the precative lū + preterite. Hebrew imprecations share the general western preference for constructions in which the agent remains undesignated and for verbs in passive form.
>
> The significance of an active construction invoking deity, as was indicated in the introductory remarks, lies in its reliance upon deity for consummation, that of the passive construction, emphasized by Prof. Blank and reiterated by us, in its reliance upon the power of the spoken word. A discussion of the religious import attaching to each of the two kinds of formulation individually, or to the differences in religious attitude between "East" and "West" expressed by these generally, properly in the domain of the history or philosophy of religion, lies beyond the scope of the present study.

Published a year before Gevirtz's dissertation, and closest to the present study in approach and results is Josef Scharbert's article, "'Fluchen' und 'Segen' im Alten

Testament."[10] In the fifteen pages devoted to "Fluchen" the attempt is made to differentiate the Hebrew terms normally translated by "curse" on the basis of etymological origin and contextual significance. Accepting suggestions of Pedersen's, but often going beyond him in interpretation, Scharbert achieves a more precise perception of the fundamental force of *ʾārar* and *qillel*. Scharbert's conclusions will appear in detail in the body of the present study, as will our convergences and divergences.

Other contiguous studies not bearing directly upon the main concern of the present study are listed in the "Selected Bibliography."

III. SCOPE AND ORGANIZATION OF THE PRESENT STUDY

The above summation discloses a variety of approaches in the treatments of the problem to date. The studies of Hempel and Blank may be characterized as "anthropological," which is to say that their primary concern is the content of curse (and blessing), the manner in which this content is expressed, and, on the basis of these, the attempt to characterize the conceptual framework of the society of which these are expressions. Hempel, as has been indicated, makes voluminous use of material from other societies and literatures in his comparative approach, while Blank implicitly bases his examination upon Hempel's study. Gevirtz's approach is classificatory and, in the same degree, analytical. While Pedersen is not oblivious of the anthropo-

---

[10] *Biblica*, Vol. XXIX (1958), pp. 1-26.

logical signification, he shares with Scharbert a basically philological methodology. The last two writers treat the biblical terms etymologically, with a consideration of corresponding cognates, and on the basis of contextual analysis they attempt to arrive at the nuances which distinguish them from one another.

The present study purposes to investigate all the pertinent occurrences of the terms for "curse" in the Bible in greater detail than has yet been attempted, with the specific objective of determining how they compare and differ in each case; to attempt to arrive at a more precise determination of the original denotation of each term, that is, of its narrowest meaning before its connotative value broadens its usage into synonymous ambiguity with other terms conceptually related but etymologically and semantically distinct.

Since the attempt to differentiate synonymous terms is essentially a study of their distribution, contextual considerations are paramount. When this approach has yielded as much as it can, analogues from neighboring societies will be consulted for help in the elucidation of texts where the context gives few clues or none to the signification of the terms under investigation. There will follow a brief discussion of analogous concepts and terminology in the literature of Israel's neighbors. While aiming at comprehensiveness in the examination of the biblical occurrences, this study does not claim the same goal in regard to the material from surrounding cultures, which is ancillary to the purpose and scope of this investigation.

The three principal terms, *ʾālā*, *ʾārar*, *qillel*, and their derivatives, will be investigated in that order; the first having the narrowest, and the last the broadest, semantic range. The last section will consider the terms which figure less prominently: *qbb*, *zʿm*, and *ḥrm*.

Within each section, insofar as it is feasible to do so without disturbing the logical development of the argument, the texts will appear in their order in the Hebrew Bible. The translations, unless otherwise noted, are the writer's. For purposes of comparison, samples of similar and differing renderings and interpretations will be cited from the ancient versions, medieval rabbinic commentaries and contemporary translations and commentaries.

IV. PRELIMINARY DISCUSSION

The Stem **ʾlw*

The consonants of this stem are certified by Arabic *ʾlw*, IV form "to swear." The final letter of Hebrew *ʾlh* is a vowel letter which represents a "weak" final sound. The verbal occurrences of the stem are not frequent: once each in the *qal* perfect, *qal* infinitive, *hiphʿil* imperfect, *hiphʿil* infinitive.[11] Of greater frequency is the occurrence of the noun *ʾālā*, pl. *ʾālōṯ*, while the byform (?) *taʾălā* occurs once.

As noun and verb it is frequently coordinate with the noun *šəḇūʿā* and with *niphʿal* and *hiphʿil* forms of the stem *šbʿ*. At times *ʾālā* and *šəḇūʿā* are used interchangeably in

---

[11]The *hiphʿil* infinitive occurs twice if the dittogram of 1 Kings 8:31 in 2 Chron. 6:22 is counted.

parallel or recurrent expressions of an identical context. Like *šᵊbūʿā* (and often together with it) it occurs in the context of a *bᵊrīṯ*. Twice, the noun occurs as a coordinate of *qᵊlālā*.

Although the term *bārūḵ* occurs once in a kind of antonymous relationship with the verb **ʾlw*,[12] the noun *bᵊrāḵā* never occurs as an antonym of the noun *ʾālā*. The verb which expresses the idea of being free of, or freed from, the effects of an *ʾālā* is the *niphʿal* of the stem *nqh* (**nqy*).

The etymology of the stem **ʾlw* is obscure. There is hardly room to doubt the correctness of Scharbert's statement:

"Manche Lexikographen stellen das hebr. *ʾlh* mit dem akkad. *ēltu* = 'Verbindlichkeit', 'Haftung' zusammen, jedoch zu unrecht, denn *ēltu* gehört zum Stamm *aʾālu*, das hebr. *ʾlh* aber zum Stam *ʾlj/w*, von dem das arab. *ʾālâ(w)*= 'schwören' abgeleitet ist."[13]

In the Targumim *ʾālā*, like *šᵊbūʿā*, is rendered by *mōmāṯā*; yet when the two terms appear together *šᵊbūʿā* seems to assert a prior claim to *mōmāṯā*, and *ʾālā* is rendered by a form of *līṭ/lᵊwāṭā* ("curse").

The Akkadian noun, cognate to Aramaic *mōmāṯā* and

---

[12]Judg. 17:2 where the utterance of "*bārūḵ*..." serves as a counter-measure to, or a withdrawal of an expressed *ʾālā*.

[13]*Biblica*, Vol. 39, fasc. 1, 1958, p. 2. I am also in agreement with his note, *ad loc.*, "Noch unwahrscheinlicher ist die Ableitung von der Negation *ʾal*, die N. H. TORCZYNER-TUR-SINAI in *Encycl. Biblica* I, Jerusalem 1955, 294, vorschlagt."

apparently sharing with it and Hebrew *ʾālā* the double sense of "curse" and "oath," is *māmītu*. Derived from the verb *aw/mū* "to speak," *māmītu* may have had the original force of "solemn pronouncement."

The Stem *ʾrr*

This stem occurs in verbal form in the active *qal* perfect, imperfect, and imperative; passive *qal* perfect and participle; *niphʿal* perfect; and *piʿel* perfect and participle. Most frequent are the occurrences of the *qal* passive participle and the *qal* imperfect. The nominal form *mᵊʾērā* occurs a few times.

Coordinate with *ʾrr* are the verbs *qll* *piʿel* and *puʿal*, *qbb*, and *zʿm*. It appears in close association with the *niphʿal* and *hiphʿil* of the root *šbʿ* and with the *hiphʿil* of **ʾlw* -- the passive participle *ʾārūr* introducing the content of the oath, adjuration, or curse. In the context of a *bᵊrīṯ* (covenant), the passive participle is the introductory rubric for the imprecations upon violators of the terms of the covenant. The antonyms of *ʾrr* in nominal and verbal occurrences are various forms of the stem *brk*.

Etymologically the Hebrew stem, as Scharbert points out, is related to the Akkadian *arāru*, "das man gewöhnlich als '(durch ein Zauberwort) binden', 'bannen' erklärt, und mit arab. *ʾarra* = 'fortjagen', 'vertreiben'.[14] The Akka-

---

[14]*idem*. pp. 6 f., Friedrich Delitzsch's *Assyrisches Handwörterbuch* (Leipzig: Hinrichs, 1896) gives two listings: "I.ʾ*rr*...Prt. *ī(!)rur*...jemanden (Acc.) fluchen, jem. verfluchen..." (p. 137) and "II. *ʾrr* Prs. *iarrur* binden, fangen (vor allem Vogel), gefangen halten." Wolfram von Soden's *Akkadisches Handwörterbuch* (Wiesbaden: Harrassowitz, 1959) gives "*arāru(m)* I (he. *arar*) 'verfluchen'" and lists no

dian cognate corresponding to m^əʾērā is arratu/erretu.

The Stem qll

The qal and hiphʿil conjugations of this stem, not translated by "curse," are not of central concern to this study; nor, for the same reason are the niphʿal and hiphʿil conjugations of the related stem qlh (*qlw/y) and its derived noun qālōn. This investigation is concerned with the piʿel (/puʿal) conjugation(s) of the stem, and with the noun q^əlālā which occurs as its nominal correspondent.

The verbal coordinate of piʿel qll is ʾrr. In secondary accounts piʿel qll occurs in the place which, in the original narrative, is occupied by qbb and zʿm; but nowhere do these last two stems appear explicitly as its coordinates.

The antonyms of qillel are the piʿel conjugations of brk and kbd.

The noun q^əlālā, as has been indicated, corresponds semantically to the verb qillel. Since, however, the noun is a formation based on the qal stem (one might reasonably expect, for example, a noun qillūl as the correspondent of qillel), it is probable that the noun derives most of its crystallized meaning by virtue of being the antonym of b^əraḵa.[15] As has been previously noted, q^əlālā and ʾālā appear twice as coordinates.

Of etymological interest is the fact that the force

---

stem ʾrr with the sense of "bind."

[15]The stem brk in Semitic languages is studied semasiologically by Thomas Plassman in The Signification of B^erāḵā (Paris: Imprimerie Nationale, 1913).

of the base-stem in virtually all Semitic languages is to "be light, swift, slight, trifling."[16] The Akkadian cognate corresponding to *qillel* is *qullulu*, for which Friedrich Delitzsch gives "schmähen...; mit Schmach anthun, o. ä."[17] CAD, which has not yet issued the "Q" volume, states that "*gullulu*, 'to commit a misdeed,' and *qalālu*, 'to take slightly, slander,' have to be strictly distinguished."[18] It lists "gullulu v.; to commit a sin;" "*gullultu* s. fem.; misdeed, crime, sin;" "*gillatu* (*gelletu*) s. fem.; crime, misdeed, sin;"[19] for occurrences which have hitherto normally been rendered by Assyriologists as *qullulu*, *qullultu*, *qillatu*.

Other Stems:[20] *qbb*, *zᶜm*, *ḥrm*

---

[16]Cf. Scharbert, *op.cit.*, p. 8: "In fast allen semitischen Sprachen ist die Wurzel, qll in den Bedeutungen 'leicht[1] (Note: Daher auch 'flink, schnell sein'), klein, unbedeutend, gering, verächtlich sein." The last-mentioned sense in Gen. 16:4 "...when she (Hagar) realized that she had conceived she regarded her mistress with contempt" (*wattēqal gᵊbirtāh bᵊᶜeynēha*) can only be fully understood in the light of CH § 145-6 (DM Vol. 2, pp. 56-57). Hagar's conduct is in violation of the law (ll. 41-2): *itti nadītim* ul *uštamaḫḫar*, "she (the second wife, who has been taken for the purpose of bearing sons) shall not regard herself as the equal of the priestess." CH § 146 specifies the penalties permitted against an amtu (= Heb. *šipḥā*, *ʾāmā*, in Gen. 21:10, both terms applied to Hagar). Although Sarah is not a *nadītu(m)*, HSS V, 67 proves that the provisions of CH § 145-6, which in Babylon may have been limited to a *nadītu(m)*, were among the Hurrians extended to a high-born lady -- which the Patriarch's wife undoubtedly was. Cf. E. A. Speiser, *Nuzi Marginalia*, Orientalia, Vol. 15, fasc. 1, 1956, p. 13 n. 3.

[17]Assyrisches Handwörterbuch, p. 585.

[18]Cf. under *gullulu* d , Vol. 5, p. 132.

[19]Vol. 5, pp. 131, 131, 73, respectively.

[20]The stems *ḥrp* and *gdp*, having well established and circumscribed meanings in clear differentiation from "curse"

The stem qbb[21] appears only as a verb and only in the qal conjugation. Coordinate with z'm and ʾrr, it occurs in antonymous relation to the noun and verb of the stem brk. Scharbert relates the Hebrew root to cognates in Tigrina and Arabic: "...liegt wohl Verwandschaft mit Tigre qb = 'schmähen, entwürdigen' ...und arab. qabiba = 'dünn sein' vor."[22]

The stem z'm comes into consideration by virtue of its occurrence, in a few instances, as a verb coordinate with ʾrr and qbb. Normally the verb is rendered as "be indignant," and the noun by "indignation."[23] Scharbert claims that, "Etymologisch verwandt ist es mit dem arab. zağama 5 = 'erschrecken'."

The stem ḥrm is treated here only because it is sometimes rendered by "curse" in English translations. Associated in the Bible with the stem qdš, it occurs in various forms in almost all Semitic languages with meanings which are identical or closely related.

---

are not treated in this study.

[21]The forthcoming analysis of the biblical texts will attempt to demonstrate that there is no reason to confuse or coordinate this root with the stem nqb.

[22]Op. cit., p. 14.

[23]Cf. BDB, p. 276.

	Etymology Cognates	Conjugation Noun	Coordinates Verb Noun	Associated Terms	Antonyms
*ʾlw	? Arab. ʾlw IV form "to swear"	Qal active Hiphʿil ʾālā	šbʿ: Niphʿal & Hiphʿil Heb. qəlālā Heb. šəbūʿā Aram. mōmātā Akkad. māmītu	bərīt ʾārūr qəlālā	bārūḵ Niphʿal nqh + prep. min
ʾrr	? Akkad. arāru arratu/erretu	Qal active & passive Niphʿal Piʿel məʾērā	qll: Piʿel & Puʿal qbb: Qal zʿm: Qal miḡɛrɛṯ məhūmā	šəbūʿā bərīṯ	brk
qll	Qal: "to be light, trifling"	Piʿel & Puʿal qəlālā	ʾrr hikkā (Hiphʿil nkh) rāʿā ḥɛrpā ḥorbā šənīnā šamma māšāl		1. Piʿel kbd 2. Piʿel brk 3. ? bərāḵā
qbb	? ? Tigr. qb "to insult"? ?Akkad. qabū "to speak"?	Qal	ʾrr zʿm		brk
zʿm	? "be angry"? ? Arab. zaǵama "to frighten"?	Qal active & passive zaʿam	ʾrr qbb		brk
ḥrm	? "forbidden, set apart, tabu"?	Hiphʿil Hophʿal	qdš		

CHAPTER II

THE STEM *ʾlw

I. THE NOUN ʾālā. THE PROBLEM AND A HYPOTHESIS

The difficulty which besets translators and commentators in their attempts to arrive at the specific content of the noun ʾālā is reflected in the variety of terms which are employed in translating it. In varying contexts this noun is variously rendered by "curse," "execration," "oath," "adjuration," and equivalent expressions. It thus becomes virtually indistinguishable from terms such as šᵊbūʿā, qᵊlālā, and mᵊʾērā.

Pedersen discusses the matter as follows:

> "Eben diese Bedeutung [that of šᵊbūʿā] hat das Wort ʾlh, das als Verbum und Substantiv benutzt wird und bisweilen mit 'Eidschwur' zu übersetzen ist. Am gewöhnlichsten ist die Bedeutung 'Fluch', Lev. 5, 1; Jdc. 17, 2. An mehreren Stellen kann man darüber im Zweifel sein, ob es mit 'Fluch' oder 'Schwur' zu übersetzen ist. Es wechselt 1 Sam. 14, 24.28 mit hišbiaʿ; ebenfalls Gen. 24, 41, vgl. V. 1. Bisweilen wird es verwendet, wo es sich um einen Bund handelt, so Gen. 26, 28; Deut. 29, 11.13. 18, 19 u.a. Aber der Begriff des Fluches bzw. der Besessenheit ist nie verlassen, selbst wo wir es anders übersetzen, und einen Unterschied im Gebrauch des Wortes bei den einzelnen Quellen nachzuweisen..., ist unmöglich."[1]

In a later chapter Pedersen continues:

> "Übrig bleibt noch ʾlh. Der Unterschied zwischen diesem Ausdruck und ʾrr wird klar, wenn man bedenkt, dass es nicht mit min verbunden werden kann, ja nicht

---

[1] Johs. Pedersen, Der Eid bei den Semiten (Strassburg: Trübner, 1914), p. 6.

einmal mit äusserem Objekt vorkommt; *ʾrr* und *qll* bezeichnen wesentlich die Wirkungsart des Fluches: den Zustand, aus welchem die Person herausgebracht, und denjenigen, in welchen sie hineingeführt wird. *ʾlh* dagegen bezeichnet das Unglück als selbständige Grösse, wie es in jemandem sitzt, und wie es auf seine Umgebungen einwirkt. Es ist somit im Hebräischen der dem assyrischen *māmītu* am nächsten kommende Begriff und kann insofern durch 'Bann', 'Besessenheit' wiedergegeben werden. Es ist ein schädlicher, unheilvoller Stoff, der im Menschen seinen Sitz haben, *Num*. 5, der ein Land 'verzehren' kann, so dass die Äcker verdorren, *Jes*. 24, 6; *Jer*. 23, 10,; vgl. *Sach*. 5,3."[2]

Despite Pedersen's negative judgment on the possibility of disentangling *ʾālā* from the closely related terms *šᵊbūʿā* and *qᵊlālā*, I believe that the terms in their original force can be differentiated. It may be convenient to begin with an analysis of our conceptions of the terms "oath, curse, covenant," with particular regard to their relations to one another; and on the basis of our study of these concepts and their biblical terminologies to attempt to arrive at a working hypothesis. This hypothesis may then be put to the test in a detailed study of these terms in their individual contexts.

An "oath" may be defined as an asseveration or promise supported by the invocation of a powerful agency (magical, divine, or human) to provide the penalty or sanction against the party making a false assertion or failing to keep his word.[3] In contemporary English usage (as in the

---

[2]*Ibid*., p.82. Pedersen expatiates on the properties of the *ʾālā*-substance in his *Israel -- Its Life and Culture* (London: Oxford University Press, 1926), Vol. I, pp. 437 ff. As will be indicated below, p.49 ff, there is little justification for such hypostatization of the *ʾālā*.

[3]The "exculpatory oath" is a special case, or subtype, of the assertory oath.

Bible), "oath" takes on the secondary meaning of "curse" -- although it is quite clear that the force of this "oath = curse" is not, as a rule, "imprecation." The mere utterance of a sacred name in an unsuitable, or "profane," context is enough to win for the ejaculation the appellation "oath" (= "curse"). Analogous to this phenomenon is the extension of the verb "to swear" -- which, properly, means "to take an oath" -- to cover the mere utterance of a sacred name in an improper context. These semantic extensions are easily explained as metonymy. The fact that every oath normally contains, explicitly or implicitly, invocation of deity and imprecation upon the taker of the oath is what makes the metonymy possible.

It is obvious that although every oath involves a curse, a curse is independent of an oath. The use of "oath" with the force of "curse"[4] is, therefore, a particular type of metonymy: it is synecdoche of the whole for the part. On the other hand, were "curse" to be used with the force of "oath," this would constitute synecdoche of the part for the whole.

Now it is abundantly clear that the basic biblical term for "oath" is *šᵊḇūᶜā*, as the basic verb for "to swear, to take an oath" is the *niphᶜal* of the root *šbᶜ*. The use of *šᵊḇūᶜā*, then, with the force of "curse" would be readily explained as synecdoche of the whole for the part. By contrast, the verb *ʾālā* is never used with the sense of "to swear = to take an oath," in the general meaning of the

[4]Whether an imprecation without any asseveration or promise, or the mere invocation of deity, by whatever name.

phrase. And yet, the noun *ʾālā*, which has unquestionably the force of "curse," appears in contexts where it seems to have the equally undeniable connotation of "oath." Is it not likely, then, that in *ʾālā* with the connotation of "oath" we have synecdoche of the part for the whole? If the answer is in the affirmative, the problem of *ʾālā* would be cleared up. An *ʾālā* would, in that case, be one part of an oath (*šᵊbūʿā*) -- namely, the sanction(s) or the invocation of the sanction(s). This would also explain the interchangeability, without effect on meaning, of the singular *ʾālā* and the plural *ʾālōṯ*. Such, indeed, is the hypothesis which is here advanced.

II. THE NOUN *ʾālā* -- IN CONNECTION WITH *šᵊbūʿā* AND *bᵊrīṯ*

Chapter 24 of Genesis relates how a wife is obtained for Isaac. Abraham has dispatched his servant to Mesopotamia to bring back for his son a wife from among his kin there, having first made the servant swear that he would not take a wife for him from among his Canaanite neighbors. The servant, arrived at his destination, has apprised Abraham's kin of his master's fortunes and of the purpose of his own mission. After telling of the oath which Abraham had made him take, he tells of his question, "What if the woman will not come back with me?" The account continues.

Gen. 24:40-41.

40) Then he said to me, "May YHWH, in whose ways I have ever walked, send his angel with you and grant success to your mission to take a wife for my son from

my kindred, indeed from my father's house.[5] 41) Only then will you be free (*tinnaqē*)

mēʾālāṯī[6]

if, when you have come to my kindred, they will not give her to you; then will you be free

mēʾālāṯī."[6]

In verse 8, where the original statement of Abraham's appears, the term *miššᵊḇūʿāṯī* occupies the place which in the above passage is filled by *mēʾālāṯī*. It is obvious, then, that the terms *ʾālā* and *šᵊḇūʿā* in these parallel passages are virtually synonymous. Yet no two terms are absolutely synonymous, and it seems clear that in the above context it is the *ʾālā* which is primary, for an oath is feared because of the imprecation(s) in it.[7]

In Chapter 26 of Genesis, Isaac moves to Beer-sheba after controversies with the inhabitants of Gerar over water wells. When Abimelech, king of Gerar, accompanied by two of his high officials, calls on Isaac, the latter asks why, in view of the recent unpleasantness between them, they have come to see him.

---

[5]The verbs in the imperfect are here rendered as precatives rather than future, contrary to AV, RSV, JPS, *et al*. If the tense were future, *i.e.*, a confident prediction, verse 41 would be superfluous, if not incongruous.

[6]AV, JPS, RSV "from my oath"; AT "(absolved) from the oath to me"; SB "(quitte) de ma malédiction"; ATD "des Schwures für mich (quitt)"; LXX ἀπὸ τῆς ἀρᾶς μου ; Targum *mimmōmāṯī*.

[7]Cf. Ibn Ezra's comment: "'Then will you be free of *ʾālāṯī*.' And he did not say '*miššᵊḇūʿāṯī*' [= "from my oath"], the sense being "because I am afraid of my master and of his *ʾālā* [= "curse"]." Scharbert refers to Gen. 24:41 in a footnote to his statement, "Durch eine Selbstverfluchung bindet man sich an ein feierliches Versprech-

Gen. 26:28-31.

> 28) They said, "We have come to the realization that YHWH is with you, wherefore we propose: let there be
>
> ʾālā[8]
>
> between our two parties,[9] you and us, and let us conclude a compact (bᵊrīṯ) with you, 29) that you will not (ʾim) do us harm, even as we have not touched you, doing you only good and letting you go safely. You now are certainly blessed of (= by) YHWH." 30) So he made them a feast, and they ate and drank. 31) Early in the morning they swore (wayyiššāḇᵊʿū) to one another, and Isaac sending them on their way, they departed in peace.

It occasions no surprise that the term ʾālā appears repeatedly in connection with a covenant (bᵊrīṯ). Every pact is sealed by an oath (šᵊḇūʿā), and every oath contains an imprecation or sanction (ʾālā). In this passage all three terms appear. The pervasiveness of metonymy is indicated by the fact that the formulaic ʾim (= that not) of the oath is immediately preceded, not by the noun or verb of the stem šbʿ, nor even by ʾālā, but by bᵊrīṯ. If the first clause of the proposal in verse 28 ("let there be ʾālā between...us") were altogether absent, the force of the proposal would still remain clear: Let there be a covenant (in which you will take an oath) that you will not harm us. There can scarcely be any doubt that the ʾālā as the sanc-

---

en..." ("Fluchen" und "Segen" im A.T., Biblica, Vol. 39, 1958, p. 4).

[8]AV, JPS, AT, RSV "an oath"; SB "un serment"; ATD "eine eidliche Verpflichtung"; LXX ἀρὰ; Targ. mōmāṯā. Scharbert, continuing the statement quoted above (cf. Note 7) that one binds oneself through a self-curse (ʾālā) to a solemn promise, refers to Gen. 26:28 (as well as to Ezek. 17:13, 16, 18), "und garantiert man bei einem Vertrag die Vertragstreue, weshalb ein Vertrag kurz ʾālā genannt werden kann."

[9]bēnōṯ, as opposed to bēn "between," deals with two

tion-clause of the oath[10] stands here for the entire oath, by synecdoche of the part for the whole, even as <u>bᵊrīṯ</u> (followed by <u>ʾim</u>) stands for oath, by synecdoche of the whole for the part.

The close association of <u>ʾālā</u> and <u>bᵊrīṯ</u> occurs again in Deuteronomy 29, in the address of Moses to the Israelites, in the territory of Moab.

Deut. 29:9-20.

> 9) You are standing, all of you, today before YHWH your God... 11) to enter
>
> <u>biḇrīṯ</u> <u>YHWH</u> <u>ʾᵉlōhεḵā</u> <u>uḇᵊʾālāṯō</u>[11]
>
> which your God YHWH concludes with you this day; 12) that he may confirm you this day as his people and that he may become your God... 13) Nor is it with you alone that I conclude
>
> <u>ʾεṯ</u> <u>habbᵊrīṯ</u> <u>hazzōʾṯ</u> <u>wᵊʾεṯ</u> <u>hāʾālā</u> <u>hazzōʾṯ</u>[12]
>
> ...17) Beware that there be not among you a man or woman, family or tribe whose heart (= intention) turns away from your God YHWH, with the intention to serve the gods of those nations; that there be not among you a root sprouting poison and wormwood, 18) who, when he hears the words of

---

respective parties.

[10]Cf. John Skinner's comment on v. 28: "The <u>ʾālā</u> is properly the curse invoked on the violation of the covenant;" Genesis (ICC. New York: Ch. Scribner's Sons, 1910), p. 367.

[11]AV, JPS "into...covenant with...and into his oath"; RSV "into the sworn covenant of..."; AT "the covenant of...and the solemn compact"; SB "dans l'alliance de... jurée avec imprécation"; HAT "in den Bund und die Eidgenossenschaft"; Targ. <u>biqyāmā</u>...<u>uḇmōmāṯēh</u>; LXX ἐν τῇ διαθήκῃ ... καὶ ἐν ταῖς ἀραῖς αὐτοῦ.

[12]AV, JPS, "this covenant and this oath"; RSV "this sworn covenant"; AT "this covenant and solemn compact"; SB "(que je conclus) cette alliance et (que je profere) cette imprécation" [Note the extent of the paraphrase.] ; HAT "diese Bund und diese Eidgenossenschaft"; Targ. <u>qiyāmā</u>...

hāʾālā hazzōʾṯ[13]

> congratulates himself in his heart,[14] thinking, "It will go well with me though I go ahead with my stubborn intention." ...19) YHWH will refuse to pardon him; rather will the angry passion of YHWH smoulder against

---

mōmāṯā; LXX τὴν διαθήκην... καὶ τὴν ἀράν.

[13]AV, JPS "this curse"; RSV "this sworn covenant" [despite the fact that *ʾālā* appears alone here!]; AT "this sacred compact"; SB "cette imprécation"; HAT "(die Worte) dieses Eides"; LXX τῆς ἀρᾶς ; Targ. *mōmāṯā*.

[14]Heb. *wᵊhiṯbārek bilᵊbāḇō*. AV, JPS, RSV render, "and blesses himself..." The occurrence of a blessing proferred subsequent to the pronouncement of a curse and as a kind of antidote to it in Judg. 17:2 would support this translation. This would, however, require that the following verb be taken as a jussive (*i.e.*, "May it go well with me...") rather than as a simple future tense. The translation "congratulates himself" which does accord with a following future tense is closer to the sense "flatters himself" (AT), which may be the intention of LXX ἐπιφημίσηται. The context supplies little help for the determination of the sense, because the meaning of *lᵊmaʿan sᵊpoṯ hārāwā ʾɛt hassᵊmēʾā* is equally in doubt. S. R. Driver (*Deuteronomy*, ICC, Edinburgh: T. & T. Clark, 3rd ed. 1902, p. 325) explains that this "clause is...to be connected with...'bless himself in his heart'; the meaning being that the idolater ...congratulates himself that he will escape all harm, *in order to destroy all together*, [italics in the original] viz. through the deleterious consequences of his sin, which ...brings down directly the Divine anger upon the entire people... The *result* of the idolater's action is represented, ironically, as being his design (*lᵊmaʿan*).." As stated, Driver's explanation makes little sense, for the idolater would be just as badly off, even if the community shared his fate. He probably has in mind the paraphrase of LXX "in order that the offender not be destroyed with the innocent," which is to say that he will be spared for the sake of the many. Driver follows up the translation of the Hebrew with a comment: "*To carry off the watered* (Is. 58: 11) *with the dry*/or *thirsty* (Ez. 19:13); a proverbial expression, denoting *all*..." Is it possible, in view of this recognized totality *per merismum*, that there is concealed here a reverse figure of speech? If *wᵊhiṯbārek* = bless himself = administer antidote = immunize himself, could the *ʾɛṯ* between *hārāwā* and *hassᵊmēʾā* be the particle introducing the direct object, and the *lᵊmaʿan* (without Driver's "ironically") introduce the putative idolater's intention: "so that the watered sweep away (= destroy) the dry," a figure of speech equivalent in meaning to "cancellation," the invoked self-blessing to cancel the effect of the *ʾālā*?

that man and

kol hā'ālā[15]

which is written in this document will settle upon him ... 20) And YHWH will single him out for calamity from all the tribes of Israel according to all

'ālōṯ habbᵊrīṯ[16]

written in this oracular record.

As is readily apparent both the ancient versions and the older English versions are literal and mechanical in translating the Hebrew expressions. RSV's translation of the conjunction of bᵊrīṯ and 'ālā by "sworn covenant" in verses 11 and 13 is a recognition of the hendiadys, which is unquestionably present in the phrases, and an improvement over the "covenant and oath" of AV and JPS. The two terms, bᵊrīṯ and 'ālā clearly do not stand for separate and independent concepts but are conjoined to express one idea. There is, however, a question as to whether RSV captures the original force of the hendiadys. In "sworn covenant" there can still be discerned the traditional rendering of 'ālā by "oath," which is not, as has been indicated, the primary meaning of 'ālā. "Sworn covenant" would be the correct rendering of bᵊrīṯ ušᵊḇūʿā. SB's solution of the problem, "l'alliance...jurée avec imprécation," restores the primary force of 'ālā (imprecation) but resorts to a paraphrase involving an insertion of something not actually present in the text. It is possible, however, to render

---

[15]AV "all the curses"; JPS "all the curse"; RSV "the curses"; AT "every curse"; SB "toute l'imprécation"; HAT "alle Flüche"; Targ. kol lᵊwāṭayā; LXX πᾶσαι αἱ ἀραὶ.

[16]AV, JPS, AT, RSV "the curses of the covenant"; SB "les imprécations de cette alliance"; HAT "...den Bundes-

the conjoined terms while retaining the primary force of *ʾālā* and omitting the absent middle term *šbʿ*. Full justice can be done to the biblical expression by "curse-enforced covenant," "curse-guarded compact," "sanction-supported covenant," or the like.

The full force of *ʾālā* as "sanction/curse" comes through in verse 18, where RSV gives "sworn covenant" despite the absence of the term *bərīṯ*. There is no reason to assume that *bərīṯ* has been accidentally omitted. The recalcitrant or fractious Israelite would respond, as he hypothetically does, not when he heard the terms of the covenant as a whole, but in defiance of the *ʾālā*, the imprecations or sanctions which are pronounced to render highly dangerous any violation of the covenant. So, too, in verse 19, the entire sanction, *kol hāʾālā*, will settle upon the violator of the covenant; and in verse 20, he will be singled out for disaster in accordance with the sanctions supporting the covenant (*ʾālōṯ habbərīṯ*), which are specifically detailed in the written record of the *bərīṯ*.

Against those who see in the working of a biblical curse, an automatic and magical (if not independent) concept, there is the evidence of Deuteronomy 30, where the promise is made that if the Israelites, having been punished for their defection, return to YHWH repentant and obedient, the sanctions (*ʾālōṯ*) applied to them will be visited upon their enemies.

---

flüchen"; Targ. *ləwāṭē qiyāmā*; LXX τὰς ἀρὰς τῆς διαθήκης.

Deut. 30:7.

And YHWH your God will dispose

kol hāʾālōṯ hāʾēllɛ[17]

against your hostile foes[18] who have persecuted you.

The connection between Deuteronomy and the *torah*-scroll found in the Temple and read before King Josiah is a staple of scholarship which requires no discussion here. Although the term *ʾālā* does not appear in the narrative in the Book of Kings, it does occur in the parallel account in Chronicles, in the oracle mediated by Huldah the prophetess.

2 Chron. 34:24

Thus says YHWH, "Lo, I am about to bring calamity upon this place and upon its inhabitants, even all *hāʾālōṯ*[19] (curses/sanctions) written in the document which they read before the king of Judah.

Of greater interest to this study, however, are two passages which make explicit reference to the *torah* of Moses, both of them containing a conjunction of the terms *ʾālā* and *šᵊḇūʿā*.

Daniel, confessing the wrongs committed by Israel and the justness of the promised retribution which has come upon them, says, in part:

Dan. 9:11.

And all Israel have transgressed your teaching

---

[17]AV, JPS, AT, RSV "all these curses"; SB "toutes ces imprécations"; HAT "Flüche"; LXX τὰς ἀρὰς ; Targ. *lᵊwāṭayā*.

[18]Taking *ʾoyᵊḇɛḵā wᵊ...śonʾɛḵā* as hendiadys.

[19]AV, JPS, AT, RSV "the curses"; SB "les malédic-

(tora), turning away from obedience to you; and so there has been poured down upon us

hā'ālā wᵊhaššᵊbūʿā[20]

written in the torah of Moses, the servant of God...

A glance at the various renderings suffices to demonstrate the superiority of AT whose translation alone expresses the force of the hendiadys. There is no question that the primary term here is 'ālā; it is the 'ālā of the šᵊbūʿā, the curse/sanction invoked in the oath which has been poured down upon Israel for its breach of the Mosaic covenant.

One feature of hendiadys is that the two terms may appear in any order without change of meaning.[21] Another feature is that either of the substantives may serve as the adjectival modifier of the other. Thus, whereas in the above passage from Daniel the primary term is 'ālā, the terms 'ālā and šᵊbūʿā, conjoined in that order, occur again but with a reversal of emphasis.

Neh. 10:29-30.

29) And the rest of the people [whose seals are not affixed to the written dcument]... 30) join with their

---

tions"; ATD "die Flüche"; HAT "die Drohungen"; LXX τοὺς πάντας λόγους.

[20]AV, JPS, RSV "the curse and the oath"; AT "the curse embodied in the oath"; SB "la malédiction et l'imprécation"; HAT "der Fluch und die Verwünschung"; LXX ἡ κατάρα καὶ ὁ ὅρκος. One wonders why RSV should overlook the hendiadys here when it recognizes it in the parallel passage in 9:29, kālā wᵊnεḥᵉrāṣā tittak, "the decreed end is poured out."

[21]As is pointed out by E. Z. Melamed, "Two which are One (ΕΝ ΔΙΑ ΔΥΟΙΝ) in the Bible," Hebrew, Tarbiz 16 (1945), p. 179.

brothers, the dignitaries, and enter

<u>bᵊʾālā</u> <u>uḇišᵊḇūʿā</u>[22]

to follow[23] the <u>torah</u> of God, which was given through Moses, God's servant...

Here, as recognized by AT the primary term is <u>šᵊḇūʿā</u> (oath) and <u>ʾālā</u> is the modifier. Perhaps an improvement upon AT's rendering would be "a penalty-fraught oath." Either translation is somewhat tautological, to be sure, since there is really no such thing as an oath which contains no curse-penalty. Such redundancy, however, is often a feature of hendiadys, the purpose of the figure of speech being to underline or emphasize the basic concept.

In two prophetic passages, one from Isaiah and the other from Jeremiah <u>ʾālā</u> occurs in similar contexts in which the noun can mean only "curse." The Isaiah passage explicitly refers to a <u>bᵊrīṯ</u>. Although the Jeremiah passage contains no reference to a <u>bᵊrīṯ</u>, the known connection between this prophet and Deuteronomy, and the centrality of <u>bᵊrīṯ</u> in his oracles, leave little doubt that the <u>bᵊrīṯ</u> between YHWH and Israel is implicit in his thought.

Jer. 23:10-11.

For the land is full of profligates[24]

---

[22]AV, JPS, RSV "into a curse and (into) an oath"; AT "oath under penalty of a curse"; SB "par imprécation et serment"; HAT "in eidliche Verpflichtung und Schwur"; ATD "(schliesst sich...an mit) Eid und Schwur"; LXX ἐν ἀρᾷ καὶ ἐν ὅρκῳ.

[23]<u>lālɛkɛṯ</u> <u>bᵊ</u> -- lit., to walk, proceed in...

[24]Taking <u>mᵊnāʾaᵃpīm</u> in a less literal sense.

Indeed, the land mourns

<u>mippe^{ə}nē</u> <u>ʾālā</u>,[25]

Dried up are the pastures of the steppe...

11) For both prophet and priest are polluted...

Isa. 24:4-6

4) The land mourns and languishes,
feeble is the world and languishing...

5) The land under its inhabitants is polluted
for they have transgressed the teachings

(<u>tōrōṯ</u>),

overstepped the laws,
violated the eternal covenant (<u>b^{ə}rīṯ</u>).

6) Therefore <u>ʾālā</u>[26]
devours the land,
and its inhabitants suffer for their
guilt.

Unless we arbitrarily deny the genuineness of the Jeremiah passage, it is important to stress, both for the

---

[25]AV, JPS "because of swearing"; as Targ. <u>mōmē dišqar</u>; For the arguments against this rendering of <u>ʾālā</u> see below pp.56 ff. R.S.V. "because of the curse"; SB "par la faute de ces gens" and marg.: "hébr. à cause de la malédiction"; HAT "wegen des Fluches"; AT "because of whom." The renderings of SB and AT as well as the preference expressed in HAT's commentary are based on LXX ἀπὸ προσώπου τούτων which would require <u>ʾlh</u> to be punctuated as <u>ʾellēh</u>. Arnold B. Ehrlich (<u>Randglossen zur Hebräischen Bibel</u>, 7. vol., Leipzig: Hinrich, 1908; vol. IV, p. 303) prefers this reading and takes the <u>m^{ə}nāʾ^{a}pīm</u> (which he emends to read <u>ḥ^{a}nēpīm</u>) of the first clause as the antecedent of the pronoun. It should be noted, however, that the entire first clause of MT verse 10 (<u>kī m^{ə}nāʾ^{a}pīm mālʾā hāʾāreṣ</u>) is absent in LXX. Ehrlich must, therefore, base his reading on Aquila and Syriac for LXX provides no antecedent. My preference for MT's <u>ʾālā</u> is supported by the remarkable parallels between this passage and the one in Isaiah (see the discussion, below) where all the versions agree on the reading <u>ʾālā</u>.

[26]AV, JPS, AT, RSV "a curse"; SB "malédiction"; KHAT "Fluch"; LXX ἀρά ; Targ. <u>mōmē dišqar</u> (as in Jer. 23:10).

exegesis of the verses and the possibility of the influence of Isaiah upon Jeremiah, the parallels between the two passages in regard to imagery and terminology. Thus, Isa. 24:4 ʾābᵊlā...hāʾārɛṣ || Jer. 23:10 ʾābᵊlā hāʾārɛṣ; Isa. 24:5 ḥanᵊpā || Jer. 23:11 ḥanᵊpū; Isa. 24:4 nābᵊlā hāʾārɛṣ, nābᵊlā tebel || Jer. 23:10 yābᵊšū nᵊʾōt midbār. The context in both passages would appear to be identical: the violation of the terms of the covenant by those who are to be Israel's leaders and teachers, and the inexorable working of the ʾālā invoked to guard the covenant's inviolability.

The sanctity of a covenant figures importantly in the thinking of the prophet Ezekiel. In Chapter 16, YHWH vows that he will punish Israel for violating its covenant with him; and in Chapter 17, for Israel's violation of the covenant between Zedekiah and the king of Babylon.

Ezek. 16:59

> For thus says the lord YHWH, "I will deal as you have done in despising
>
> ʾālā[27]
>
> to break a covenant (bᵊrīt).

Ezek. 17:11-19

> 11) Then the word of YHWH came to me: 12) "Say now to the rebellious house:...The king of Babylon did come to Jerusalem and, taking her king and her officers, brought them to himself in Babylon. 13) Then taking one of the seed royal he concluded a covenant with him bringing him

---

[27]AV, JPS, AT, RSV "The oath"; SB "le serment"; HbAT "den Schwur"; LXX ταῦτα (= ʾellē); Targ. mōmē.

b'ʾālā[28]...

15) But he rebelled against him, sending agents to Egypt that it should provide him with horses and men in force. Shall he succeed? Shall one who does such a thing escape punishment -- to break a covenant and go free? 16) By my life,[29] says the lord YHWH, in the place of the king who crowned him, whose

ʾālā(ṯō)[30]

he despised in breaking his covenant with him, in Babylon, he shall die... 18) Having despised

ʾālā[31]

to break a covenant, though he had given his hand (on it), yes, having done all this, he shall not escape. 19) On the contrary,[32] the Lord YHWH speaks thus, By my life

ʾālāṯī[33]

which he despised in breaking a covenant concluded in my name (bᵊrīṯī) I will requite upon his head."

The term ʾālā in every one of these passages appears in its basic meaning without metonymic force. Properly speaking, it is not the promissory statement in an oath

---

[28]AV, JPS, AT, RSV "oath"; SB "serment"; HbAT ("verflichtete ihn) unter Eid" and the note in the commentary: "Wörtlich 'unter einen Fluch bringen', der bei Vertragsbruch wirksam wird." LXX (ἐν) ἀρᾷ ; Targ. bᵊmōmē.

[29]For the demonstration that ḥay/ḥe in the Hebr. oath formula is a noun in the construct, see Moshe Greenberg, "The Hebrew Oath Particle ḤAY/ḤE," JBL Vol. LXXVI, Part 1 (March 1957) p. 34 ff.

[30]AV, JPS, AT, RSV "(whose) oath"; SB "le serment"; LXX τὴν ἀράν μου ; Targ. mōmāṯeh.

[31]AV, JPS, AT, RSV "oath"; SB "serment"; LXX ὁρκωμοσίαν. Targ. mōmē.

[32]For this force of lāḵen, cf. Gen. 4:15.

[33]AV "mine oath"; JPS "Mine oath"; AT, RSV, "my oath"; LXX τὴν ὁρκωμοσίαν μου ; Targ. mōmāṯī. Scharbert (op.cit., p. 4): "das wir etwa 'Eid unter Anrufung meines Namens' wiedergeben können."

which one fears, but the curse or sanction invoked in support of the promise. To break a covenant one must indeed defy (/despise) the sanctions; or, conversely, contempt of the sanctions is implicit in any act of breaking a covenant. Since it was YHWH who was invoked to punish the violator of the covenant,[34] it is YHWH who will effectuate the imprecations. In 17:19 the rendering of *ʾālāṯī* and *bərīṯī* respectively by "my oath" and "my covenant" is as wrong as it is confusing to a reader of the English Bible, for it is not YHWH's covenant and its attendant sanctions that are involved (as in 16:59), but the covenant made with the king of Babylon. Clearly *ʾālāṯī* means "the sanctions invoked of me,"[35] and *bərīṯī* can only be, "the covenant made in, or sworn to by, my name."

In 17:13 the expression *wayyāḇēʾ ʾōṯō bəʾālā* reflects the basic force of *ʾālā* = curse, sanction. For, properly speaking, one does not bring anyone into or under an oath; but one does bring him under the threat of sanctions or penalties. It is worth stressing that even in the English expression "under oath" the word "oath" stands by metonymy for that part of the oath which is a curse, for English idiom does not admit of "being under" a statement or promise.

---

[34]For a discussion of the invocation of YHWH in treaties imposed by both Assyrians and Neo-Babylonians, see Matitiahu Tsevat, *The Neo-Assyrian and Neo-Babylonian Vassal Oaths and the Prophet Ezekiel*, JBL, Vol. LXXVIII, Part III (Sept. 1959) pp. 199 ff.

[35]Cf. Scharbert's statement quoted in Note. 33.

The term *ʾālā*, or rather the plural *ʾālōṯ* (if, indeed, the form is nominal rather than verbal) occurs once more in the context of *bᵊrîṯ*. Unfortunately the passage presents too many problems to be of value for this study.

Hos. 10:4

dibbᵊrû dᵊḇārîm ʾālōṯ šāwʾ kārōṯ bᵊrîṯ
upārāh kārōʾš mišpāṭ ʿal talmē śāḏāy[36]

RSV They utter mere words;
with empty oaths they make covenants;
So judgment springs up like poisonous weeds
in the furrows of the field.

Ehrlich comments as follows:

"Dieser Vers, der den Zusammenhang durchbricht, scheint von anderswoher versprengt zu sein. Der Text ist hier heillos beschädigt. Nicht nur lässt sich mit dem neutralen *dbrym* nichts anfangen, sondern es ist auch der Pl. von *ʾlh* zu spät für Hosea, und *šwʾ* kann den Eid als einen falschen bezeichnen; *šqr* ist das einzige Wort dafür. Ausserdem ist der Vergleich im zweiten Halbvers nicht recht verstandlich und der Ausdruck *ʿl tlmy śdy* mit Bezug auf *mšpṭ* unpassend."[37]

Translators of the Bible are compelled by their very task to translate every passage, however obscure or textually corrupt. In the absence, however, of answers to the difficulties cited by Ehrlich, it would be preferable to avoid forcing meaning onto a dubious text. Scharbert re-

---

[36] AV "They have spoken words, swearing falsely in making a covenant"; JPS "They speak words, /They swear falsely, they make covenants"; AT "They speak mere words; they swear false oaths; /They make leagues"; SB "Ils disent des paroles, faux serments alliances"; ATD "Worte machen, Falscheid schwören, Bunde schliessen"; LXX λαλῶν ῥήματα προφάσεις ψευδεῖς διαθήσεται διαθήκην ; Targ. *mᵊmallîn milîn dᵊʾōnes yēmān lišqar lilmā gāzᵊrîn qᵊyam*.

[37] Arnold B. Ehrlich, *Randglossen*, Vol. V, p. 196.

marks "ʾālōṯ šāwʾ in Hos. 10, 4 können wir nur umschreiben, etwa: 'unter einer Selbstverfluchung einen Vertrag mit dem Hintergedanken beschwören, ihn bei nächster Gelegenheit zu brechen'." A number of considerations, however, are to be adduced against this paraphrase: 1) A self-curse in an oath, even if expressed with the mental reservation to break the promise at the first opportunity, would not necessarily constitute an ʾālaṯ-šāwʾ, literally "an empty curse". 2) Even Scharbert's paraphrase imputes to the noun ʾālā the sense of "oath" and to the corresponding verb the sense of "to swear, take an oath," which, as I hope to show, is a force never demonstrably attested for the term. 3) There remains still the problem of dibbᵊrū dᵊḇārīm and the general awkwardness of the entire verse in its context.

III. ʾālā -- VERB AND NOUN AS ADJURATORY IMPRECATION

In the preceding discussion it was shown that in every passage analyzed the basic meaning of the noun ʾālā is curse, imprecation, sanction; that in those passages where it has been rendered by "oath" (or even by "covenant"), the translation was made possible by metonymic extension, specifically by synecdoche of the part for the whole. It must be remembered that although every oath involves (explicitly or implicitly) a curse, not every curse implies an oath. The term "oath" has frequently, and correctly, been defined or characterized as a conditional or contingent curse. There is, however, another type of conditional or contingent curse, differing from "oath" in that the conditional/contingent curse is invoked not upon the person speaking but upon a party in the second or third (grammatical) person.

Such a conditional curse is best expressed in English by the term "adjuration." When addressed to a second person the adjuration often has the nature of a charge or command delivered together with the invocation of a curse in the event of non-compliance; it may have the same nature, when directed to or against a third person, in which case the charge or command is expressed as a jussive. When the contingency lies in the past -- that is, if the deed has already been committed -- the adjuration is similarly directed against a possible perpetrator of the deed. In all the cases here listed the purpose of the adjuration is to induce someone to perform an action, or to undo a deed, or to preclude the taking of an anticipated action. One more possibility remains: an address to a second person from whom no response is desired or indicated, i.e., the simple pronouncement, or invocation, of a curse against that person if he has committed a given act. This latter address, too, falls under the heading of "adjuration." There is one case of conditional/contingent imprecation which does not fall under the purview of "adjuration": that is, the invocation of a curse against an unknown party from whom no response is desired or expected; in this last instance the contingency lies only in the unidentifiability of the third party, e.g., "May such-and-such befall anyone who has done such-and-such."

In the succeeding section, the thesis will be advanced that the term ʾālā, as noun or verb, covers every instance listed in the preceding paragraph, which is to say, every instance of conditional curse, not directed against oneself.[39] It will be further argued that the stem šbʿ, verbal or nominal, when it extends beyond the range of conditional curse, does so by metonymic extension and represents an invasion of the area which originally and properly belongs to ʾālā.

A. ʾālā -- In Summons of Witnesses and Malefactors.

The institution, in the ancient near-East, of public proclamation, to advertise or elicit information in regard to the status of property, the commission of crimes, etc., is too well known to require extensive comment here.[40] Whatever the form or nature of the proclamation in neighboring societies, it is clear that in Israel it took the form of a conditional imprecation (ʾālā) against the per-

---

[39]It should, perhaps, be indicated that the ʾālā in every analyzable occurrence in Section II, is essentially not an unconditional, but a conditional or contingent, curse. As the curse-part of an oath (šᵊbūʿā), the condition is expressed by the "if" or "if not" clause of the oath with the subject always in the first grammatical person.

[40]To cite just a few examples: 1) The formula in legal documents from Nuzi which deal with property transactions: tuppi ina arki šudūti ina bab abullim šaṭir, "the tablet was inscribed after proclamation in the city gate." 2) The Talmudic term hakrāzā, "proclamation," specifically with regard to the obligation of a finder of lost property to advertise for the owner. 3) CH § 16, where public proclamation is made to elicit information concerning, or the actual producing of, a fugitive slave. The šisīt nagīri(m), "call of the herald," is the Babylonian parallel to qōl ʾālā in Lev. 5:1, although there is no indication as to whether the former involved an imprecation. Cf. G. R. Driver and J. C. Miles, The Babylonian Laws (Oxford: Clarendon Press, 1956), Vol. II, p. 19. 4) The public pronouncement among contemporary Bedouin of an imprecation against any finder withholding an item of lost property. Cf. T. Canaan, The Curse in Palestinian Folklore, JPOS 15,

petrator of a crime, as well as against accessories after the fact and witnesses withholding material evidence.

Lev. 5:1

> If any person has committed an offense, in that he hears
>
> <u>qōl ʾālā</u>,[41]
>
> and he has evidence, whether first-hand or indirect, if he does not speak out he shall bear his penalty.[42]

Of the English translations, RSV's would appear to express the concept most felicitously. Yet a thorough understanding of the institution of the <u>ʾālā</u> requires the awareness that every "adjuration" involves a contingent curse. A full, if awkward, exposition of <u>qōl ʾālā</u> would be "a public summons backed by a contingent curse."

The verse above and one in Proverbs reflect light upon each other.

Prov. 29:24.

> He who shares (the loot) with a thief
> is his own enemy (lit. hates himself);
> he hears
>
> <u>ʾālā</u>,

(1935), p. 240.

[41]AV "the voice of swearing"; JPS "the voice of adjuration"; AT "the oath of adjuration"; RSV "a public adjuration"; SB "la formule d'adjuration"; HAT "eine laut ausgesprochene Verwünschung"; LXX φωνὴν ὁρκισμοῦ ; Targ. <u>qāl mōmē</u> and var. <u>mōmāṯā</u>. Other interesting variations: Scharbert (<u>op.cit.</u>, p. 3) "den lauten Fluch"; KHAT "eine feierliche Beschwörung."; D. Hoffman "die Stimme eines Beeidigung" (<u>Das Buch Leviticus</u>, 2 Vol., Berlin: Poppelauer, 1906).

[42]The term <u>ʿāwōn</u> like Akkad. <u>arnu(m)</u> means both "crime" and "punishment..." For a novel interpretation of this verse, and of the entire passage through v. 13, cf.

yet cannot speak out.[43]

Here, too, "the adjuratory curse" best expresses the meaning of ʾālā. The traditional rendering of ḥōleq ʿim gannāḇ "partner of a thief" misses the point of the apothegm. The gannāḇ, the professional thief, is beyond instruction. The saying is directed to anyone who may be tempted on occasion to benefit from a share in stolen goods. Though not a party to the theft itself, he is warned that he will become implicated after the fact and that, unable to respond to the adjuration without convicting himself, he will remain subject to the curse.

In Judges 17 the stem *ʾlw occurs as a verb in the qal perfect. The context makes it perfectly clear that the action involved is the pronouncement of a curse, conditioned only by the fact that the object of the imprecation is the unknown perpetrator of a crime. The purpose of the pronouncement is to induce the offender to confess and to make restitution.

Judges 17:2

...And he said to his mother, "The eleven hundred pieces of silver which were stolen (lit., taken) from you,

---

Abram Spiro, A Law on the Sharing of Information, AAJRP, Vol. 28, (1959), pp. 95-101.

[43]AV "cursing"; JPS "the adjuration"; AT, RSV "the curse"; SB "l'adjuration" and marg. note, "c'est-à-dire la malédiction que l'on prononcera contre le criminel inconnu ou les témoins demeures cachés." HAT "die Verfluchung" and comment: "Von Beschwörung ist weder hier noch Lev. 5 die Rede, sondern man hat an eine öffentliche feierliche Verfluchung des unbekannten Thäters und seiner Helfer zu denken, die man der Strafe Gottes übergab."; LXX ὅρκου ; Targ. mōmāṯā.

<u>w$^{\partial}$ʾat</u> <u>ʾālīṯ</u>[44]

> indeed, expressing it in my hearing -- that silver is in my possession. It was I who took it."; whereupon his mother declared, "Blessed be my son by YHWH."

It should be noted that the mother's response to her son's confession -- an invocation of blessing to counteract her preceding curse -- is necessitated by the fact that the only question (or contingency) in the imprecation had been that of the thief's identity. It appears likely that the mother had suspected her son all along. Nevertheless, the moment it becomes certain that the "whoever..." of her curse is her own son, she must cancel her imprecation, which otherwise would remain in effect.

B. <u>*ʾlw -- In Adjuration Designed to Preclude an Action.</u>

As was seen in the immediately preceding passage, the verb <u>*ʾlw</u> appears in the qal as an intransitive. The verb in a finite tense appears only twice, once in Kings 8:31-32,[45] and once in I Samuel 14:24. In both instances it appears as a <u>hiphʿil</u>, <u>i.e.</u> transitive = "impose an <u>ʾālā</u> upon." In I Samuel 14 the Israelites, in a hard-fought battle, have put the Philistines to rout. King Saul is eager to make the defeat as crushing as possible, and, anxious lest the pursuit of the fleeing enemy be interrupted by the eagerness of his own men to loot the latter's aban-

---

[44] AV "about which thou cursedst"; JPS "about which thou didst utter a curse"; AT "concerning which you uttered a curse"; RSV "about which you uttered a curse"; SB "au sujet desquels tu proféré une malédiction"; ATD..."einen Fluch ausgestossen"; LXX καί με ἠράσω ; Targ. <u>w$^{\partial}$ʾat</u> <u>yēmīṯ</u>.

[45] See below, p. 52.

doned supplies (Cf. v. 32)...

I Sam. 14:24-28.

24) Now the men of Israel were hard-pressed at that time, but

<u>wayyō'ɛl</u>[46]

Saul the people, as follows: "Cursed be the man who partakes of food before evening, when I shall be avenged on my enemies!" ...[There follows a corrupt passage, the sense of which can be restored with the help of LXX: honeycombs, abandoned by their bees, are found in the field,[47]] 26)...but no one put his hand to his mouth for the people feared

<u>'ɛṯ</u> <u>haššᵊḇūʿā</u>.[48]

27) But Jonathan had not heard

<u>bᵊhašbīaʿ</u>[49]

his father the people, so, reaching out the tip of the staff in his hand, he dipped it into the honey-comb and brought it (lit., his hand) back to his mouth... 28) Then one of the men spoke up, saying

"<u>hašbēaʿ</u> <u>hišbīaʿ</u>[50]

---

[46]AV "had adjured"; JPS "adjured"; AT "put (the people) under oath"; RSV "laid an oath on the people"; SB "avait prononcé (sur le peuple) cette imprécation"; ATD "legte...(dem Volk) 'einen Eid' auf"; LXX ἀρᾶται (τῷ λαῷ) ; Tar. <u>wᵊ'ōmī</u>. Scharbert (<u>op.cit</u>. p. 4, n. 6) "<u>wayyō'ɛl</u> = "er liess dass Volk eine Selbstverfluchung sprechen."

[47]For a full discussion of the problems and an attractive solution, cf. S. R. Driver, <u>Notes on the Hebrew Text of the Books of Samuel</u>, 2nd ed. (Oxford: Clarendon Press, 1913), p. 113 f.

[48]AV, JPS, AT, RSV "the oath"; SB "le serment juré"; ATD "den Schwur"; LXX τον ὅρκον ; Targ. <u>(miš)šᵊḇūʿāṯā</u>. Pedersen (<u>Der Eid bei den Semiten</u>, p. 108), "Sauls Verfluchung desjenigen, der etwas essen würde, wird ein dem Volke auferlegter Eidschwur gennant (I Sam. 14, 26.27; vgl. Jdc. 21, 18)."

[49]AV, JPS, RSV "when...charged (the people) with the oath"; AT "when...adjured"; SB "(n'avait pas entendu son père) imposer le serment sur..."; ATD "wen...(dem Volk) den Schwur auferlegte hatte"; LXX ἐν τῷ ὁρκίζειν ; Targ. <u>kaḏ 'ōmī</u>.

[50]AV, JPS "straitly charged...with an oath"; AT "strictly adjured"; RSV "strictly charged...with an oath";

your father the people, explicitly, 'Cursed be the man who eats anything today!'"...

The key to the entire passage lies, of course, in the term wayyōʾɛl in verse 24;[51] but for that verb we might not be alert to the existence of an ʾālā in the passage, for all the other terms relating to it are various forms of the stem šbᶜ. And yet it is highly probable that the entire passage revolves around the concept of ʾālā, adjuratory imprecation, and not šᵊbūᶜā, oath/conditional self-curse. It would seem that this distinction between the two nominal terms was, originally , quite clear; and, furthermore, that the niphᶜal of šbᶜ was used for the utterance of a conditional self-curse (oath), the qal of *ʾlw for the utterance of a contingent imprecation (intransitive), and the hiphᶜil of *ʾlw for the utterance of an ʾālā against someone (transitive). Interchange of the two basic stems would then be due to metonymy -- but it would be wrong to assume

---

SB "a impose ce serment"; ATD "einen heiligen Schwur auferlegt hatte"; LXX ὁρκίσας ὥρκισε ; Targ. ʾomāʾā ʾōmī.

[51]It is, therefore, of interest that Ehrlich (Randglossen, Vol. 3, p. 213 f.) does not accept wayyōʾɛl as original. His objection lies not in this word but in niggaś which he regards as impossible in the context. His involved reconstruction of v. 24 would read wᵊʾīš yiśrāʾel niggaš bayyōm hahūʾ {wy(y)} ʾɛl <place name lost> <wayyašbaᶜ> šāʾūl...And the men of Israel approached <place-name> <and (Saul) adjured>... In view of the occurrence of the verb elsewhere, particularly the hiphᶜil infinitive in I Kings 8:31, which Ehrlich accepts as original, there seems to be no compelling reason to question the originality of wayyōʾɛl here. For the parsing of the verb, see Gesenius-Kautzsch-Cowley, Hebrew Grammar (2nd Eng. ed., Oxford: Clarendon Press, 1910) §76d, where the verb is taken as imperfect apocopated hiphᶜil on the presumed process wayyōʾɛl <wayyōʾlɛ̄ < wayyāʾlɛ̄ < wayyaʾᵃlɛ̄ < wayyaʾlɛ̄. A simpler explanation ascribes the vocalization to the influence of hōʾīl by an error in the tradition. G. Bergstrasser, Hebräische Grammatik (Leipzig, 1929) II 31 e, p. 172.

metonymy in any given instance unless the context excludes the original force.

In any case, there can be no question of the presence of an oath in this passage. There is none. The *nipĥʿal* of *šbʿ* does not appear. The verb *wayyōʾɛl* means that Saul pronounced a conditional curse upon his army. No one was made to take an oath or was laid under oath; Jonathan is subject to the curse although not party to the imprecation nor even aware of it. The word *šəbūʿā* in verse 26 is "curse" by metonymy and the *hiphʿil* of *šbʿ* is everywhere in this passage, by metonymy, equal to the *hiphʿil* of **ʾlw* and is best translated by "adjure."

C. Excursus -- *hiphʿil šbʿ* = *hiphʿil *ʾlw*

It may be of value to stress here that in the majority of instances the *hiphʿil* of *šbʿ* has the causative force, *i.e.*, to cause someone to take an oath. The exceptions, in addition to I Sam. 14:27, 28, where it is equal to *hiphʿil *ʾlw*, and is to be translated by "adjure," are:

Num. 5:19, 21. See below, pp. 50 f.

Josh. 6:26 I Sam. 14:28

I Kings 2:42-43. Solomon to Shimei ben Gera. Cf. *wāʾāʿid bəkā* || *hišbaʿtikā* and *hammiṣwā ʾᵃšɛr ṣiwwītī ʿalɛka* || *šəbūʿat YHWH*

I Kings 22:16 (II Chron. 18:15)

Neh. 13:25. See below, p. 124.

Cant. 2:7, 3:5, where the strong force of "adjure" is a poetic license; and 5:8, 9, where the "adjuration" is in the form of a question.

D. *ʾālā* -- *An Appeal to the Divine/Supernatural to Punish Violations of the Moral Code.*

The two cases to be discussed here have these features in common: 1) the breach of law or morality is supposed to have already taken place; 2) a response by the target of the imprecation is either unnecessary or not to be expected; 3) the effectuation or non-effectuation of the curse is to serve an oracular function: to disclose guilt and/or innocence, condemnation and/or vindication.

The first case, in Numbers 5, purports to be YHWH's instructions on the procedure to be followed when a wife is suspected by her husband of having committed adultery, but evidence is lacking. The several perplexing textual and semantic difficulties in this passage are not of significant hindrance to the purposes of this study.[52] After describing the preparation of the sacrificial offerings attending the ritual, the preparation of the "holy" water, and the disposition of the woman, the text goes on:

---

[52]For a detailed discussion of the problems and the history of scholarly speculation upon them, see G. B. Gray, *Numbers*, ICC (New York: Ch. Scribner's Sons, 1903), pp. 43-57. Briefly the problems are 1) the conflate nature of the text; 2) the enigmatic syntax of *mē hammārīm* and the highly dubious derivation of the latter word from *mrr* "to be bitter"; 3) the meaning of *yɛrɛk nōp̄ɛlɛt* and *bɛṭɛn ṣāḇā*. To the numerous conjectures, ancient and recent, I would add the following: If, as is likely, the "falling away of the thigh" is an expression for sterility, and if the traditional rendering of *ṣāḇ(ā)* as "swelling" is correct, the spell would consist of the phenomenon known as "false pregnancy." This would obviate the question as to the *śōṭā*'s pregnancy (which is nowhere suggested in the text), and explain v. 28, where *wᵊnizrᵊʿā zāraʿ* would mean that the woman would be able to bear children (if innocent of adultery). If the *hiphʿil* participle of *yārā* could be shown ever to have the force of "to give an oracle" (Cf. Gen. 12:6, Deut. 11:30 and the sense of *tōrā* = "oracle" everywhere in First Isaiah), one might be tempted to read *mōrīm* everywhere for *mārīm*, the water then operating with

Num. 5:19-27.

19) Then the priest is to charge (*wəhišbīaʿ*)[53] the woman, saying to her, "If no man has lain with you...be immune to this *mārīm* -- water which brings on the spell,[54] 20) but if you, on the other hand ...have contracted defilement in that any man other than your husband has had intercourse with you," 21) then shall the priest adjure (*wəhišbīaʿ*) the woman (with the)

bišəḇūʿaṯ hāʾālā[55]

speaking to her exactly so, "YHWH make you

ləʾālā w lišəḇūʿā[56]

among your people making your thigh fall away and your belly swell; 22) thus may the water which brings on the spell enter your vitals to make your belly swell and your thigh fall away." And the woman is to answer, "Amen, Amen." 23) Then the priest shall write

hāʾālōṯ hāʾellē[57]

---

oracular efficacy in being *məʾārərīm* or not. The traditional "bitter" makes little sense and has a weak foundation, hence my preference for leaving it untranslated. It is in any case probable that the confusion attending the entire passage is due to the desuetude of one of the few biblical practices smacking so strongly of the magical.

[53]AV "(shall) charge her by an oath"; JPS "cause her to take an oath"; AT "have her take an oath"; RSV "make her take an oath"; SB "déférera le serment à..." HAT "nehme... die Beschwörung...vor"; LXX ὁρκιεῖ ; Targ. *wəyōmē*.

[54]For a discussion of *məʾārərīm*, see below, p.111 ff.

[55]AV, JPS, "oath of cursing"; AT "oath of execration"; RSV "the oath of the curse"; SB "un serment imprécatoire"; HAT "einer feierlichen Verwünschung"; LXX ἐν τοῖς ὅρκοις τῆς ἀρᾶς ; Targ. *bəmōmāṭā dilwāṭā*. Scharbert (*op. cit.*, p. 3, no. 5) "einer...auferlegte Eid..."

[56]AV, JPS "a curse and an oath"; AT, RSV "an execration and an oath"; SB "(te fasse servir...) aux imprécations et aux serments"; LXX ἐν ἀρᾷ καὶ ἐνόρκιον ; Targ. *lilwāṭā ulmōmē*.

[57]AV, JPS, AT, RSV "these curses"; SB "ces imprécations"; HAT "diese Flüche"; LXX τὰς ἀρὰς ταύτας ; Targ. *yaṯ ləwāṭayā hāʾillēn*.

> on a document and blot them out in the <u>mārīm</u>-water; 24) and make the woman drink the <u>mārīm</u>-water which brings on the spell so that the spell-producing water may enter her for <u>mārīm</u>... 27) And when she has been made to drink the water, it shall come about that if she has contracted defilement in having indeed been unfaithful to her husband, then the spell-producing water shall enter her for <u>mārīm</u>, so that her belly swell, her thigh fall away and the woman become an
>
> <u>ʾālā</u>[58]
>
> among her people.

It should be apparent now that despite the traditional translations, <u>hišbīaʿ</u> in verses 19 and 21 is not a causative and that the woman does not take an oath. Aside from the fact that the words of the priest are direct discourse (<u>i.e.</u>, the priest does all the talking),[59] the translation of <u>hišbīaʿ</u> by a causative would have the woman taking two separate oaths, a highly unlikely procedure; furthermore, verse 19 does not conform to the oath-formula at all, for it contains no curse (<u>ʾālā</u>) -- on the contrary, it has, in place of a curse, a statement proposing vindication. What is present, as indicated in the translation offered here, is a solemn address listing the alternatives of innocence and vindication or guilt and retribution. In verse 19 the former is pronounced, in verse 20 the protasis of the latter, and in verse 21 the apodosis, which contains the <u>šᵊbūʿaṯ hāʾālā</u>, the adjuratory curse. The spell, "the falling away of the thigh and the swelling of the belly"

---

[58]AV, JPS "a curse"; AT, RSV "an execration"; SB "elle servira d'example dans les malédictions"; LXX εἰς ἀρὰν Targ. <u>lilwāṭā</u>.

[59]Except for the woman's answering "Amen," which does not constitute proof that the woman takes an oath.

is the content of the *ʾālā*. In verse 23, *hāʾālōṯ hāʾellē* may, despite the plural, be rendered "this entire curse." The meaning of the woman's becoming an *ʾālā ušᵊḇūʿā* in verse 21 is, of course, that as victim of the spell she will be the embodiment or a visible example of the efficacy of the adjuratory curse.[60]

I Kings 8:31-32 (and II Chron. 6:22-23)

> 31) If a man offend against his fellow,
>
> *wᵊnāśā ḇō ʾālā lᵊhaʾᵃlōṯō ubāʾ ʾālā*[61]
>
> before thine altar in this temple, 32) then hear thou in heaven and execute judgment upon thy subjects, condemning the guilty by requiting his conduct upon his own head, and vindicating the righteous by rewarding him according to his honesty.

---

[60]So understood in Sifré to Numbers (18:2), "*lᵊʾālā* [as a curse] means that people shall curse by her [pointing to her and saying] 'May it befall thee as it befell so and so'... Scharbert (*Biblica* 39, 1, p. 5): "Die Person, die eine durch Fluch gesicherte Ordnung verletzt hat und daher vom Unheil ereilt wurde, wird zu einer *ʾālā*. Hier ist der Ausdruck metonymisch gebraucht." It should be noted that in the summarizing subscript (vv. 39-31) the traditional translation of *ʿāwōn* as "iniquity" is pointless and, when understood to refer to the *śōṭā*'s husband, misleading. The woman, if convicted, suffers the penalty; but there is no provision for punishing her adulterous consort. To be free of penalty is, however, not to be "free from iniquity." He remains an adulterer. See above, p. 43, note 42.

[61]AV "and an oath be laid upon him to cause him to swear, and the oath come"; JPS "and an oath be exacted of him to cause him to swear, and he come and swear"; AT "and an oath be laid upon him compelling him to swear...and he come in and swear"; RSV "and is made to take an oath, and comes and swears his oath"; SB "...prononce sur lui un serment imprécatoire et le fasse jurer"; HAT "man einen Fluch uber ihn ausspricht und ihn verflucht, und er muss vor deinen Altar...den Fluch über sich aussprechen lassen" and note in commentary "und lese *ubāʾ bᵊʾālā*"; LXX καὶ ἐὰν λάβῃ ἐπ᾽ αὐτὸν τοῦ ἀράσασθαι αὐτον καὶ ἔλθῃ καὶ ἐξαγορεύσῃ "and make confession"(!); Targ. *wᵊyeršē* (var. rdg. *wdrš*) *bēh mōmē lᵊʾōmāyūṯēh wᵊyēṯē yōmīnēh*.

As is evident from the citations in note 61, the translators, ancient and modern, are virtually unanimous in understanding the text as referring to the exaction or imposition of an exculpatory oath. The commentators are in similar agreement. Thus Rashi, understanding the offense in question as adultery, identifies the context here with that of Numbers 5:18 ff. and, drawing parallels between the two passages, interprets the text here as the subjection of the suspected adulterer to a procedure corresponding to that which is prescribed in Numbers for the *śōṭā*. Nor is there any question in Scharbert's mind that the text deals with the imposition of an oath, "Ein solcher mit einer Selbstverfluchung verbundene Eid gilt bei Gericht als Beweismittel. Er kann vom Ankläger...dem Angeklagten auferlegt werden..."[62]

Rashi's comment on *wᵊnasaʾ* (*lšwn* *nsh*)does not make it clear whether the sibilant in his text was *ś* or *š*; while Kimchi's allusion to *maššaʾṯ* *mᵊʾūmā* in Deut. 24:10 would seem to indicate an *š* sibilant in his text. Most commentators prefer the reading *nšʾ*[63] and it is clear that the rendering of the text as involving the exaction of an oath is based on *nšʾ* with an understood sense of "to exact." Against this I would urge the following considerations: 1) The preference of *nšʾ* is obviously influenced by a preconception of the intention of the passage. 2) The occurrence

---

[62] Scharbert, *Biblica* 39, 1, p. 3.

[63] S. Bär, *Libri Regum*, 1895; Rudolf Kittel, *Biblica Hebraica*, 3rd ed.; and among many, A. Ehrlich, *Randglossen*, Vol. VII, p. 233.

of <u>nś'</u> in manuscripts and printings, despite the preference of <u>nš'</u>, establishes the former as the <u>lectio</u> <u>difficilior</u> and warrants the invocation of the principle <u>lectio</u> <u>difficilior</u> <u>praestat</u>. 3) The Greek λάβῃ supports <u>nś'</u>. 4) The verb <u>nš'</u> is never used in the sense of exacting anything but a loan or interest. 5) The <u>hiphʿil</u> of <u>'ālā</u> (though occuring altogether only two times) is not used in the sense of causing someone to take an oath, whereas this is the normal sense of <u>hiphʿil</u> <u>šbʿ</u>. 6) Finally, the primary meaning of <u>'ālā</u> as herein set forth.[64]

The meaning of the passage becomes quite clear if <u>'ālā</u> is taken in its basic force of "contingent imprecation." The translation would be as follows, "If someone commit an offense against his fellow and the latter takes up an imprecation against him to bring him under the power of a curse, may (or, and) that (conditional) imprecation come(s) before your altar in this temple..."[65]

This interpretation is in keeping with the entire context of Solomon's prayer, which is to the effect that

---

[64]Against the preferences of the majority cf. James A. Montgomery, <u>The Book of Kings</u>, ICC (New York: Ch. Scribner's Sons, 1951), p. 202: "This rdg. [<u>nś'</u>] is generally preferred; but Akk. <u>nīšu</u>, "oath" (= Heb. root <u>nś'</u>, used of 'lifting up' hands at an oath), suggests that <u>nš'</u> is here much more tenable." Also J. Pedersen, <u>Der Eid bei den Semiten</u>, p. 103: "Bei den Israliten sprach man vor dem Altar einen Fluch gegen den unbekannten Verbrecher aus, der dann durch diesen Fluch getroffen wurde (I <u>Reg</u>. 8, 31)."

[65]Biblical idiom permits a passive force like the French "on..." An alternate translation would then be, "If an offense be committed by a man against his fellow and an <u>'ālā</u> is taken up..." The force of <u>wᵊnāšā</u> <u>bo</u> puts one in mind of the English "to swear out (a warrant)," where what is involved is not an oath but a charge.

YHWH should maintain the prestige of his temple in Jerusalem by answering all prayers directed toward that shrine. (It makes it clear, incidentally, that the imprecation is basically regarded as a prayer.) The only textual objection to this interpretation is that u<u>ḇā'</u> would have to be emended to read <u>uḇā'ā</u>. That <u>'ālā</u> does not require the definite article may be seen by comparing Lev. 5:1, Prov. 29:24 (see above, pp. 43, 44). On the other hand the standard interpretation requires either an emendation of <u>'ālā</u> to <u>'ālō</u> (the infinitive), or to <u>bə'ālā</u>, or to <u>wə'ālā</u>.

The force of <u>'ālā</u> as both imprecation and prayer -- or better, as imprecatory prayer now comes through vividly in its context in Job 31. The entire chapter consists of Job's protestation of his undeviating righteousness. So sure is he of his rectitude, so sure that he is free of any guilt -- whether in relations with his fellow man or God -- that he does not hesitate to resort to a series of exculpatory oaths, calling down disaster upon himself if he should be wrong in any of the particulars.

Job 31:29-30

> 29) If I have rejoiced at the ruin of my enemy
> or exulted when calamity befell him--
> 30) I have not even let my mouth offend
> by asking for his life
>
> <u>bə'ālā</u>[66]

---

[66]AV "(by wishing) a curse (to his soul)"; JPS, RSV "with a curse"; AT "(by calling down) curses (upon him)"; SB "(de la vouer a la mort) dans une malédiction"; HbAT "(seine Seele verwünschend) durch Fluch"; Targ. <u>bəmōmāṯā</u>; LXX bears little resemblance to the Heb.: Ἀκούσαι ἄρα τὸ οὖς μου τὴν κατάραν μου, θρυλληθείην δὲ ἄρα ὑπὸ μου κακούμενος -- "may my ear then hear my curse, may I be a by-

There is no indication here or anywhere in the Bible that the utterance of an imprecation constituted a violation of a social norm. On the contrary, the preceding discussion would indicate the acceptance of the employment of an *ʾālā* for the achievement of redress of wrongs. In the above passage Job reaches a climax in the claim that he has never been vindictive even in regard to his enemies, never having resorted to that legitimate but injurious institution -- the *ʾālā*.

D. *ʾālā* -- Employed, Improperly, as an Accusation.

Once it is recognized that the *ʾālā* was an established institution in Israel, that every *ʾālā*, employed as a contingent imprecation upon an adversary suspected of wrongdoing is *ipso facto* an accusation, it becomes easier to appreciate the significance of a number of passages, the meanings of which have been in doubt. In two texts, one from Hosea and the other from Psalms, the term *ʾālā* appears in juxtaposition with the term *kḥš*.

Hosea 4:1-2.

> 1) Hear the word of YHWH, O people of Israel,
> for YHWH has a case (*rîḇ*) against
> the inhabitants of the land:
> for there is no integrity (*ʾᵉmɛṯ*) and no
> fidelity (*ḥɛsɛḏ*)[67]
> and no awareness of God in the land.

---

word in my affliction." Cf. Scharbert, *Biblica* 39, 1, p. 4: "Job beteuert, dass er durch eine *ʾālā* niemals das Leben eines Mitmenschen gefordert habe. *ʾālā* ist hier kein Fluchzauber durch den man jemandem schaden will..., sondern die Selbstverfluchung eines falschen Zeugen, der ein Todesurteil gegen einen Unschuldigen erzwingen will."

[67]Despite the interposition of *wᵉʾēn*, the two terms *ʾᵉmɛṯ* and *ḥɛsɛḏ*, constitute a case of hendiadys, the former

2) ʾālō wᵊkaḥeš,[68]

killing, stealing, and adultery
have broken all bounds,
and murder follows hard upon murder.

Ps. 59:13.

(For) the sin of their mouths, the words of their lips
may they be trapped in their arrogance

umēʾālā umikkaḥaš yᵊsappērū[69]

The confusion over the meaning of both passages is confounded by the fact that both verbs ʾālā and kiḥeš have been elusive in their connotations. Ehrlich, declaring, correctly that kiḥeš does not mean "to lie," prefers Veruntreuung (faithlessness) or Fehlgehen (going astray). The

---

defining the latter, the force being "constant/unwavering loyalty."

[68]AV, JPS, "swearing and lying"; RSV, "swearing, lying"; AT "cursing, lying"; SB "parjure et mensonge"; ATD "(Sie) fluchen und lügen"; LXX ʾΑρὰ , καὶ ψεῦδος ; Targ. yēmān lišqar wᵊkadbīn. Thus AT is supported by LXX and the other Vss. by Targ. as T. K. Cheyne (Hosea, Cambridge, 1889, p. 63): "The 'swearing' meant is of course 'false swearing.'" A. Ehrlich (Randglossen, Vol. V, p. 172) puts one in mind of a contemporary detective-story plot. Taking ʾālā as perjury and pointing out "kḥš aber heisst nicht lügen, sondern veruntreuen," he continues, "Danach ist der Sinn wie folgt: Meineid bei Veruntreuung und Mord bei Diebstahl und Ehebruch sind gang und gäbe oder nehmen überhand. Gemeint ist, dass der der Veruntreuung Angeklagte falsch schwört, um die Anklage zu entkräften, und der ertappte Dieb und Ehebrecher sich durch eine Mordtat retten."

[69]AV, JPS "for cursing and lying which they speak"; AT "for the curses and lies which they utter"; RSV "For the cursing and lying which they utter"; SB "pour le blasphème, pour le mensonge qu'ils débitent"; ATD "ob des Fluchs und der Lüge, welche sie reden"; LXX καὶ ἐξ ἀρᾶς καὶ ψεύδους διαγγελήσονται ; Targ. ʾarūm min mōmāṯā umin šiqrā yištaʿyān. A. Ehrlich, (Die Psalmen, p. 136) "und man sich von ihrem Fluche und seinem Fehlgehen erzähle." Scharbert (Biblica 39, 1, p. 4), "In Ps. 10, 7...und 59:13...kann es sich ebenfalls nur um einen Meineid handeln." E. J. Kissane (The Book of Psalms, Dublin: Browne & Nolan, 1954, Vol. 1, p. 264), emends the last word to yissāpū, rendering it "let them be caught."

meaning of kiḥeš, however, seems to lie closer to "deny falsely, dissemble" as in Genesis 18:5, where Sarah, having been caught out by YHWH in a jeer over the prediction that she will yet bear a son, dissembles or falsely denies her skepticism -- wattᵊkaḥeš śārā... The verb kiḥeš would appear to have just this force in Leviticus 5:21 ff., a passage dealing with false oaths in regard to property and atonement made for such oaths after restitution is made to the owner.

Lev. 5:21-24

> 21) If any one sins committing a trespass against YHWH in that he denies his fellow's claim (wᵊkiheš baᶜᵃmītō) in the matter of a bailment or security or robbery; or he has defrauded his fellowman; 22) or, having found a lost item and dissembled about it (wᵊkiḥeš bāh), swears falsely in regard to any one of such offenses which men commit ...

If kiḥeš is given this force, the sense of both passages is enhanced considerably. In Hosea, verse 1 receives its explication in verse 2. Thus 1) there is no honesty, no fidelity, no awareness of God: 2) accusations (by imprecatory adjuration), false denials/dissembling, murder, theft, obscene behavior break all bounds. In Psalm 59, despite the semantic-textual problems which remain, we would at least understand the conjunction of ʾālā and kaḥaš.

In support of this interpretation and against the standard translations and commentaries I would adduce the following considerations: 1) The verb ʾālā never appears with the force of "swearing," and 2) never with the sense of "perjury". 3) Cursing or imprecation, if circumstances warrant, is not in itself a moral breach. On the positive side, there is 4) the proved connection between ʾālā and theft or other crime, and 5) the excellent sense which <u>ʾālā</u> as adjuratory imprecation, involving accusation, yields in the context of <u>kiḥeš</u>.

The sense yielded above for <u>ʾālā</u> as a legitimate institution, which may, however, be employed deceitfully and as an instrument of oppression does full justice to

Ps. 10:7.

His mouth is filled with
<u>ʾālā</u>[70]
and deceit and oppression,
under his tongue are mischief and crookedness.

Against the traditional rendering is the consideration that mere "cursing" is not a natural member of a series which includes deceit and oppression, mischief and crookedness. On the other hand, all these terms are associated with the mouth and tongue. A conditional imprecation which, if it does nothing else, impugns the honesty of the person who is its target, fits the context admirably.

F. <u>Excursus on Exodus 20:7 and Psalm 24</u>.

The third "word" or "commandment" of the decalogue has long presented a semantic problem.

Exod. 20:7 (and Deut. 5:11)

You shall not take up the name of your God, YHWH,
<u>laššāwʾ</u>

---

[70]AV, JPS, RSV "cursing"; AT "curses"; SB "il maudit", attaching it to the end of verse 6 and making the preceding <u>ʾašɛr lōʾ bᵊrāʿ</u> its object; ATD "Fluch"; LXX ἀρᾶς; Targ. <u>lūṭīn</u>. Kissane in <u>The Book of Psalms</u>, Vol. I, pp. 39, 44, would emend <u>ʾlh</u> to <u>ʾēlek</u> and attach it to the preceding verse.

for YHWH will not acquit (/hold guiltless) anyone who takes up his name laššāwʾ.

In the Holiness Code, Lev. 19:12 explicitly forbids the taking of a false oath by God's name: wᵉlōʾ tiššābᵊʿū bišmī laššāqɛr. Does the command in Exod. 20:7 represent merely a stylistic variant of Lev. 19:12? If it does not, if laššāwʾ is not the same as laššāqɛr, what is the meaning of the prohibition?

The LXX rendering of laššāwʾ by ἐπὶ ματαίῳ "idly, in a trifling or meaningless way," suggests a definite distinction between šāwʾ and šɛqɛr = "false." Targum Onkelos renders the first laššāwʾ by lᵉmaggānā "in vain," and the second occurrence of the term by lᵉšiqrā "falsely." Rashi, in keeping with rabbinic tradition, says that the first laššāwʾ refers to an oath demonstrably false, such as swearing that a pillar of stone is actually a pillar of gold; the second laššāwʾ refers to a pointless oath, e. g. swearing that wood is wood, or that stone is stone.[71] Even in Rashi's first category it can be seen that a distinction is present between an oath laššāwʾ and what is normally understood by a false oath. Among modern commentators we may cite S. R. Driver who comments "take... [in vain] properly, take up...for unreality...i.e. make use of it for any idle, frivolous, or insincere purpose. The root idea of shāwʾ, is what is groundless or unsubstantial: hence in a material sense it means unreal, vain...and in a moral sense

[71] The Talmud lists two other categories of "vain" oaths: an oath to transgress a religious obligation, and an oath to perform an impossible act. Cf. Bab. Tal., Shebuoth, 25a, ff.

it denotes what is empty, frivolous, or insincere... God's name is to be treated with reverence..."[72] Pedersen assumes that the decalogue refers to false swearing, "Verbot und Warnung gegen das Falschschwören steht...in unmittelbarem Zusammenhang mit dem Verbot des Götzendienstes (Jer. 7, 9; vgl. Ex. 20, 7).[73] Ehrlich does not hesitate to confess, "Was hier verboten wird, ist nicht ganz klar. Wahrscheinlich steht tś' fur tś' ʿl śptyk, und lšw' heisst, wie Jer. 2, 30 und öfter, zwecklos, umsonst."[74]

It would appear that although the basic distinction between šāwʾ "vain" and sɛqɛr "false" is suggestive -- it can not in itself be regarded as decisive evidence that the decalogue does not refer to false oaths. Where the ninth commandment in the decalogue, Exod. 20:16, reads: "Thou shall not speak up against your neighbor as a false witness (ʿeḏ šāqɛr)," the corresponding precept in Deut. 5:18 is identical except for the last word which is šāwʾ.[75]

We may, however, find a clue to the problem in two questions. The first: if Exodus 20:7 does not refer to false oaths, how account for the omission from the decalogue of a proscription of a highly serious offense? The second

---

[72] S. R. Driver, The Book of Exodus (Cambridge: University Press, 1953), p. 196. Cf. also ATD "nicht zum Truge aussprechen," and explanation in commentary, "wie bei Zauberei, Wahrsagerei, Lästerung, Meineid."

[73] Johs. Pedersen, Der Eid bei den Semiten, p. 142.

[74] A. B. Ehrlich, Randglossen, Vol. I, p. 341 and cf. his discussion, not of prime importance here, continuing on pp. 342-43.

[75] Cf. also I Sam. 25:21 where laššɛqɛr appears in a context where one would normally expect laššāwʾ.

question, independent of the first: what is the need for the second clause in 20:7? Why, in connection with this prohibition alone, are the Israelites warned that "YHWH will not acquit (i. e., absolve from punishment) anyone who takes up his name laššāwʾ"?

A likely answer to the first question arises from the very nature of the oath: it is a conditional self-curse. If the asseveration implicit in the oath is false, the condition is thereby fulfilled, and the taker of the oath knows that he has thereby invoked a curse (ʾālā) upon himself. There is no need for a prohibition against a false oath, because self-interest alone would be enough to preclude it. The very nature of the oath -- for those who put any stock at all in its efficacy -- is that it has an inherent device (the ʾālā) which precludes a false statement.[76]

The answer to the second question may also provide the solution to the meaning of "Thou shall not take up my name laššāwʾ." What institution is there in Israel which is so closely akin to the oath as to be mistaken for it; which has so many feature in common with the oath that the same terms may be applied to both (nāśāʾ, bāʾ bᵊ-, hinnāqē min); and, finally, whose nature is such that one might think that one could employ it laššāwʾ, groundlessly, with-

---

[76]It is of interest that the prohibition against false swearing in Lev. 19:12 is tied in with the profanation of God's name, which is to say that the command is given not from the point of view of the taker of the oath, not with a primary concern for the penalty which he will incur; but from a theological point of view -- a concern that the name YHWH not be profaned.

out incurring punishment?

The institution is, of course, the *ʾālā*, the conditional curse, employed as an accusation of wrongdoing against one's fellowman. No more effective device for character assassination has been conceived than the *ʾālā* used *laššāwʾ*. Let us imagine an example. A invites B, against whom he harbors a secret spite, to his home. After B's departure, A pretends that a small but valuable item is missing. He "swears out" the *ʾālā*: "If A has taken my such-and-such may YHWH do this-and-that to him." B may feel compelled even to take an exculpatory oath in denial of the charge, without proving his innocence conclusively. Yet A acts with impunity. Should the truth become known, what, after all, has he done? He has not uttered a curse. He said merely that *if*... It is against such a groundless *ʾālā* that warning would have to be given: Despite the fact that the words of the *ʾālā* are, technically, free from falsehood -- the intent is evil, the taking up of YHWH's name is unwarranted, *laššāwʾ* -- and YHWH will, though men may not, see to it that he is punished.

The force of *ʾālā* as unwarranted conditional imprecation was originally discerned, to be sure, in Hosea 4:1-2, Psalm 59:13 and Psalm 10:7. If, however, the above solution be accepted for the meaning of Exodus 20:7, it would, in turn reinforce the interpretation of *ʾālā* in those three passages. And, finally, it becomes clear how close the traditional translations of *ʾālā* by "false swearing, perjury" come to the meaning of the term -- and how far away they remain.

Our attention turns now to Psalm 24.[77]

1) A mizmor of David's
The earth is YHWH's and the fullness thereof
the world and those who dwell therein;
2) For it is He who founded it upon the seas,
and fixed it firmly upon the floods
3) Who may ascend the mountain of YHWH's?
and who will stand in his holy place?
4) He whose hands are innocent of wrongdoing
and whose heart is pure

ʾašɛr lōʾ nāśāʾ laššāwʾ napšō [Qᵊrē:napšī]

and has not sworn deceitfully
5) He will receive a blessing from YHWH
uṣᵊdāqā from God who grants him victory
6) This is the generation of those who seek him
who seek thy presence [Gk: O God of] Jacob.

The relevance of this psalm to this study centers, immediately, around the second half of verse 4, and particularly around the first clause of the second half-verse. Two problems present themselves. First, which is original, the Kᵊtīb: napšō (his life, soul), or the Qᵊrē: napšī (my life, soul)? If it is the latter, the speaker could only be YHWH and the reference only to Exod. 20:7. Second, supposing the Qᵊrē to be original, in what sense is it to be taken? Does the pronominal suffix ("his") refer to the subject of nāśāʾ, in which case the meaning of the phrase would be the negative correspondence to Ps. 25:1 (ʾēlɛkā

77"Psalm 24" as discussed here refers only to verses 1-6. Most modern commentators regard vv. 1-6 and vv. 7-10 as representing two originally separate compositions. Thus G.H.A. v. Ewald regards vv. 7-10 as the song of victory sung when the Ark of the Covenant was removed to Zion (II Sam. 6); and vv. 1-6 as a purely didactic song. Commentary on the Psalms, transl. by E. Johnson (London: Williams & Norgate, 1880), Vol. I, p. 82. This opinion is quoted and accepted by Franz Delitzsch (The Psalms, transl. by Francis Bolton, Edinburgh: T. & T. Clark, 1871), Vol. I, p. 334. T. K. Cheyne: "Two striking little chants." The Book of Psalms (London: Paul, Trench, Trubner, 1904), Vol. I, p.101.

YHWH napšī ʾeśśāʾ "to thee, O YHWH, do I lift up my soul") i.e. who has not lifted up his soul to vanity (false values, or even false gods)? Or could napšō refer to YHWH and the reference be to Exod. 20:7.

Jewish tradition, of course, accepts the Qᵊrē. Targum Jonathan renders dᵊlāʾ ʾōmē ʿal šiqrā lᵊḥay(y)āḇā napšēh "who has not sworn falsely incurring guilt/penalty." Rashi, taking the phrase in the sense of Exodus 20:7, refers to Amos 6:8 where nišbāʿ ʾᵃdōnāy YHWH bᵊnapšō "the Lord YHWH has sworn by his life," shows beyond a doubt that napšī is a simple alternate to šᵊmi. Ibn Ezra indicates that even the Kᵊṯīḇ would refer to the deity. LXX renders the clause according to the Kᵊṯīḇ: ὃς οὐκ ἔλαβεν ἐπὶ ματαίῳ τὴν ψυχὴν αὐτοῦ,[78] but it may be of significance that whereas it renders nāśāʾ here by the same verb as in Exod. 20:7, in Ps. 25:1 it employs ἦρα to render ʾeśśāʾ. JPS translates, "who hath not taken My name in vain." Most translations, on the other hand, accept the Qᵊrē and render laššāwʾ by "unto vanity" (AV), "to what is false" (RSV), "aux vanités" (SB), ATD "nach Bösem."

The parallelism of the second clause of the half-verse wᵊlōʾ nišbaʿ lᵊmirmā "and has not sworn deceitfully," virtually guarantees that the first clause is a reference to the prohibition of Exodus 20:7. It will further be argued that verse 4 is the key to the understanding of the entire psalm (vv. 1-6), which is to say that the psalm is

[78]Except for Cod. Alex. which reads τὴν ψυχήν μου.

not merely "a poem of didactic character,"[79] but has as its Sitz-im-Leben the misuse of the ʾālā and the šᵊbūʿā.

It may not be inappropriate to raise a number of questions about the semantic unity of the psalm: 1) What does YHWH's ownership of the world have to do with the character of the person who may ascend YHWH's holy mountain? 2) What is the significance of the juxtaposition of "hands innocent of wrong-doing" and "pure heart," and the relation of these qualities with the specific and defined content of verse 4? 3) Is there any particular reason why this person should carry off a bᵊrākā rather than another expression for "reward"? 4) What is the meaning of the ṣᵊdāqā which is parallel to bᵊrākā? The traditional translation "righteousness" is surely pointless; and if the well-attested meaning "vindication" (so RSV) is correct here, vindication in regard to what? 5) Finally, what in the context of the foregoing, is the meaning or significance of this being the generation which "seeks" YHWH?

The suggested interpretation of this psalm is as follows. Its Sitz-im-Leben is the ʾālā as imprecatory adjuration or prayer publicly pronounced against a supposed malefactor -- an institution lending itself to misuse or abuse, the latter specifically prohibited in Exodus 20:7. The association of the ʾālā with YHWH's temple in Jerusalem is explicit in I Kings 8:31-32 (see above, p.52 f.)

Verses 1-2 introduce the theme of the psalm: property. The world and all its contents are the property of

---

[79]See above, note 77 and cf. ATD, "Dass Lied... gehört vermutlich zur Liturgie des Herbstfestes..."

YHWH, for it is he (and not Marduk or Aššur as in the Babylonian or Assyrian versions of the *Enuma eliš* epic) who has founded it firmly upon the nether waters. As the ultimate owner, distributor, and legitimizer of property,

(Verse 3) YHWH will not tolerate in his sanctuary any thief or cheat. He will permit only that person

(Verse 4) who is innocent of actual malfeasance and free of deceitful intent (*ba*(?)*r lēḇāḇ*), *i.e.*, one who neither employs an empty/unwarranted *ʾālā* against his fellow, nor swears deceitfully. Note that the latter refers not to a false oath but to a misleading one, in which the asseveration of the oath is technically true but cunningly evades the issue.

(Verse 5) The *bᵊrāḵā* "blessing," which the honest man carries away with him from YHWH's temple is the antonymous contrast to the curse (non-explicitly, but certainly present) of the *ʾālā*; and *ṣᵊḏāqā* is his vindication of the charge of the *ʾālā*, at the hands of *ʾᵉlōhē yišʿō* God who delivers him/makes him triumphant. (Cf. in I Kings 8:32 *lᵊharšīʿ rāšāʿ*...*ulᵊhaṣdīq ṣaddīq lāṯeṯ lō kᵊṣiḏqāṯō*.)

(Verse 6) *zɛ dōr dōršāw* is not merely a protestation of piety, a declaration of longing for communion with God, but, rather, *dāraš* is used in its technical force, to seek an oracle (here an oracular verdict) from God. This is the generation that looks to Him for his victory-assuring favor.

So interpreted, the six verses constitute a logically ordered unit which is, except for poetic parallelism, free of redundancy.

G. The "flying ʾālā" in Zechariah 5:1-4.

One of the visions seen by Zechariah and interpreted for him by the angel of YHWH is a scroll (mᵊgillā) of enormous dimensions flying through the air. This scroll, says the angel, represents the ʾālā which is going out over all the land. "I have sent it forth," says YHWH, "and it shall enter the house of the thief and of him who swears falsely by my name; and, lodging in his house, it will destroy it down to the timber and stones."

The difficulty in the text, centering around the interpretation of kī kol haggōneḇ mizzē kāmōhā niqqā wᵊkol hannišbaᶜ mizzē kāmōhā niqqā in verse 3[80] does not seriously affect our study of the ʾālā.[81] The "curse" is written on a scroll, comparable to the document (sep̄er) upon which the sanctions of the covenant (ʾālōṯ habbᵊrīṯ) were inscribed (see above p. 9). The embodiment or personification of the ʾālā here is obviously a poetic conceit and the text hardly warrants reading any additional significance into a figure of speech.

We may cite Scharbert, as the most recent commentator on this verse.

---

[80]For a detailed discussion of the problem and the various solutions offered, see the discussion by H. G. Mitchell in Haggai and Zecharia, ICC, (New York: Ch. Scribner's Sons, 1912) pp. 168-171. The problem, briefly, centers on the force of niqqā -- whether it is past or future in tense, with the respective alternatives in meaning of "to have gone unpunished" or "to be expiated"; and whether mizzē means "from this time on" or whether together with the following kāmōhā is to be emended to zē kammē (as in 7:2) "already how long."

[81]Renderings: AV, JPS, AT, RSV "the curse"; SB "la malédiction"; ATD "der Fluch"; LXX ἡ ἀρά; Targ. dā mōmāṯā.

> Hier sind einfürallemal Flüche über Diebe, Meineidige, und andere Übeltäter in einem himmlischen Buch schriftlich verzeichnet, die dann aktualisiert werden, sobald sich jemand eines Rechtsbruches schuldig macht. Damit ist in prophetischer Darstellungsweise das Axiom von der immanenten Sanktion des Sittengesetzes ausgesprochen, das besagt: Ein Vergehen gegen die sittliche Ordnung wirkt sich mit inneres Folgerichtigkeit für den Frevler selbst zum Schaden aus.[82]

What may, at the risk of prolixity, be stressed here is the intimate association of ʾālā with property-offenses and the taking of false oaths, the latter being surely of an exculpatory nature. It would be difficult to exaggerate the extent to which the ʾālā as accusatory conditional imprecation, and the šᵊḇūʿā as exculpatory conditional self-curse were employed in ancient Israel in connection with disputes over property.

The noun *taʾᵃlā appears only once, in Lam. 3:65, with the pronominal suffix of the second person (taʾᵃlāṯᵊḵā). Even if derived from ʾālā "curse," it would possess little value for our study. The weight of the evidence, however, indicates a derivation from another stem. LXX renders it by μόχθον (toil, distress, trouble), as in Lam. 3:5 it renders uṯlāʾā by ἐμόχθησεν. The Targum also renders the noun in both passages by a form of šlʾh (to weary). Rashi understands the term to derive from ʾūl/yʾl and refers to the niphʿal nōʾᵃlū (to become foolish) in Is. 19:13. The context too offers little support for a term as strong as "curse." All things considered, therefore, we are offered little choice but to let the passage lie undisturbed.

---

[82] Biblica, Vol. 39 (1958), p. 3.

IV. SUMMARY

The term *ʾālā* has the basic force of curse, in the sense of imprecation or malediction, which is to say curse as approached from the point of view of pronouncement/utterance, vocal or recorded in writing. As such it is present, explicitly or implicitly, in every *šᵉḇūʿā* "oath" which by definition is a conditional self-curse; and similarly -- and in turn -- in every *bᵉrīṯ* "covenant" which is by definition an agreement solemnized by oath(s). When joined to *šᵉḇūʿā* or *bᵉrīṯ* by the conjunctive *waw*, the conjunction is invariably a hendiadys with the force of the imprecation/sanction guarding the statement in the oath or the terms of the covenant. When appearing independently, *ʾālā* may stand for both *šᵉḇūʿā* and *bᵉrīṯ* by synecdoche of the part for the whole; as, indeed, *šᵉḇūʿā* occasionally stands for *ʾālā* by synecdoche of the whole for the part.

As an institution kindred to the *šᵉḇūʿā* but independent of it, the *ʾālā* is an adjuration or conditional curse addressed to another in the second or third person, for the purpose of evoking a desired action or precluding an anticipated action; or it is a conditional imprecation, basically a prayer-form, addressed to the deity, and asking for punishment of a malefactor whose guilt cannot be proved. When publicly pronounced, in the temple of YHWH or elsewhere, such an *ʾālā* *ipso facto* constituted an accusation of wrongdoing. Since the person employing the *ʾālā* in such a manner made no unconditional statement of fact, it was thought the *ʾālā* could be used with impunity to impugn the character of an innocent person. The absence from the decalogue of a clear prohibition against false swearing (a prohibition understood as rendered unnecessary by the very nature of the oath as self-curse), and the known distinction between the term *šɛqɛr* "false" and *šāwʾ* "empty/baseless," suggests that the third statement of the decalogue constitutes a prohibition against the use of an unwarranted *ʾālā*, and warns that such use of an *ʾālā* invoking the name YHWH will be punished by YHWH. In the light of this suggestion, verses 1 to 6 of Psalm 24 are interpreted as a poem whose *Sitz-im-Leben* is the sanctuary on Zion where, by means of his oracular response(s) to the contents of *šᵊḇūʿā* and *ʾālā*,[83] YHWH vindicated the innocent and condemned the guilty.

In a few instances *ʾālā* stands for the material curse (misfortune) itself, or the person suffering a curse, by metonymy of cause for effect.

V. AKKADIAN *māmītu*

The Akkadian noun *māmītu*, cognate to Aramaic *mōmāṯā* by which the Targumim render Hebrew *ʾālā*, conveys unquestionably the meanings of both "curse/ban" and "oath." Which one of these meanings, however, is primary, and which secondary? Pedersen seems to regard "oath" as the primary meaning.[84] The primary term for "oath," however, despite

---

[83]The phrase "oracular response(s)" is not to be understood as necessarily implying a spoken judgment. The judgment of YHWH may very likely have been seen in the fortunes of accuser and accused subsequent to the appeal made in the sanctuary.

[84]"*Māmītu* bezeichnet nicht nur, was wir unter Eid verstehen; es kommt ebenso häufig in der Bedeutung Besessenheit oder Fluch vor, und dies ist wichtig für unser

its occasional metonymic extension to mean "curse,"[85] must be nīš (ili or šarri) "by the life of (god or king)," analagous to the Hebrew oath-formula ḥē-hammɛlɛḵ or ḥay-YHWH.[86] It would seem that māmītu, having the same semantic range as Hebrew ʾālā, might yield to the very analysis that has herein been applied to the ʾālā, i.e. that māmītu has "curse" as its basic meaning, and particularly with the force of "imprecation, malediction;"[87] that it came to have the force of "oath" by synecdoche of the part for the whole; and by metonymy of cause for effect, received the meaning of "curse" in its material, operative, sense.

Erica Reiner in the Commentary on the edition and translation of Šurpu has this to say of māmītu.

> māmītu has been translated throughout this tablet wherever else it occurs in Šurpu as "oath." This is the first meaning of the word, and is clearly its meaning in the first thirteen lines of this tablet Tablet III . In its other occurrences in Šurpu, as in religious texts in general, māmītu means something evil. This meaning can be defined more closely precisely from this tablet which lists various actions and objects known to be connected with taking an oath. We suppose, then, that those māmītu's too whose significance escapes us refer to symbols and symbolic actions accompanying an oath. It was feared, it appears from this tablet, that the numen inherent in

---

Verständnis des assyrischen Eides. Gelegentlich wird es von der mit dem Eid eingegangenen Verpflichtung gebraucht." (Der Eid bei den Semiten), p. 2.

85As e.g. in Šurpu V-VI 67, (ditto: 77, 87, 97, 117, etc.), VII 28. All references to Šurpu are to the edition by Erica Reiner, AfO, Beiheft 11 (1958).

86Cf. the discussion of E. A. Speiser, "Nuzi Marginalia," Orientalia, Vol. 25, fasc. 1 (1956), pp. 21-23.

87This force is virtually certified by etymology. As indicated in the Introduction (see above, p. 17), derived from amū/awū, its original sense must have been close to "solemn pronouncement."

these, once invoked, would stay unbound and afflict the person who had sworn the oath.[88]

Since the thesis presented here is that "oath" is not "the first meaning of the word" *māmītu*, we shall have to examine the first thirteen lines of Tablet III in Dr. Reiner's translation and see whether "oath" is "clearly its *māmītu*'s meaning."

1. Incantation. The effect of any *māmītu* this man, son of his god, is under (m...*ša*... *iṣbatū*).
2. *Asalluhi*, exorcist among the gods, will undo;
3. the *māmītu* of father and mother he is under (*ṣabat[i]*),
4. the *māmītu* of his father's father, the oath of his mother's mother,
5. the *māmītu* of brother or sister,
6. the *māmītu* of seven generations of (his) father's house he is under
7. the *māmītu* of old or young,
8. the *māmītu* of family or in-laws,
9. the *māmītu* of offspring or sucklings,
10. the *māmītu* of friend or companion,
11. the *māmītu* of comrade or associate,
12. true or false *māmītu* (*m*. *ketti* *u* *sarti*)
13. heavy or light *māmītu* (*m*. *kabitti* *u* *qallati*)

The analysis of the oath (see above p.23 and 24) as conditional self-curse disclosed that it involves I) an utterance -- asseveration or promise; II) a sanction invoked upon the person making the utterance; III) the power invoked to effectuate the sanction. None of the nouns in the lines above can refer to III, for the powers invoked to effectuate the sanctions are limited as far as we can tell to a magical agency, god(s), or king. (Cf. below p. 153 f). The substantives in line 9 rule out I altogether, for sucklings do not speak. Normally II would rule out the possibility of oath here in any case, since the person making the utterance is the one who is to be affected by the sanc-

---

[88] *Šurpu*, p. 55, col. 2.

tion. We know, however, that the imprecation upon self may extend to include people and objects dearer than self (hence such oaths as "upon my child's head," "upon my mother's grave" etc.). This possibility is, nevertheless, ruled out by lines 10 and 11 for the relationships here are too distant to be meaningful in such use.

It has been further suggested that one is never, properly speaking "under" or "clutched by" (ṣabit) an oath, but rather under the power, gripped by the power, of the curse part of an oath. And, with reference to line 2, the function of an exorcist is not to annul oaths but to loosen (puššuru) the grip of misfortune, curse. Thus, the sense of "curse" for māmītu is as apposite in the context above as "oath" is irrelevant. The substantives associated with the māmītu's would then not be "symbols and symbolic actions accompanying an oath," but people or things to whom (/which) the curse (māmītu) is in some way etiologically related. Indeed, lines 54 ff. are virtually explicit in relating the māmītu to the violation of ethical norms, transgressions of divine commands, and ritual or cultic trespass.[89]

In Maqlū V 72 the sorcerer is accused ina nīši u māmīt tuqattainni ina nīši u māmīt pagarkunu liqtī, which Meier renders, "Durch Eid und Bann wolltet ihr mich vernichten: durch Eid und Bann nehme euer Leib ein Ende!"[90] What-

---

[89]It must be said that l. 12 (māmīt ketti u sarti) fits "oath" better than it does "curse." But the contrast of opposites as in l. 13 indicates that this may be a "literary" or formulaic device. In any case, why should an oath which is true or "firm" (kettu) result in misfortune?

[90]Gerhard Meier, Die assyrische Beschwörungssamlung Maqlū, (AfO, Beiheft 2, 1937), p. 37.

ever is meant by the conjunction of the two terms in the context of sorcery, there can be no doubt that in the following line the meaning is "a curse contracted in connection with oath or prayer": *Maqlu* VII 134 *māmīt nīš ili nīš qātā*^{II} *māmīt*.[91]

It would seem that the cause of the perplexity concerning the meaning of *māmītu* is exactly that which lies behind the problem of *ʾālā*, namely the metonymic extension (by synecdoche of the part for the whole) of the basic term for "imprecation" to stand for "oath," and in turn for "compact, covenant, treaty." Thus the basic Akkadian terms for "curse," "oath," "pact" (Hebrew, respectively *ʾālā*, *šᵊbūʿā*, *bᵊrīt*) would appear to be, respectively *māmītu*, *nīš*(*ili*), *adē*.[92] Thus in such expressions as *etepuš* [*m*]*āmīta*,[93] *la itter māmīta*,[94] *itmūni u ištanī māmīta ina bērišunu*[95] there can be no question but that the concept involved is either an oath or a pact. But in the oft-occurring expression *adē*

---

[91]Rendered by Meier " Bann durch Eid bei einem Gott, durch Eid bei der Schwurhand." (*AfO*, Beiheft 2), p. 51.

[92]D. J. Wiseman, *The Vassal-Treaties of Esarhaddon* (London: British School of Archaeology in Iraq, 1958), translates *adē* by "treaty, treaty-terms, vassal-treaty stipulations" (p. 3). Cf. his discussion of the terminology used in connection with *adē*, and "the more exact meaning" of the term: "a law or commandment solemnly imposed in the presence of divine witnesses [actually the powers invoked to effectuate the sanctions] by a suzerain upon an individual or people who have no option but acceptance of the terms. It implies a 'solemn charge or undertaking on oath'..." (P. 81, n. 1).

[93]TA 67, l. 13 rendered by Knudtzon, "er hat einen Schwur-Bund gemacht."

[94]TA 148, ll. 36-37. Knudtzon: "so hat er nicht *erfüllt* den Schwurbund."

[95]TA 149, ll. 59-60. Knudtzon: "haben geschworen

u māmīt Speiser has noted that we are confronted by a case of hendiadys.[96] He compares the expression to ʾālōṯ habbᵊrīṯ in Deut. 29:20, and suggests "pact adjurations." It would appear, however, that a closer parallel would be Deut. 29:11 (bi)ḇrīṯ (YHWH) u(ḇᵊʾ)ālā(ṯō), and the force of the Akkadian, "a curse/sanction-guarded pact."

It may be noted, in conclusion, that whereas Hebrew ʾālā occurs in the majority of cases with the force of "imprecation" and a few times with the force of a material "curse," Akkadian māmītu occurs very frequently in the sense of the operative curse itself derived though it is from a stem meaning "to speak, utter."

---

und den Schwurbund wiederholt untereinander."

[96]"An Angelic 'Curse': Exodus 19:20," JAOS, (July-Sept. 1960), p. 198, n. 1.

CHAPTER III

THE STEM ʾrr

I. PASSIVE PARTICIPLE ʾārūr, AS RUBRIC IN IMPRECATIONS.

Every scholar who has had occasion to comment on biblical passages dealing with curses has noted that the most common rubric introducing a malediction is the qal passive participle of the verb ʾrr. This first section will deal with those texts in which ʾārūr appears in a context so general as not to provide any clues to a connotation narrower or more specific than the general sense "cursed" = destined for misfortune.

Thus in Isaac's blessing of Jacob little can be deduced about ʾrr except its antonymous relationship to brk.

Gen. 27:29.

ʾōrᵊrε̄ḵā ʾārūr[1]

and blessed be they who bless you.

In Balaam's blessing of Israel the formula is identical except for the reversed order of the phrases.

Num. 24:9.

Blessed be they who bless you,

---

[1]AV, JPS "Cursed be everyone that curses you"; AT "Cursed be they who curse you"; RSV "Cursed be everyone who curses you"; SB "Maudit soit qui te maudira"; ATD "Verflucht seien, die dich verfluchen"; LXX ὁ καταρώμενός σε ἐπικατάρατος ; Targ. līṭāḵ yᵊhōn līṭīn.

<u>wᵊʾōrᵊrɛ̄ḵā ʾārūr.</u>[2]

In Deuteronomy 27, the ʾārūr rubric is again employed with self-sufficient force against anyone who will be guilty of specific breaches of various provisions of the covenant.

Deut. 27:15-26.

15) ʾārūr[3] be the man who makes a graven or molten image...[4]
16) ʾārūr be he who dishonors his father or mother...
17) ʾārūr be he who removes his neighbor's landmark...
18) ʾārūr be he who misleads a blind man on the road...
19) ʾārūr be he who perverts the justice due to the alien, widow, or orphan...
20) ʾārūr be he who lies with his father's wife...
21) ʾārūr be he who lies with any beast...
22) ʾārūr be he who lies with his sister...
23) ʾārūr be he who lies with his mother-in-law...
24) ʾārūr be he who attacks his fellow clandestinely...
25) ʾārūr be he who takes a bribe that an innocent man may be slain...
26) ʾārūr be he who does not fulfill in his actions the words of this tōrā.

In Deuteronomy 28, the ʾārūr rubric is supplemented by the areas in which the curse will be operative; in effect the passage expresses the ubiquity of the curse: in

---

[2]The versions are substantially the same as on the previous verse.

[3]Eng. vss. "cursed"; SB "maudit"; HAT "zum Fluch"; LXX Ἐπικατάρατος ; Targ. liṭ.

[4]Each imprecatory pronouncement is followed by the response "Amen," on the part of the Israelites. For similar features in the conclusion of Hittite and Assyrian treaties, cf. G. E. Mendenhall, "Covenant Forms in Israelite Tradition," B. A. XVII, pp. 50-76, and D. J. Wiseman, The Vassal-Treaties of Esarhaddon, p. 26.

every enterprise connected with the necessities of life, fertility, and the conduct of the affairs of the polity.

Deut. 28:16-20.

16) ʾārūr[5] shall you be in the city and ʾārūr in the countryside.
17) ʾārūr shall be your harvest-basket and your kneading-trough.
18) ʾārūr shall be the fruit of your body and the fruit of your soil, the increase of your herds and the young of your flocks.
19) ʾārūr shall you be in your coming in and ʾārūr shall you be in your going out.[6]

After the destruction of Jericho, Joshua pronounces an ʾālā (wayyašbaᶜ)[7] invoking YHWH's punishment on anyone who will undertake to rebuild Jericho.

Josh. 6:26.

... ʾārūr[8]

at the instance of YHWH (lipnē YHWH)[9] be the man who ventures to rebuild this city, Jericho. At the cost of his first born shall he lay its foundation, and at the cost of his youngest son shall he rear its gates.

---

[5]The versions substantially the same as cited in note 3. HAT "verflucht."

[6]For the meaning of this verse, cf. E. A. Speiser, "'Coming' and 'Going' at the 'City' Gate," BASOR, No. 144 (Dec. 1956), pp. 20-23.

[7]See above p. 22 f. It is noteworthy that wayyašbaᶜ is intransitive. Properly speaking there is no adjuration here, but only an imprecation upon anyone who anytime in the future will rebuild Jericho. The effectuation of the ʾālā is narrated in I Kings 16:34. The renderings of wayyašbaᶜ: AV "adjured them"; JPS "Charged the people with an oath" [despite the absence of ʾeṯ hāᶜām]; AT "had an oath taken"; RSV "laid an oath upon them"; SB "fit prononcer ce serment"; ATD "liess J. (das Volk) folgenden Schwurtun"; LXX καὶ ὅρκισεν ; Targ. wᵊʾōmī.

[8]Eng. vss. "Cursed"; SB "maudit"; ATD "Verflucht"; LXX ἐπικατάρατος ; Targ. liṭ.

[9]For this force cf. Num. 14:37, 32:20 ff.

In I Samuel 14, King Saul, in his eagerness to inflict maximal losses on the routed Philistines, seeks to insure an unflagging pursuit of the enemy by an ʾ<u>ālā</u> (<u>wayyōʾɛl</u>) pronounced against an Israelite who eats before evening.

I Sam. 14:24.

...ʾ<u>ārūr</u>[10]

be the man who partakes of food before evening,
when I shall be avenged on my enemies...

The specific meaning of ʾ<u>ārūr</u> in this passage eludes us but not the awful inexorability of the curse once pronounced. Jonathan, unaware of the solemn prohibition, tastes honey, and God's displeasure becomes known when he refuses an answer to a question put to his oracle. When the offense is traced to Jonathan's action Saul announces -- sadly -- that Jonathan must die. It would be wrong, however, to assume from this narrative that ʾ<u>ārūr</u> necessarily involves a sentence of death. Ample evidence to the contrary will be presented in the next section. Furthermore, the death sentence against the offender may be traced not to the ʾ<u>ārūr</u>-formula which is general, but to verse 39, an oath taken by Saul (after he has learned that an offense of some sort has been committed) to the effect that the offender will die -- be he even his own son Jonathan.

In Jeremiah 11 the ʾ<u>ārūr</u> rubric spoken by YHWH against violators of his covenant, can only be understood as a

---

[10]Eng. vss. "Cursed"; SB "Maudit"; ATD "Verflucht"; LXX ἐπικατάρατος ; Targ. <u>lîṭ</u>.

statement of fact or a decree, but hardly as a wish.

Jer. 11:3...Thus says YHWH, the God of Israel,

<u>ʾārūr</u>[11]

is the man who does not obey the words of this covenant.

Just what <u>ʾārūr</u> can mean as applied to a day, as it is in Jeremiah 20, is difficult to conceive, although it is clear enough that Jeremiah's basic idea is the wish that he had never been born. The second <u>ʾārūr</u>, applied to the man who brought the glad tidings of the birth of a son, can be regarded only as poetic hyperbole unless we are willing to impute to the prophet an imprecation against a well-intentioned innocent.

Jer. 20:14-16.

14) <u>ʾārūr</u>[12]

the day on which I was born!
The day my mother bore me --
may it not be blessed!

15) <u>ʾārūr</u>

the man who brought the news to my father,
"A son has been born to you -- a male,"
making him rejoice indeed.

16) May that man be like the cities
which the Lord mercilessly overthrew;
May he hear a cry of anguish in the morning
and an alarm at noonday...

Unquestionably out of place and interrupting the flow of a pericope on Moab is

---

[11] Eng. vss. "Cursed (be)"; SB "Maudit (soit)"; KAT "verflucht(ist)"; LXX ἐπικατάρατος; Targ. <u>lîṭ</u>.

[12] Eng. vss. "Cursed be"; SB "maudit soit"; KAT "Verflucht"; LXX ἐπικατάρατος ; Targ. <u>lîṭ</u>. And so, also in v. 15. Scharbert: "In Jer 20, 14 f allerdings ist das <u>ʾārūr</u> zu einem blossen Affektausbruch abgeblasst." (<u>Biblica</u>, Vol. 39, fasc 1), p. 7.

Jer. 48:10.

> <u>ʾārūr</u>[13]
>
> is he who is slack in doing the work of YHWH,
>
> <u>wᵊʾārūr</u>
>
> is he who keeps back his sword from shedding blood.

In Malachi 1, since YHWH is speaking, the <u>ʾārūr</u> should be taken as a pronouncement of doom rather than as a wish.

Mal. 1:14.

> <u>wᵊʾārūr</u>
>
> is the conniver, who has a male in his flock, but vows and sacrifices one that is blemished ...[14]

II. <u>ʾārūr</u> IN ITS BASIC DISCERNIBLE SENSE

The English term "curse," in its material sense, has a broad connotation ranging from a simple synonym for misfortune to a condition of unrelieved hopelessness brought on by supernatural forces, magical or divine. The contexts in which <u>ʾārūr</u> occurs, however, provide adequate evidence that the term has its own specific denotation. This can be discerned in several striking passages in Genesis.

God's sentence pronounced upon the serpent for his part in "man's first disobedience" is told in:

---

[13]The renderings substantially the same as in note 12.

[14]The renderings of <u>ʾārūr</u> as above note 12.

Genesis 3:14.

> Thereupon YHWH, God, said to the serpent,
> "For having done this,
>   *ʾārūr ʾattā mikkol*[15] beasts
>   and all the animals of the steppe;
> Upon your belly shall you move,
>   and earth shall you eat
>   all the days of your life.

The traditional translations of *ʾārūr mi(n)-* (as AT's "most cursed of," in particular) require the assumption that all the beasts were cursed. Such an assumption has no basis whatever in the biblical narrative. What the text does explicitly state is a manner of differentiation between the serpent and all other species of animals. Whereas all other species have legs for locomotion and feed on vegetation, the serpent is deprived of his limbs and sentenced to eat earth. E. A. Speiser, in the most recent comment on the verse, expresses it this way: "With the preposition (*mi(n)*) the verb *ʾārar* denotes 'to anathematize, ban'." Thus in Gen. 3:14, ...the traditional translation 'cursed...are you above all...the beasts of the field' is totally out of place, since the other animals have done nothing to draw a curse upon themselves. What the syntax and context require is 'you are banned from all the other animals.'[16] Apparently the first to feel the inadequacy of the traditional translation was Johs. Pedersen, who, influenced by the Arabic analogy of punishing an offender by expelling him from his tribe, writes concerning this verse,

---

[15]AV "thou *art* cursed above all"; JPS "cursed art thou from among all"; AT "the most cursed of all"; SB "Maudit sois-tu entre tous"; ATD "sei verflucht vor allem"; LXX ἐπικατάρατος σὺ ἀπὸ ; Targ. *lîṭ ʾat mikkol*.

[16]*JAOS*, Vol. 80, No. 3 (July-Sept. 1960), 198.

"das bedeutet: du bist aus der Gesellschaft, zu der du gehörst, verstossen."[17]

We are now in a better position to understand another passage where <u>ʾārūr</u> occurs again with the preposition <u>mi</u>(<u>n</u>). Addressing Cain, who has denied knowledge of his brother's whereabouts, YHWH retorts that Abel's blood, shed by Cain, is crying out to him (for redress) from the ground, and proceeds to pass sentence.

Gen. 4:11.

11) Now, therefore,

<u>ʾārūr</u> <u>ʾattā</u> <u>min</u>[18]

the earth which has opened its mouth to receive from your hand the blood of your brother.

One wonders just what the traditional "cursed from the ground" was understood to convey. Pedersen, though not improving on the translation (he renders "verflucht von"), explains that "<u>ʾārar</u> <u>min</u> bedeutet hier ganz deutlich 'ausstossen aus', und es ist die Rede von einer Ausstossung aus seinem Stammgebiet."[19] Pedersen's explanation thus elicits some sense from the expression, as do the paraphrases of AT "cursed shall you be in banishment from," and SB "sois maudit et chassé du (sol fertile)." The objection to a paraphrase, however, is that the insertion of an ele-

---

[17]<u>Der Eid bei den Semiten</u>, p. 68. Scharbert cites and accepts Pedersen's interpretation.

[18]AV, JPS "thou art cursed from"; RSV "you are cursed from"; ATD "verflucht seist du von"; LXX ἐπικατάρατος σὺ ἀπὸ ; Targ. <u>līṭ</u> <u>ʾat</u> <u>min</u>.

[19]<u>Der Eid bei den Semiten</u>, p. 68.

ment which does not occur in the original leaves the suspicion that the force of the original may not have been wholly grasped. And the objection to Pedersen's interpretation is that the force of "expulsion" (ausstossen) is not borne out in the other occurrences (see, e.g., the following discussion on Gen. 3:17-18). Furthermore, to trace the force of the verb to the specific "Rede von einer Ausstossung aus einem Stammgebiet" would require more evidence than Pedersen is able to adduce. It would seem, therefore, that Speiser's suggestion is the one which most satisfactorily supplies both the basic force and a meaningful translation: "The...basic meaning of supernatural spell underlies Heb. *ʾārar* in several unambiguous passages...in Gen. 4:11, ...both the plain text and sense agree on 'you are banned from the soil'."[20]

Actually the ban is not from contact with the soil, but from enjoyment of its productivity. Verse 12 makes it clear that Cain, who was hitherto a tiller of the soil, will now find only frustration in his labors and will, perforce, become a homeless fugitive. "When you till the earth, it shall no longer yield its vigor to you -- a wandering fugitive shall you be on the earth."

Further support for *ʾārūr* with the force of "to be in the grip of a spell," or literally "spellbound" is provided in YHWH's sentencing of the man for his disobedience.

---

[20] *JAOS*, Vol. 80, No. 3, 198.

Gen. 3:17-18.

17) ...Because you obeyed your wife's bidding and ate of the tree of which I expressly enjoined you not to eat

ʾᵃrūrā[21]

is the earth on account of you. By travail shall you eat of it all the days of your life; 18) thorns and thistles shall it sprout for you and the plants of the steppe shall you eat.[22]

The penalty imposed on the man is almost identical to that which in 4:11 is pronounced against Cain. In both instances the earth will not respond to cultivation, yielding nothing to Cain, and little to "the man." But whereas in Chapter 4, ʾārūr is applied to Cain, here it is applied to the soil. Precisely speaking, the earth cannot even "be banned," as, despite the traditional translations, it certainly is not "cursed." The only sense which can apply to the term ʾārūr in both passages with equal meaningfulness is "to lie under a spell or ban." In 4:11 the spell is on Cain, barring (or banning) him from the earth's fertility; in 3:17-18 the spell is on the soil, rendering it recalcitrant to the ministration of the first man and his descendants. In both cases the colloquial expression "hexed" could be applied to that which is ʾārūr.

It is not unlikely that the force "banned" is the

[21]AV, JPS "cursed...(for thy sake)"; AT "Cursed...(through you)"; RSV "cursed...(because of you)"; SB "Maudit ...(à cause de toi)"; ATD "verflucht...(um deinetwillen)"; LXX ἐπικατάρατος ...(ἐν τοῖς ἔργοις) Targ. līṭā...(bᵃḏīlāḵ).

[22]The last clause is part of the punishment: When the tilled earth produces thorns, man will be driven to eat the plants which grow wild on the steppe.

basic denotation of <u>ʾārūr</u> in the pronouncement of Noah.

Gen. 9:25-26.

9) ...<u>ʾārūr</u>[23]

be Canaan

an abject slave shall he be to his brothers!

10) ...Blessed of YHWH, my God, be Shem...[24]

Whereas Shem and Japheth will dwell together as freemen and equals Canaan shall be banned from free association with them -- his will be the role of the most abject of slaves.

In the words imputed to the partriarch Jacob concerning the fate of the tribes in time to come the status of Simeon and Levi is given an etiology traceable to the ruthless attack of their eponymous ancestors upon Schechem.

Gen. 49:7.

<u>ʾārūr</u>[25]

be their anger so fierce,
their wrath so relentless
I will divide them in Jacob,
I will scatter them in Israel.

At first glance it would seem that the force of <u>ʾārūr</u> as disclosed in the preceding passages is not germane

---

[23]Eng. vss. "Cursed (be)"; SB "Maudit (soit)"; ATD "Verflucht (sei)"; LXX ἐπικατάρατος ; Targ. <u>līṭ</u>. Cf. Pedersen (<u>Der Eid</u>..., p. 79), "<u>ʾrr</u> kann auch gebraucht werden, um die soziale Erniedrigung, die Ausstossung aus der Gesellschaft der freien, vollberechtigten Manner zu bezeichnen. So z. B. <u>Gen</u>. 9, 25, wo <u>Kᵉnaʿan</u> für <u>ʾārūr</u> erklärt wird, indem er der Knecht seiner Brüder wird..."

[24]Reading with Ehrlich and other, <u>bᵊrūk YHWH ʾᵉlōhay</u>.

[25]Eng. vss. "cursed (be)"; SB "Maudite"; ATD "Fluch (über)"; LXX ἐπικατάρατος ; Targ. <u>līṭ</u>.

here. It must be understood, however, that the *ʾārūr* as applied to the passions of Simeon and Levi applies by metonymy to the tribes themselves.[26] The explication of *ʾārūr* leaves no doubt as to what status is to be denied to them: the role of independent tribes exercising hegemony in their own respective territories. By the time of the monarchy Levi was hardly a tribe in any sense of the term, and Simeon had been assimilated into Judah. Thus the ban here relates to territorial integrity and ethno-political independence.

The recovered force of *ʾārūr* may now serve to enhance in considerable measure our appreciation of the status of the Gibeonites among the tribes of Israel. After the destruction of Jericho and Ai and the extirpation of their populations the Gibeonites resort to a ruse to save themselves from a similar fate. A number of them, wearing worn-out clothes and patched sandals, carrying provisions moldy with age, arrive as envoys from a distant land despatched to conclude a treaty with the conquering Israelites. The Israelite chieftains are taken in by the stratagem,[27]

---

[26] As implied in Rashi's comment: "Even at the time of chastening he cursed only their anger..."

[27] The traditional renderings of v. 14, *wayyiqqᵊḥū hāʾᵃnāšīm miṣṣēḏām wᵊʾɛt pī YHWH lōʾ šāʾālū* as *e.g.*, RSV, "So the men partook of their provisions and did not ask direction from the Lord," misses the point of the story. If "the men" are Gibeonites, why should they have inquired of YHWH's oracle. If they are Israelites, why should they partake of the wretched fare. The subjects of the sentence are, of course, the Israelite chieftains, who did not partake at all, but took some of the provisions, and satisfied by their inspection, failed to ascertain the truth by means of YHWH's oracle; thereupon falling for the ruse and concluding a

conclude a pact, swearing by YHWH not to kill the Gibeonites. They then learn to their dismay that they have granted immunity to a people slated for extermination. The narrative continues:

Josh. 9:22-23.

> 22) Joshua then summoned them and addressed them, "How dared you deceive us[28] saying, 'We are far distant from you,' when you dwell right in our midst? 23) Now, therefore,
>
> ʾarūrīm ʾattɛm,[29]
>
> never shall there be any among you who are not slaves, hewers of wood and drawers of water for the temple of my God.

The oath cannot be undone, nor the pact violated without incurring YHWH's wrath,[30] and the Israelites are committed to tolerating the Gibeonites in their midst for all succeeding generations. But Joshua is not altogether without recourse: the status of the Gibeonites has not been determined. Here, then, the force of Joshua's declaration becomes apparent. ʾarūrīm ʾattɛm is a decree and not an imprecation. The Gibeonites are not cursed, they are banned. Never will they be permitted to mingle with, and become assimilated to the people of Israel. The tradition-

---

a compact with the tricksters.

[28]Hebr. lāmmā rimmīṯɛm ʾōṯānū. Joshua certainly knew "why" the Gibeonites resorted to the deception.

[29]AV, JPS, (/RSV) "ye (/you) are cursed"; AT "Cursed are you"; SB "vous êtes maudits"; ATD "So sollt ihr nun verflucht sein"; LXX καὶ νῦν ἐπικατάρατοί ἐστε ; Targ. liṭīn ʾattūn.

[30]Cf. II Sam. 21:1-3. Saul did break the pact; the qɛṣɛp of YHWH expressed itself by means of a three-year famine in the time of David, who had to ask the Gibeonites what amends they would accept to remove the curse (ʾālā, to be sure), the expression for the latter being ūḇārᵊḵū.

al translations clearly miss the point. The Gibeonites are to constitute a special class -- or, to be more exact -- a caste, outside the pale of Israel; and never will there be a Gibeonite who is not destined from birth to be a servant bound to the menial services required by YHWH's sacrificial cult.[31]

A significant distinction between "class" and "caste" is the hereditary feature of the latter. The continuance of the Gibeonites as a caste could be assured only by a ban against their intermarrying with Israelites. Such a ban in regard to intermarriage was directed against the entire tribe of Benjamin in the narrative of Judges 21 and 22.

Judges 21:18.

> ...for the Israelites had taken an oath, to wit
>
> *ʾārūr*[32]
>
> be he who gives a wife to Benjamin.

Although, as indicated earlier, *ʾārūr* is the general rubric for the curse-formula, the context here suggests an added force. Just as Benjamin has been declared an outlaw tribe, banned from fellowship with its confederate cognate tribes, so anyone who would violate and marry into the tribe of Benjamin will be *ʾārūr*, banned, cut off from the favor of men and heaven.

---

[31]Cf. Pedersen's comment (cited above, n. 23), which applies equally to Josh. 9:23 as to Gen. 9:25.

[32]Eng. vss. "Cursed (be)"; SB "Maudit (soit)"; ATD "verflucht (sei)"; LXX ἐπικατάρατος ; Targ. *līṭ*.

In I Samuel 26, David, who has just proved by his sparing of Saul's life that he is innocent of treasonable intentions, remonstrates with the king.

I Sam. 26:19.

> Now, therefore, let my lord the king hear the words of his subject: If it is YHWH who has incited you against me, let him accept an offering; but if it is mortals --
>
> <u>ʾᵃrūrīm</u> <u>hem</u>[33]
>
> at the instance of YHWH, for they have now driven me away -- denying me contact with YHWH's land -- saying, in effect, "Go -- serve other gods."

Despite the traditional translations, David is not concerned with hurling imprecations. He is making out a case for his own innocence and against Saul's gratuitous suspicion and persecution of him. The responsibility for Saul's suspicion and harrassment of David can lie in either divine or human agency. The Deity's anger against the victim can be placated by means of a sacrifice. If human beings are at fault they incur the Deity's wrath, for the effect of their lies is to deprive YHWH of a worshipper by driving him out of the territory where alone YHWH can be worshipped. There is almost perfect symmetry in the protasis and apodosis of David's second statement -- so that the former's <u>gērᵊšūnī</u> <u>hayyōm</u> <u>mēhistappēᵃh</u> <u>bᵊnaḥᵃlaṯ</u> <u>YHWH</u> almost defines the term <u>ʾᵃrūrīm</u> in the latter. By the act of driving David out of YHWH's presence,[34] David's accusers

---

[33]AV, JPS, AT "cursed be they"; RSV "may they be cursed"; SB "qu'ils soient maudits"; ATD "seien sie verflucht"; LXX ἐπικατάρατοι ; Targ. <u>liṭīn</u>.

[34]Cf. v. 21. <u>wᵊʿattā</u> <u>ʾal</u> <u>yippol</u> <u>dāmī</u> <u>ʾārᵊṣā</u> <u>minnɛgɛd</u> <u>pᵊnē</u> <u>YHWH</u>, "Now, therefore let not my blood fall to the ground away from YHWH's presence."

are themselves ʾᵃrūrîm lipnē YHWH "banned at YHWH's instance," barred from YHWH's favor.[35]

The Book of Kings supplies enough information concerning Jezebel to allow for speculation as to what is meant by the characterization of her as ʾᵃrūrā. Thrown to her death from a palace window by her own attendants at the command of the victorious rebel Jehu, her corpse lies unattended while Jehu takes his dinner. Jehu then gives the command:

II Kings 9:34

> ..."Attend now to
>
> ʾɛṯ hāʾᵃrūrā hazzōʾṯ[36]
>
> and bury her, for she is (after all) daughter of a king."

The epithet ʾᵃrūrā in the mouth of Jehu may signify no more than a natural reaction to her dire end. Or, as is more likely, Jehu may be making reference to the fact that, years before, Jezebel's doom was sealed by the oracle of YHWH delivered by Elijah (I Kings 21:23), "The dogs shall

---

[35]Cf. Scharbert's comment on this passage as well as upon most of the passages treated hitherto (Biblica 39, 1) p. 7, "In all diesen Fällen handelt es sich um mehr als bloss um einen Wunsch; man vollzieht damit einen Ausschluss aus der Gemeinschaft und erwartet, dass den Betroffenen wirklich das Unheil ereilt." It is difficult to tell whether Pedersen understands David's words as a statement of fact (as it is here taken) or as a wish, hence imprecation. Cf. the following two sentences (Der Eid, p. 79), "David sagt I. Sam. 26, 19, dass, wenn Menschen Saul gegen ihn aufgereizt haben, dann sind sie ʾᵃrūrîm lipnē YHWH, denn sie haben ihn aus dem Lande Jahwes vertrieben. David ist also selbst ein Verstossener und wird wohl seinen Feinden nichts Geringeres wunschen."

[36]AV, JPS, AT "This cursed woman"; RSV "This accursed woman"; SB "cette maudite"; HAT "dieser Verfluchten"; LXX

eat Jezebel within the territory of Jezreel." It is possible, however, that even in this instance the more specialized force of ʾārūr can be discerned. When Jehu hears the report that only the skull, hands and feet of Jezebel have been found, he quotes the above oracle with the expansion, "and the corpse of Jezebel shall be as dung upon the surface of the fields in the territory of Jezreel, so that no one shall be able to say, 'This is Jezebel.'" Even in death a person can be ʾārūr "outcast," barred from proper burial. For examples of this not uncommon threat, compare the exchange between David and Goliath (I Sam. 17:44-46); the words of Isaiah to Shebna (Isa. 22:15-18); and Jeremiah's prophecy that bones already buried shall be disinterred to become dung on the surface of the earth (Jer. 8:1-3).

Both Pedersen and Scharbert[37] have noted that the term ʾārūr in Jeremiah 17:5 receives an explication in verse 6, which is virtually a warrant for the force "banned."

Jer. 17:5-7.

5) Thus says YHWH:

ʾārūr[38]

is the man who trusts in mortals,
and considers mere flesh his strength,[39]

τὴν κατηραμένην ; Targ. yāṯ ʾaʾrūrǝṯā.

[37]Pedersen, Der Eid, p. 79; Scharbert, Biblica, 39, 1, p. 6.

[38]Eng. vss. "Cursed"; SB "Malheur(à)"; KAT "Verflucht"; LXX ʾΕπικατάρατος ; Targ. līṭ.

[39]Heb. zǝrōʿō, his arm; but so often in the connota-

his heart thus turning away from YHWH.

6) He shall be like a shrub in the wasteland,
never witness to the approach of anything good
He shall dwell in the parched places of the wilderness,
a land of salt, and uninhabited.

7) Blessed is the man who trusts in YHWH...

While it is true that the imagery of a shrub in a parched wasteland may be nothing more than the poetic contrast to the simile of the man who is blessed, in verses 7 and 8, like a tree planted by an unending supply of water -- it is nevertheless a picture of both loneliness and barrenness. And the texts so far studied have provided ample evidence that high on the list of dreaded misfortunes are those of being banned from fellowship and denied fecundity.

The term <u>ʾarūrīm</u> is applied in Psalm 119:21 to those who stray from YHWH's commandments. The verse is cited in its entirety in the Hebrew.

<u>gāʿartā</u> <u>zēḏīm</u> <u>ʾarūrīm</u> <u>haššōgīm</u> <u>mimmiṣwōṯɛḵā</u>.[40]

This verse as rendered by the traditional translations is hardly meaningful and somewhat incongruous in the context of the psalm as a whole. <u>ʾārūr</u>, it is clear, is an extremely strong term; its meaning, indeed, approaches the

---

tion of "strength" that <u>BDB</u>, p. 283, lists this word as one of its meanings.

[40]AV (/JPS) "Thou hast rebuked the proud that are cursed, which (/That) do err from thy (/Thy) commandments"; AV "Thou dost rebuke the arrogant, the accursed..."; RSV "Thou dost rebuke the insolent, accursed ones..." SB "Tu t'en prends aux superbes, aux maudits,..."; ATD "Die Frechen hast du bedroht. Verflucht, ver..."; HAT "Du bedräust die verfluchten Übermütigen, die..." LXX Ἐπετίμησας ὑπερηφάνοις ἐπικατάρατοι οἱ ἐκκλίνοντες ...; Targ. <u>nəzaptā</u> <u>zədonīn</u>, <u>līṭīn</u>...

force of "damned." Now to apply the verb gāʿar "rebuke," to those already damned is to impute bathos to the verse. On the other hand, the structure of the psalm is discernible at a glance. It is a series of affirmations on the part of the psalmist concerning his loyal devotion to the Deity and his commandments, alternating with entreaties for YHWH's favor. The subject of virtually every sentence is the psalmist, in the first person; the Deity appears only as the one addressed usually by an imperative. Thus there is in the psalm no parallel to, or precedent for, a statement about YHWH's treatment of those who stray from his ways.

Because of these considerations, Ehrlich's suggestions that gāʿartā be emended to gāʿartī is most persuasive.[41] Equally agreeable is his conclusion that, contrary to the conjunctive accent of MT, and with the majority of the ancient versions, ʾᵃrūrīm belongs to the second clause. Erhlich's translation is:

> Ich fahre die frechen Uebertreter an,
> verflucht sind mir, die sich freuen, deine Gebote zu missachten.
> (I rebuke the insolent transgressors,
> cursed to me are those who rejoice in disregarding your commandments.)

---

[41] "Für gāʿartā, welches keinen befriedigenden Sinn gibt, is ohne Zweifel gāʿartī zu lesen." Arnold B. Ehrlich, Die Psalmen (Berlin: Poppelauer, 1905), p. 303. The adoption of Ehrlich's emendation is based on the structure of the psalm, not on the assumption that gāʿar is in meaning so much weaker than ʾārar. Prof. Moshe Greenberg has brought to my attention that gāʿar means more than "rebuke." In Zechariah 3:2 and Malachi 2:3 the verb might best be rendered by "exorcise," and "blight" respectively; in Deut. 28:20 migʿɛrɛt is parallel to mᵊʾērā (cf. below p.112f); and in the Genesis Apocryphon XX 28, for wttgʿr mnnh dʾ bʾyštʾ he suggests the rendering "let this evil be exorcised/banished from us." The term gʿr would thus be very close in meaning to ʾrr.

His translation of the second clause is explained by his note, "Doch muss das zweite Versglied, welches sonach einen vollständigen Satz bildet, nichtals Verwünschung, sondern als einfache subjektive Behauptung gefasst werden."[42]

If we now apply to *ʾarūrīm* the force of "ban, exclusion," which has been amply attested heretofore, the entire declaration will be seen to assume a sharper force -- with the second clause being a climactic parallel to the first: The psalmist repulses the ungodly; they are, indeed, anathema to him.

III. OTHER FORMS OF THE VERB *ʾārar*

Until E. A. Speiser's discussion of Exodus 14:20[43] the concealment of a form of *ʾārar* in that verse remained unsuspected. It would be pointless to reproduce the discussion here *in toto*, but the main outlines of the argument will be given.

The pursuing Egyptians are about to overtake the fleeing Israelites when the angel of God (in one source) or the cloud-pillar (in another source) moves from a position in the van of the Israelites to one at their rear, in interposition between the pursuers and the pursued.

Exodus 14:20.

> And it (/he) thus came between the army of Egypt and the Israelite host, so that there was the cloud and the darkness

---

[42] *Op.cit.* Ehrlich, *Die Psalmen*, p. 303.

[43] "An Angelic 'Curse': Exodus 14:20," *JAOS*, Vol. 80, No. 3 (July-Sept. 1960), pp. 198-200.

wayyāʾɛr *ʾɛṯ* *hallaylā*[44]

so that one did not come close to the other all that night.

The ostensible meaning of the Hebrew, the verb understood as *hiphʿil* causative of *ʾōr*, is "it caused the night to be light," a feat as improbable for a cloud-pillar to perform as it would have been useless as a protection for the Israelites. The translations of the Targum, AV, JPS, which have it that light was provided for the Israelites and denied the Egyptians depend upon the introduction of pronouns or adverbs which are not present in the text. The Greek version is an attempt to make sense out of a perplexing verb, but offers no assurance that its translators possessed a "Vorlage" reading *wyʿbr* in the place of MT's *wyʾr* *ʾt*. A further indication that the protection of the Israelites consisted of "darkness" and not "light" is provided by Josh. 24:7 which, referring to the incident, says explicitly that God "put darkness (*māʾᵃpel*) between you and the Egyptians."

The form *wayyāʾer* need not, however, be derived from *ʾōr*. As it stands it can be the apocopated *hiphʿil* of *ʾrr* or, since the *hiphʿil* of *ʾrr* is not otherwise attested, a slight change in vocalization yields the imperfect *qal* *wayyāʾor*. The verse would then read "And it [the pillar of cloud] came between the Egyptian camp and the Israelite camp. Thus there was the cloud with the darkness, and it

---

[44]AV "but it gave light by night *to these*"; JPS "yet gave it light by night there"; RSV "and the night passed" with marg. note "Gk: Heb. *and it lit up the night*"; LXX καὶ διῆλθεν ἡ νύξ ; Targ. *ulyiśrāʾel* *nᵉhar* *kāl* *lēlyā*.

cast a spell (wyʾr) upon the night, so that one side could not make contact with the other all through that night."

Support for this force of ʾārar, and for Speiser's interpretation of Exodus 14:20, comes from a neighboring culture. In a private-communication to Speiser,[45] Rudolf Anthes writes of the article that it "particularly appeals to me...it is closely related to a recent study of mine (to be published in ZAeS 86) in which I have tried to show that the usual Egyptian word for 'beschwoeren,' 'to put a spell upon,' is not differentiated in the Pyramid Texts from the same word in its meaning 'umkreisen,' 'encircle'; therefore, the Egyptian word for 'beschwoeren' originally means 'bannen,' 'in einem Bannkreis festhalten.' It struck me first that by chance we both tried to get at the bottom of words like 'beschwoeren,' 'fluchen'; moreover it happens that exactly the meaning 'in einem Bannkreis festhalten' would fit very well indeed in Exodus 14:20 as well." As an afterthought, Professor Anthes wonders whether "although 'cast a spell upon the night' appears to contradict this understanding."

There is, however, no contradiction. "Night" and "darkness" are not synonyms. The night might well have afforded enough light to allow for an Egyptian assault upon the Israelite camp had it not been for the supernatural cloud which did grip the night in a "bannkreis" of unnatural darkness, making impossible any contact between the two forces. It is, moreover, more than likely that the words

---

[45] Dated: April 27, 1961.

<u>hɛʿānān</u> <u>wᵊhaḥošɛḵ</u> (the cloud and the darkness) are not two separate elements but constitute a case of hendiadys, the latter being the product or effect of the former.[46]

In Chapter 22 of Numbers the verb <u>ʾārar</u> occurs in the <u>qal</u> imperative and in the <u>qal</u> imperfect -- active and passive. Balak, king of Moab, has witnessed the Israelite conquest of the Amorite kingdom. Aghast now at the prospect that the horde will overcome him, too, he summons to his aid the redoubtable Balaam from Mesopotamia. Balak's envoys deliver the summons.

Num. 22:6-12.

6) Come then now

<u>ʾorā lī</u>[47]

this people, too strong in number for me; perhaps I shall be able to inflict a defeat upon them and drive them from the land; for I know that he whom you bless is blessed and he whom

<u>tāʾor yūʾār</u>.[48]

vv. 7-11. The envoys, having delivered their summons to Balaam, are invited to spend the night while Balaam inquires of YHWH for instructions. God appears to Balaam and is told by Balaam of the Moabite mission. 12) God

---

[46]For a striking analogy, cf. Gen. 1:14, where the heavenly luminaries are to be <u>lᵊʾōṯōt</u> <u>ulᵊmōʿᵃḏīm</u> <u>ulᵊyāmīm</u> <u>wᵊšānīm</u>, not as <u>e.g.</u>, RSV, "for signs and for seasons and for days and years," but rather, "for time markers of days and years."

[47]AV, JPS "curse me"; AT "curse"; RSV "curse...for me"; SB "maudis-moi"; HAT "verfluche mir"; LXX ἄρασαι μοι Targ. <u>lōṭ lī</u>.

[48]AV, JPS "thou cursest is cursed"; AT, RSV "you curse is cursed"; SB "tu maudis est maudit"; HAT "du aber verfluchst, der wird (auch wirklich) verflucht"; LXX ἂν καταράσῃ συ, κεκατήρανται Targ. <u>(wᵊḏī)ṯlūṭ līṭ</u>. Scharbert (P. 6): "Wer von den Zauberformeln solcher Leute getroffen

said to Balaam, "You are not to go with them;

lōʾ tāʾor[49]

the people, for it is bārūk (blessed = immune).

One could hardly desire a context more helpful for the deduction of the force of ʾārar. "Curse" is far too general a term to convey the effect that Balak desires: The Israelites are too numerous for me. In their present condition I cannot hope to defeat them. But if you put them under a spell / hem them in (a "Bannkreis"), immobilize them, then they will be so paralyzed that I shall stand a good chance to defeat them.

It should be noted that the term "curse" is frequently employed in translations of several different terms whenever they occur in a context with the antonym brk. Here, however, it must be clear that the primary concept is that of ʾrr and the term brk must derive its antonymous connotation from the former. "Blessed" is here too vague a term to convey the force of bārūk here, which is: immune to a spell/unhampered by obstacles/possessed of freedom of action.[50]

---

ist, ist nach dem Glauben der Moabiter unrettbar dem Fluch verfallen (yūʾār)." In the absence of any hiphʿil occurrence of the stem, there is no reason to suppose that yūʾār is other than qal passive.

[49]AV, JPS "thou shalt not curse"; AT (/RSV) "you must (/shall) not curse"; SB "Tu ne maudiras pas"; HAT "Du darfst...nicht verfluchen"; LXX οὐδὲ καταράσῃ ; Targ. lāʾ tᵊlūṭ.

[50]Num. 23:17, where ʾorā occurs again is discussed below; cf. p. 201.

In the "Song of Deborah" (Judges 5:2-31), the angel or "messenger" of YHWH is pictured as giving a command, the imperative together with the emphasizing infinitive absolute of *ʾārar* directed against the inhabitants of Meroz who did not respond to the summons for battle against the Canaanites.

Judges 5:23.

ʾōrū[51]

Meroz, commands the angel of YHWH,

ʾōrū ʾārōr[52]

its inhabitants,
because they came not to the aid of YHWH,
to the aid of YHWH among the heroes.[53]

Whether the command is given by an angel of YHWH, or, as Rashi understands it, by Barak, it is far more likely that the command would involve the imposition of a specific penalty rather than the comparatively tame call "to curse" = "to hurl imprecations," which the *malʾāḵ* could, in any case, do on his own. It is much more probable that the verb *ʾārar* here has the basic force which was discerned in the discussion of Josh. 9:23, Judg. 21:18, etc. The sense

---

[51]AV, JPS "Curse ye"; AT, RSV "Curse"; SB "Maudissez"; ATD "Fluchet"; LXX καταράσασθε ; Targ. *lūṭū*.

[52]AV, JPS "curse ye bitterly"; AT "Curse utterly"; RSV "curse bitterly"; SB "maudissez, maudissez"; ATD "mit Flüchen fluchet"; LXX καταράσει καταράσασθε ; Targ. *lūṭū uṯᵊḇārū*.

[53]Or "the mighty/valiant warriors." There is no reason to translate (with AV, JPS, RSV) the preposition *bᵊ-* governing *(hag)gibbōrīm* by "against." Whatever the force in v. 13 of this chapter, cf. the usage in I Chron. 12:1; Amos 2:16; and I Sam. 17:12 where Jesse is probably too old (read: *mibbōʾ bāʾᵃnāšīm*) to join the fighters.

of the command would then be: Put a ban upon the inhabitants of Meroz. The force of the imperative strengthened by the infinitive would not be "curse bitterly," but, rather, banish utterly/make anathema..." Since the offense of the people of Meroz was that they sundered themselves from the rest of Israel at a time of crisis, punishment by "banning/exclusion/excommunication" would be poetic justice.

An example of a passage where the general term "curse" for the verb ʾārar yields semantic incongruity is

Mal. 2:2.

> "If you will not listen, if you will not lay it to heart to pay homage to my name," says YHWH-Hosts, "I will dispatch against you
>
> ʾεṯ hammᵊʾērā wᵊʾārōṯī[54]
>
> your blessings,
>
> wᵊgam ʾārōṯīhā[55]
>
> because you do not take it to heart.

Just what does it mean "to curse a blessing"? That it meant little is evidenced by the translations of AT and HAT. But "turn/change a blessing into a curse" is here a paraphrase, not a translation. And Deut. 23:6 (wayyahᵃpok YHWH...ʾεṯ haqqᵊlālā libṟāḵā) shows that Hebrew can, if it desires, say just that. Then, there is the question of just what is meant by "your blessings." SB states confidently in a footnote, "Il s'agit, au sens concret, des

---

[54]AV, JPS, RSV "(a/the) curse...and I will curse"; AT "curse...and I will turn (your blessings) into a curse"; SB "la malédiction et maudirai"; HAT "den Fluche und (wandle ...in) Fluch"; LXX τὴν κατάραν, καὶ ἐπικαταράσομαι; Targ. yaṯ mᵊʾerta wᵊʾēlōṯ.

[55]AV (/RSV) "yea (/indeed) I have...cursed them"; JPS "yea, I will curse them"; AT "make it a curse"; SB "Et déjà je l'ai maudite"; HAT "ja ich verfluche"; LXX καὶ καταράσομαι αὐτήν; Targ. wᵊʾap ʾalūṭinēh.

biens matériels départis aux Lévites." Other suggestions are the priestly benedictions, the priestly revenues, the priestly privileges, not to mention the highly favored Draconic solution which, regarding the whole sentence as superfluous, relegates it to the limbo of "marginal annotation."[56]

If, with Rashi and Ibn Ezra, we understand the b^ərāḵōṯ as the earth's produce, as indeed verse 3 states in explication hinᵊnī gōʿer lāḵɛm ʾɛt hazzɛraʿ (I am rebuking the seed for you = to your disadvantage); and restore to ʾārar its basic sense of "ban, block off," the entire sentence will be seen to yield excellent sense. As in Gen. 3:17-18, the blessing of earth's fertility was denied to man by a divinely-imposed spell, so here too in Malachi, the threat is that the conditions requisite for fertility will be barred to man by a mᵊʾērā, a spell, unless proper respect is paid to YHWH and his worship. Indeed, the spell is already working in that the fertility has already been diminished. The entire matter is made explicit in the following chapter. The translation is RSV.

Mal. 3:9-11.

9) bammᵊʾērā ʾattɛm nēʾārīm,[57]

for you are robbing me; the whole nation of you.

---

[56]For the various speculations, see J.M. Powis Smith, The Book of Malachi (ICC, New York: Ch. Scribner's Sons, 1912), pp. 36-37. Smith, SB, Vulgate prefer the LXX ὦμον (= Heb. zᵊrōaʿ) to MT's zɛraʿ in v. 3.

[57]AV, JPS, RSV "Ye (RSV, you) are cursed with a (JPS, the) curse"; AV "with a curse are you accursed"; SB "La malédiction vous atteint"; HAT "Von dem Fluche seid ihr getroffen"; Targ. bᵊlūṭā ʾattūn miṯlāṭīn; LXX is discussed in the text.

> 10) Bring (*hāḇîʾū*) the full tithes into the storehouse (*bêṯ hāʾōṣār*), that there may be (*wîhî*) food (*ṭɛrɛp*) in my house; and thereby put me to the test, says the Lord of hosts, if I will not open the windows of heaven for you and pour down for you overflowing blessing (*bᵊrāḵā*). 11) I will rebuke the devourer (marg.: Or *devouring locust*) for you, so that it will not destroy the fruits of your soil; and your vine in the field shall not fail to bear, says the Lord of hosts.

It is difficult to accept the traditional interpretation of verses 9 and 10 as reflected above. While it is true that LXX seems to have some formation of *rāʾā* (to see, look) rather than MT's forms of *ʾrr*, we may still keep the *ʾrr* terms and permit the LXX version to strengthen our doubts about the traditional interpretation of what follows. LXX, beginning with the last two words of verse 8 reads: 8)... ὅτι τὰ ἐπιδέκατα καὶ αἱ ἀπαρχαὶ μεθ᾽ ὑμῶν εἰσιν; 9) καὶ ἀποπλέποντες ὑμεῖς ἀποβλέπετε, καὶ ἐμὲ ὑμεῖς πτερνίζετε. τὸ ἔθνος (var. ἔτος = year) συνετελέσθη. 10) καὶ εἰσηνέγκατε πάντα τὰ ἐκφόρια εἰς τοὺς θησαυρούς, καὶ ἐν τῷ οἴκῳ αὐτοῦ ἔσται ἡ διαρπαγὴ αὐτοῦ. An English translation would be: 8) ...because the tithes and the first fruits are in your possession. 9) and you surely look away, and supplant (or deceive) me. The nation (var. "year") is brought to an end. 10) And you have brought all the produce into the storehouses, but in the house shall be its plunder.

Against the traditional interpretation are the following considerations: *bêṯ hāʾōṣār* is never used elsewhere for the temple (or its granaries); and if it were so used here, the clause immediately following would express a rather obvious reason for the command. Moreover, Malachi's complaint throughout is not in regard to the quantity but the quality of the offerings. The support for the rendering of *ṭɛrɛp̱* by "food" is weak.[58] On the other hand it is well established that *ṭɛrɛp̱* or *ṭᵊrēp̱ā* does not constitute first-class food. I suggest, therefore, that the first two clauses of verse 10 be attached to the preceding verse, that *hāḇīʾū* be read as *hāḇīʾ* (the infinitive), and *ṭɛrɛp̱* understood as analogous to *mošḇaṯ* in 1:14 (cf. above, p.51). The passage would then read:

> 9) You are in the grip of a curse/spell, for it is me whom you are scanting (?) -- the whole lot of you -- 10) bringing the full tithes into (your own) storehouses, while in my temple there is but carrion. But try me in respect to his, and see if I do not open for you the sluices of heaven, pouring down for you blessing without limit...

What, in any case, comes through clearly in this passage is that the *bᵊrāḵōṯ*, the blessings of 2:2, which come under the *mᵊʾʾērā* of the Deity, are identical with the *bᵊrāḵā* of 3:10 -- and both are synonymous with the rains required to fructify the soil. Rains can be barred, re-

---

[58]Only Ps. 111:5, where God provides *ṭɛrɛp̱* for those who fear him; and Prov. 31:15 where the housewife *par excellence* does the same for her household... Despite the prohibitions against eating flesh of prey (*ṭᵊrēp̱ā*) in Exod. 23:30, and against eating the flesh of an animal which dies a natural death (*nᵊḇēlā*) in Deut. 14:21, the priestly tradition in regard to these prohibitions seems qualified. Lev. 17:15 and 22:28 indicate that the absolute prohibition applies only to the priests, who may not render themselves ritually unclean (the effect of eating such meat). Lev. 7:24 confirms this by prohibiting to the non-priest Israelite the *ḥelɛḇ* ("fat") of a *nᵊḇēlā*. Normally this "fat" was burned on the altar; since *nᵊḇēlā* could not be used as an offering, it was necessary to make it explicit that though the flesh of *nᵊḇēlā* might be eaten, its "fat" was nevertheless interdicted. It is striking that Ezekiel, certainly post-Deuteronimic, forbids *nᵊḇēlā* and *ṭᵊrēp̱ā* only to the priests (Ezek. 4:14, 44:31). In view of the foregoing, allusions to "prey" (*ṭɛrɛp̱*) eaten by men, even in what some critics regard as "late" literature, need occasion no surprise. On the contrary, since *ṭɛrɛp̱* could not be arranged for by human agency, the force of Ps. 111:5 may indeed be

strained, held back -- but hardly "cursed."

That a day can be <u>ʾārūr</u> was seen in Jer. 20:14 (see above, pp. 80-81); Speiser's interpretation of Exod. 14:20 makes it clear that a night can be the object of <u>ʾārar</u> (see above, pp. 64-66). In the former instance the absence of explication makes it impossible to determine the specific force of the verb; in the latter instance the context was shown to require that the connotation of the verb is the laying of a spell on the night, rendering it an impenetrable darkness. The most extended passage in which both day and night are explicitly or implicitly <u>ʾārūr</u> is Job 3:1-9; indeed, it contains occurrences of three different terms (<u>piʿel qll</u>, <u>ʾrr</u>, <u>qbb/nqb</u>) which in translations are rendered by "curse." For reasons of economy and simplicity a translation of the text is offered first, followed by an explanation to justify the various points of interpretation.

Job. 3:1-9.

1) After this Job opened his mouth
   and railed at (wayyᵉqallel)[59] the
   day of his birth.
2) Taking up his theme, he declared:
3) "Would that the day had perished on which I
   was born,
   and the night that announced, 'A man-child
   is conceived.'
4) Would that that day had been darkness,
   unsought by God above,
   no light shining down upon it.
5) Would it had been polluted by darkness and
   gloom,
   that clouds had settled down upon it
   that the blackening (?) of day (?) had
   terrified it.

---

that God arranges a windfall for his faithful.

[59]For the force of this verb, cf. below, p. 129.

6) That night -- would that pitch blackness had seized it,
that it had not been joined to the days of the year,
in the number of the months it had not entered.
7) If only that night had been barren,
unvisited by a joyful sound!
8) Would it had been cursed by the
ʾōrᵊrē yōm,[60]
the warriors roused by Leviathan.
9) Would that the stars of its dusk had been darkened,
that it had looked for light and found none,
and had not glimpsed the flicker of dawn."

The key to the understanding of Job's speech lies in the construction of the tenses -- a key provided by both Rashi and Ibn Ezra, i.e., the imperfects are to be rendered as past conditional, or past optative.[61] As in Jer. 20:14, the passage is a poetic hyperbole expressing the wish that the speaker had never been born, so as never to have lived to experience his unbearable misfortune.

In verse 8, the ʾōrᵊrē yōm, traditionally rendered "those who curse the day" is followed by a semantic non-sequitur in its appositional phrase, "those who are ready/skillful to arouse Leviathan." There is therefore consid-

---

[60]AV, JPS, (/AT, RSV) "that (/who) curse the day"; SB "qui maudissent les jours"; ATD "Der Tagverflucher"; LXX ὁ καταρώμενος ; Targ. nᵊbīyāʾa dī lāṭᵊṭīn.

[61]Rashi on 3:2, "a 'future' expression in the sense that he said, 'Would that the day had perished on which I was to be born, for then I should not have been born.'"; Ibn Ezra on the same verse: "He wishes that from the first the day on which he was born had perished -- if he was born in the daytime -- or, if he was born at night, that the night had perished." The preference for gʾl "to defile," in v. 4 rather than gʾl "to redeem," is shared by Rashi and Ibn Ezra, while in v. 5 Rashi favors deriving yhd from hdh "to rejoice," and Ibn Ezra rejects this root in favor of yḥd, "to be united."

erable merit to the suggestion of H. L. Ginsberg (private communication), to restore the parallelism by reading Yām in the place of yōm; the phrase, then, a subjective genitive, would have reference to a mythological primeval battle of (the) Sea (Yām), its spell casting allies, the ʿaṯīdīm roused by Leviathan to battle (in a lost cause) against the Deity.[62]

Even if yōm is not original in v. 8, Jer. 20:14 is proof enough that a day could be ʾārūr, and this passage, in the last two clauses of verse 6 would provide virtual definition of the force of ʾārar in the sense of "to ban, to exclude from the company of." If further evidence is required, we need only compare the parallelism in verse 6 here with that in Gen. 49:6-7, where the term ʾārūr does occur.[63]

---

[62]Cf. in the Ugaritic myth, the victory of Baal over Yamm, "Poems about Baal and Anath," III AB A, ANET pp. 130-131; and in the Akkadian Creation Epic, the victories of Ea and Marduk over Tiamat and her allies. For the employment of spells as weapons cf. ANET (pp. 60 ff.) I 60-66, II 117, IV 61, 91. Leviathan, Rahab, Tannin are various names for the same Sea-creature defeated by God in the primordial battle. For other allusions to this battle and to the allies of the Sea, cf., Job 7:12, 9:13, 26:12-13; Isa. 51:9-10; Ps. 74:13-14. For the sense of ʿaṯidīm cf. Job 15:24, Isa. 10:13, 14:9 and, possibly, Esther 8:13. N. H. Tur-Sinai explains the ʾōrᵊrē yōm, "the cursers of the day" as allies of "Leviathan, prince of the sea and the depths, who reigned also over Sheol...in his war against God of heaven and light. It was a natural part of their fight against the light-god to curse daylight, over which he ruled." (The Book of Job, Jerusalem: Kiryath Sepher, 1957), pp. 56-57. Although 24:13 ff. with its explicit allusion to the "rebels against the light," provides strong support for Tur-Sinai's interpretation, the suggestion of H. L. Ginsberg is attractive for the neatness of the parallelism it restores.

[63]Cf. above, p. 55 f.

Job 3:6.

ʾal yiḥad [rd. *yēḥad*] *bī(y)mē šānā*

bᵊmispar yᵊrāḥīm ʾal yābōʾ

Gen. 49:6.

...*bᵊsōdām ʾal tābōʾ napšī*

biqhālām ʾal tēḥad kᵊbōdī

Speiser notes the parallel of *ʾōrᵊrē yōm* to the "magical treatment of the night" in Exod. 14:20.[64] Actually, the passage in Job seems to provide explicitly the effect of the spell on the night which Speiser discovers in the Exodus passage. Verse 6: *hallaylā hahūʾ yiqqāhehū ʾopɛl* -- "that night -- would that pitch blackness/thick darkness had seized it."

The *piᶜel* factitive of *ʾrr* appears in two passages. The first is:

Gen. 5:29.

> And he [Lamech] named him Noah, having in mind: this one will bring us relief from the agonizing toil of our hands[65] required by the soil which YHWH
>
> *ʾērᵊrāh*.[66]

In this passage J, the author also of the account in Chapter 3, is referring back to the sentence passed on mankind in 3:17[67] and ahead to

---

[64]*JAOS*, Vol. 80, No. 3, p. 200.

[65]Taking *mimmaᶜᵃśēnū umēᶜiṣṣᵊbōn* (*yādēnū*) as hendiadys.

[66]AV, JPS (/AT, RSV) "hath (/has) cursed"; SB "a maudit"; ATD "verflucht hat"; LXX κατηράσατο; Targ. *dᵊlāṭah*.

[67]Cf. above p. 55.

Gen. 9:21-22.

> Now Noah, the farmer, was the first to plant a vineyard,[68] (21) and, drinking the wine, he became drunk...

As the biblical "wine-hero" (cf. Dionysios/Bacchus), Noah introduces to mankind the potion in which it may find surcease from the hard labor which is required to make the soil productive. (As the first to drink the heady brew, it is only natural that he imbibes without caution and succumbs.) The <u>piᶜel</u> of <u>ʾrr</u> in 5:29 yields satisfactory sense only when taken as a factitive and rendered by "had put under/subjected to a spell."

It may now be emphasized that <u>ʾārar</u> as an active verb governing an object, and certainly the <u>piᶜel</u> factitive of the verb, do not, primarily, constitute an oral or spoken action. Although incantations are employed to cast spells and pronouncements are made to effectuate a ban, either activity can be performed independent of words (spoken or written) as necessary or sufficient cause. It is this consideration which helps us to understand why the term "curse," which has for us the primary force of "imprecation," is so often misleading when used to render the term <u>ʾrr</u>. It is due to a failure to grasp this that Scharbert

---

[68]The traditional translations of v. 21 make little sense when they are not misleading or demonstrably wrong. Cf. AV "And N. began <u>to be</u> a husbandman"; JPS "And N. the husbandman began and..."; RSV "N. was the first tiller of the soil." Gen. 4:2 clearly states that "Cain was a tiller of the soil." Thus, SB comes close to the sense with, "Noé, le cultivateur commenca de planter la vigne." But the <u>hiphᶜil</u> of <u>hll</u> often has the sense of to do something for the first time. Cf. <u>e.g.</u>, I Sam. 22:15 "Was this the first time that..."; I Sam. 14:35 "...that was the first altar he built..."; and the <u>hophᶜal</u> in Gen. 4:26 "...then for the first time was YHWH invoked by name."

can be both right and wrong, perceptive yet (in the last sentence) somewhat anti-climactic in his observation concerning the various instances of <u>ʾrr</u>:

> ...In all diesen Fallen wird man nicht an ein privates Verfluchen, das jeder beliebige Mensch vornehmen könnte, zu denken haben, sondern an ein Verfluchen, das nur bestimmten Personen obliegt... Wir werden am besten bei der üblichen Übersetzung 'verfluchen' bleiben, werden uns aber immer vor Augen halten müssen, dass es sich dabei um besonders wirksame Fluchformeln handelt, die in der Regel nur gewissen mit ungewöhnlichen Fähigkeiten ausgestatteten Personen zugeschrieben werden. Allerdings hat auch Gott die Macht zu einem derartigen Verfluchen.[69]

It would be strange indeed if God did not have the ability or power to "curse," or to do anything else of which men are capable. But the reason for the fact that not everyone can be the subject of the <u>ʾrr</u> activity is also the reason why we cannot rest with the translation "to curse." Anyone can curse, which is to say that anyone can deliver himself of maledictions, but it is not given to everyone to impose a spell or a ban. God, or one who derives his power from God, or a magician who is privy to the secrets of the occult -- these can bind with a spell. And a community or a society, or its representative authorities can ban an individual or a group from relations with it. And, finally, a spell may be brought on, effectuated or implemented, through the instrumentality of, say, a specially prepared potion.

This last possibility is, of course, what we encounter in the <u>mayīm</u> <u>hammᵊʾārᵊrīm</u> of Num. 5:11 ff.[70] This potion

---

[69]<u>Biblica</u>, 39, 1 (1958), p. 6.

[70]Discussed above, p. 50 ff.

is not water that causes the curse (AV, JPS), nor that brings the curse (AT, RSV); it is not "les eaux de malédiction" (SB), nor "Fluchwasser" (Scharbert)[71] nor "fluchbringendes Wasser" (KHAT). It is, rather, precisely what Speiser describes:

> ...Nor can 'curse' be made to fit the passage that deals with the woman accused of adultery... The form there is mᵊʾārᵊrīm (factitive participle of ʾārar). It is applied to a specific potion,...which could not in any circumstances voice a violent denunciation (the customary meaning of 'curse'). The potion is utilized as an agent 'that implements the spell/ordeal,' which is exactly how it is described.[72]

IV. THE NOUN mᵊʾērā

The noun mᵊʾērā occurs only five times, and in contexts which, on the whole, offer few clues to its specific force, other than its association with the verb ʾrr.

In Deuteronomy it follows the series of pronouncements, each of which begins with the term ʾārūr (Cf. above, p. 48).

Deut. 28:20

YHWH shall send against you

ʾet hammᵊʾērā...[73]

---

[71]Biblica 39, 1 (1958), p. 7.

[72]JAOS, Vol. 80, No. 3 (July-Sept., 1960), pp. 198-199. The only modification I would suggest in Speiser's expression is the omission from the last sentence of "/ordeal." The potion is actually and literally understood as "bringing on the spell" if the woman is guilty.

[73]AV, JPS "cursing"; RSV, AT "curses"; SB "malédictions"; HAT "Fluch"; LXX τὴν ἔνδειαν ; Targ. yāt mᵊʾertā.

Since this noun is followed by two terms which are even more general m^ehūmā "discomfiture," and migʿɛrɛṯ "rebuke," it is likely that we have hendiadys here, the primary term being mᵊʾērā, "a curse sent to chastise and confound." It should at all events be clear that mᵊʾērā is not constituted of words. There is no indication of anything spoken nor dependence on anything spoken. The best indication, in consideration of the force of the verb, is that it is a curse in the material, operative sense.[74]

It is just this force which was seen to inhere in both verb and noun in two passages in Malachi.[75]

Mal. 2:2.

...and I will dispatch against you

ʾɛṯ hammᵊʾērā[76]

Mal. 3:9.

bammᵊʾērā[77] ʾattɛm nēʾārīm

The remaining occurrences are in Proverbs.

---

[74]Scharbert, though he grasps this on the whole, still finds it necessary to tie the mᵊʾērā to an imprecation (Fluchwort), but what indication is there that the latter is necessary? "Das nomen mᵊʾērā ist die vom Fluch ausgehende unheilwirkende Kraft, die geradezu mit dem eingetroffenen Unheil selbst identisch ist; es bezeichnet also nicht das Fluchwort, sondern das Ergebnis desselben." (Biblica, 39, 1, 1958), p. 7.

[75]Cf. above, pp. 102 f.

[76]Eng. vss. "the curse"; SB "malédiction"; HAT "den Fluch"; LXX τὴν κατάραν ; Targ. yaṯ mᵊʾertā.

[77]AV, AT, RSV "with a curse"; JPS "with the curse"; SB "La malédiction (vous atteint)"; HAT "von dem Fluche"; Targ. bᵊlūṭā. For LXX, see above, p. 103 (n. 57).

Prov. 3:3.

m^{ə}ʾērat YHWH[78]

is on the house of the wicked, but the abode of the righteous he blesses (y^{ə}bārek).

Prov. 28:27.

He who gives to the poor does not experience want,

but he who hides his eyes

rab m^{ə}ʾērōt[79]

In neither of the above passages is there any hint of anything spoken as necessary to the concept of m^{ə}ʾērā; therefore, SB's "malédiction" should be ruled out. The m^{ə}ʾērā, in short, is the operating curse, or spell.

V. SUMMARY

The stem ʾrr in both its verbal and nominal occurrences has the force of "curse" only in the operative sense of the word. As such, its basic sense is best rendered by "spell." If a spell is imagined as something like a magic circle, which bars what is within from that which is without, it becomes clear what the denotation and connotation of ʾrr is in all its occurrences. When applied to earth or rain it is a spell which bars fertility to men. When applied to men (or animals), it bars them from the benefits

---

[78] AV, JPS, AT "the curse of the Lord"; RSV "The Lord's curse"; SB "Malédiction de Yahve"; HAT "Der Fluch des Herrn"; LXX κατάρα θεοῦ ; Targ. l^{ə}wāṭ^{ə}tā dεʾelāhā.

[79] AV, JPS (/AT) "shall (/will) have many a curse"; RSV "will get many a curse"; SB "sera maudit"; LXX ἐν πολλῇ ἀπορίᾳ ἔσται ; Targ. sagiʿin l^{ə}wāṭātē.

of fertility or association with their fellow creatures. As applied to a night it means the barring from the night of any illumination whatsoever.

Since the power to bind with a spell or to impose a ban is not given to everyone, the subject of the active verb ʾrr is always the Deity or an agency endowed by God or the society with unusual powers.[80] Anyone, however, has the power to imprecate -- and since an imprecation is strongest when it invokes a supernatural power, the term ʾārūr is the natural rubric for imprecation. This is not to say, however, that the occurrence of this rubric necessarily implies the presence of an imprecation (ʾālā). It may be the expression of a fact already present, but not yet generally recognized; or the prediction of an inevitable consequence of a certain action or inaction; or it may be the expression of a decree.

VI. AKKADIAN arāru AND arratu/erretu

As was cited earlier, the basic force of Akkadian stem ʾrr is "to bind (by means of incantation), to ban;"[81] hence, the frequent occurrence of the noun and the verb together with a negation of the antonym pašāru "to loosen," in the phrase which seems to have become a stereotype arrat la napšuri...lirur(ū), "may the (god or gods) ban (someone)

---

[80]It is noteworthy that except for the reference to the mythological ʾōrᵊrē yōm in Job 3:8, no one has the power to ʾrr in the sense of "bind with a spell" unless that power stems from a special relationship with God. Even the foreigner, Balaam, is conceived as owing his powers to YHWH.

[81]Cf. above, p. 17.

with an unloosenable ban." As Speiser has emphasized, this phrase "shows that *arratum* was something that could be 'loosened, unbound' (verb *pašārum*), hence a form of restraint or bond. Accordingly, the stem *ʾRR* connotes 'to bind, hem in with obstacles, render powerless to resist.' When such an effect was achieved by magical means, the counteraction (*pašārum*) required corresponding supernatural intervention; hence the *lipšur* formulae in the series *Šurpu* and related texts..."[82]

It would seem that despite the more extensive operation of metonymy in Akkadian the functions of *arāru* and its cognate noun *arratum*/*erretum* parallel rather closely those of *ʾārar* (and possibly *mᵊʾʾērā*) in Hebrew. Whereas *māmītu* parallels *ʾālā* as being "curse" from the point of view of "utterance," Akkadian *arāru*(*m*) parallels Hebrew *ʾārar* in reflecting "curse" in its operative sense. Thus as in the Bible, not anyone could be the subject or agent of the verb *arāru* although anyone could call upon the gods to *arāru* someone else. Thus B. Landsberger, "Während *arāru* der nur unter Anrufung der grossen Götter wirksame formelle Fluch ist..., umfasst das schwächere *nazāru* auch die Beschimpfung,

---

[82]It should be noted that the term *pašāru* is used together with other terms for magic, offenses, and retributive punishments: *Šurpu*, II 187-191 *l*[*ipašši*]*rū* with *arnu*, *ḫiṭātu*, *gillatu*, *ennītu*; III 183-184 [*ar*]*an idū la idū* [*u*]*paššar*...; VIII 80-82 *nišu māmīt arni ḫi*[*ṭitu*]...*lū patrānikka lū pašrānikka*; Maqlū I 20 *kišpuša ruḫuša rusūša lippašrū*; II 72 *pušur kišpišunu limnūti*; E. Ebeling, "Die Akkadische Gebetsserie 'Handerhebung'," (Berlin: Akademie-Verlag, 1953), VAT 13637, 13-15 (p. 36) *u mimmū mala ana iliya*[...*egū*] *aḫṭū lipp*[*ašra*]; King Magic Nr. 11, 19 (p. 72) *anni puṭur šērti pušur*. That any kind of evil should "grip" one is, however, not a consideration against the well-attested force of *ʾrr*.

Verbalinjurie."[83]

Hence in the Epilogue to CH, l. 23-24 _errētiya imešma errēt ilī lā idurma_ is not as DM renders, "has despised my curses and has not feared the curses of the gods,"[84] which implies two separate sets of curses, but rather, "the curses/spells (invoked by me), namely the curses (effectuated) by the gods." A comprehensive study of all the occurrences of _arāru_ and _erretum_/_arratum_ might prove of value, but is beyond the scope of this investigation.

---

[83]Benno Landsberger, "Das 'gute Worte'," _MAOG_ 4 (1928/29), p. 319.

[84]DM, Vol. 2, p. 101.

CHAPTER IV

I. *qillel* ≠ IMPRECATION. WITH VARIOUS SUBJECTS AND OBJECTS.

As has been indicated in the preliminary discussion in Chapter I,[1] the *qal*, *niphᶜal*, and *hiphᶜil* of the stem *qll*, since they are not rendered by "curse" or its equivalents, are not of central concern to this investigation. Nevertheless, it would be remarkable indeed if there were no relation between the base-stem and the D-stem (*piᶜel*). It may therefore simplify matters to quote Scharbert's introduction to the problem, especially since the similarity of approach between his study and this one should make the convergences and divergences in interpretation of special interest.[2]

> In fast allen semitischen Sprachen ist die Wurzel *qll* in den Bedeutungen "leicht,[3] klein, unbedeutend, gering, verächtlich sein" o.a. nachzuweisen. Im Hebr. finden wir die gleichen Bedeutungen im Qal vor. Für Nif sind die Bedeutungen "sich als schnell erweisen,"[4] "leicht, ohne Schwierigkeit sein,"[5] "leichtfertig,"[6] "gering sein" oder "sich geringschätzen";[7] für das Hif

---

[1]P. 18.

[2]Footnotes 3-13 correspond to Scharbert's 1-11; hence the German system of biblical references.

[3]"Daher auch 'flink schnell sein'; vgl. 2 Sm 1, 23; Jer 4, 13; Hab 1, 8; Job 7,6; 9, 25."

[4]"Is 30, 16."

[5]"4 Kg 3, 18; 20, 10; Spr 14,6."

[6]"Jer 6, 14; 8, 11."

[7]"1 Sm 18, 23; 2 Sm 6, 22: Is 49,6: Ez 8,17."

"leicht machen,"[8] "verachten, schmähen"[9] belegt. Das Pilp und Hitpalp bedeutete wohl ursprünglich "schnell hinundherbewegen" und daher "schütteln" bzw. "geschüttelt, erschüttert werden,"[10] (eine Schneide) wetzen."[11] Für das Pi, Pu und das Substantivum q^elālā geben die Wörterbücher allgemein die Bedeutungen "(ver) fluchen," "verflucht werden," "Fluch" an.[12] Wir werden aber auch hier von der Grundbedeutung "leicht, unbedeutend, gering sein" auszugehen und das Pi zunächst wörtlich "als unbedeutend hinstellen, geringschätzen, für klein und unbedeutend erklären" o.ä. wiederzugeben haben. Diese Bedeutung ist zweifellos im AT noch an manchen Stellen erhalten.[13] Wir brauchen uns hier nur mit Pi, Pu und dem Nomen q^elālā zu beschäftigen.

As indicated by the heading, the texts discussed in this section have a variety of subjects and objects in connection with qillel (or its passive form), and in no instance will the verb be seen to have the force of "curse" = "imprecation."

The deluge having ceased and the waters having receded, YHWH smells the fragrance of the sacrifices offered up by Noah and promises himself,

Gen. 8:21.

...I will never again

(l^e)qallel[14]

---

[8]"Ex 18,22; 1 Sm 6, 5; 3 Kg 12, 4.9 f; Jon 1, 5; 2 Chr. 10, 4.9 f."

[9]"2 Sm 19, 44; Is 8, 23; 23, 9; Ez 22, 7."

[10]"Jer 4, 24; Ez 21, 26."

[11]"Koh 10, 10"

[12]"Vgl. GES.-BUHL; KOEHLER, ZORELL."

[13]"Vgl. PEDERSEN, Der Eid bei den Semiten, 80."

[14]Eng. vss. "curse"; SB "(je ne) maudirais (plus)"; ATD "verfluchen"; LXX καταράσασθαι; Targ. limlāṭ. Pedersen, "...bezeichnet qll die Erniedrigung, die Beraubung der Ehre und des Glückes,...des Fluches. Diese Bedeutung

> the earth on man's account...nor will I ever again destroy all living things as I have done.

Unless one came to this verse with the prejudice that qillel means "to curse," one would never be led by the context to render l^{ə}qallel by means of this term. The verb suggests no pronouncement whatever, and, to the contrary, the reference is to a known non-oral action: the bringing on of the flood disaster. That the force of l^{ə}qallel here is "to abuse/treat harshly or injuriously" is clear from the parallel and complementary final clause, where the verb l^{ə}hakkōt has the basic meaning "to smite/to inflict injury upon."

The Holiness Code contains the following prohibition: Lev. 19:14.

lōʾ t^{ə}qallel[15]

> the deaf nor shall you put a stumbling block before the blind...

It is evident that the purport of this verse is to prohibit abuse of the handicapped. The question is what specific force the verb qillel has in this context. I cannot agree with Hempel who takes the verb as referring to "ein gesprochener Fluch" and explains that the reason for

---

bewährt sich überall im A. T. Jahwe sagt z. B. Gen. 8, 21: ..." (Der Eid) p. 80. Scharbert, "Auffallend selten hat das Verbum in der Bedeutung 'verfluchen' Gott als Subjekt" and note referring to Gen. 8:21 (Biblica 39, 1, p. 10).

[15]AV, JPS (/RSV) "Thou shalt not (/you shall not) curse"; AT "You must not curse"; SB "Tu ne maudiras pas"; HAT "Du sollst...nicht fluchen"; LXX Οὐ κακῶς ἐρεῖς ; Targ. lāʾ t^{ə}lūṭ.

the prohibition is that a deaf person, being unable to hear the curse pronounced against him, will be unable to take counter-measures to ward it off.[16] There is no evidence that an unjustified curse was regarded as efficacious, nor that curses had to be pronounced in the hearing of the victim; in view of the latter consideration, the deaf person would be no more vulnerable than one in full possession of his auditory sense.

It does appear likely that in contrast to the mentally afflicted, who were regarded as possessed by a spirit, hence under the special protection of heaven,[17] the physically afflicted were often regarded as suffering the Deity's displeasure, hence, as fair game. In any case, the verse singles out the particular areas of vulnerability of the respective victims in prohibiting abusive treatment. The word qillel would then be particularly apposite owing to its connotation of abuse, in general, and verbal abuse specifically. Scharbert says of the verb here, "So wird

---

[16]ZDMG, Neue Folge, Band 4 (1915), p. 38 f.; so also A.R.S. Kennedy in the Century Bible, Leviticus & Numbers, (Edinburg: Jack) p. 131. Cf. the comment in the Cambridge Bible, Leviticus (Cambridge, 1914), p. 108: "Though the deaf cannot hear, the curse must not be uttered"; D. Hoffman, Das Buch Leviticus, 2 vols. (Berlin: Poppelauer, 1906), Vol. 2, p. 40: "Den einfachen Sinne nach ist hier...verboten, den Wehrlosen, der nicht vor dem Richter klagen kann, anzugreifen"; SB, taking ḥēreš as "un muet" ("Autre traduction: 'un sourd'") explains in the margin: "Il ne peut répondre en maudissant à son tour." The Gallic sense of fair play!

[17]Cf. I Sam. 21:12 ff. David's ruse of feigning madness can be understood only on the presumption of the inviolability of the person of one possessed. Cf. the term məšuggaʿ in this passage, its application in contempt to the nābīʾ in Hos. 9:7; and, possibly with no connotation of contempt, in Jer. 29:26.

qll Pi...wohl nicht 'verfluchen', sondern einfach 'beschimpfen, schimpfen über' o.ä. bedeuten."[18] Although in agreement with Scharbert, I would caution that *qillel* (as in Gen. 8:21) need not involve a spoken element, and that in English the more general term "embarrass" is closer to the force of *qillel* than is "insult."

The *puʿal* imperfect of *qillel* occurs in Isaiah 65. In a pericope which celebrates the future felicity of Jerusalem and her inhabitants, the promise is made that the latter will enjoy exceptional longevity.

Isa. 65:20.

> No more shall there be anyone of that place
> who does not fill out his years (lit."days")
> Indeed a man shall die still young at a hundred years,
> and he who falls short of a hundred
> *yəqullāl*.[19]

The above translation follows the punctuation of MT, whose accents join *ʿūl yamīm wəzāqen*, yielding *per merismum* "anyone." (Actually *ʿūl* alone with *wəzāqen* would yield that sense, but *ʿūl yāmīm*, "a short-lived infant" is poetic redundance, since that meaning is expressed in *ʾašɛr lōʾ yəmallēʾ ʾɛṯ yāmāw*.) The rendering of *ḥōṭɛ̄ʾ* as "fall short of" is the basic sense of the stem *ḥṭʾ* and is so understood by AT, SB, Buhl, Ehrlich, and many others. The passage is

---

18 *Biblica* 39, 1, p. 10.

19 AV, JPS, RSV "shall be accursed"; AT "shall be accounted accursed"; SB "sera signe de malédiction"; KAT "geht mit raschem Schritt"; LXX ἐπικατάρατος ; Targ. *yiṯrak*. The Aramaic is interesting, in that it has the force "banished," which was seen to be that of *ʾārūr*.

hardly deserving of Skinner's comment, "The expression of the thought is unaccountably labored and obscure."[20]

Scharbert's rendering of <u>yᵊqullāl</u> is "geringgeschätzt, verachtet." In English, it might be rendered by "unfavored, unfortunate." If "accursed" be kept, it must be understood that the term is used in its broadest sense, implying neither imprecation nor malediction.

Jeremiah's complaint of the unjustified treatment which is accorded to him features the verb in question.

Jer. 15:10.

> Woe is me, mother mine, that you have given birth to me -- a man of suits and quarrels with the whole land. Though I make exactions of no one, nor anyone of me -- yet all
>
> <u>mᵊqalᵊlā⟨w⟩nī</u>.[21]

Despite Scharbert who accepts the sense of "verfluchen" here,[22] there is no cogent reason for rendering the verb here by "curse." Jeremiah, as is well known, was subjected to all kinds of abuse. Indeed a person who characterizes himself as a lamb being led to the slaughter (Cf. 11:19) would probably have welcomed anything as tame as malediction.

---

[20] J. Skinner, <u>Isaiah</u>, Cambridge Bible (Cambridge: University Press, 1954), p. 241.

[21] AV, JPS "doth curse me"; AT, RSV "curse me"; SB "me maudit"; HAT "fluchen"; <u>LXX</u> (ἡ ἰσχύς μου ἐξέλιπεν ἐν τοῖς καταρωμένοις με) Targ. <u>mᵊlaṭṭīn lī</u>.

[22] <u>Biblica</u> 39, 1, p. 10: "In der Regel sind es Menschen, die andere verfluchen" and note referring to Jer. 15:10; also to Josh. 24:9; Ps. 62:5; 109:28; Prov. 30:10; Neh. 13:2, 25.

Nehemiah reports his reproof of those Jews of Jerusalem who had taken wives from the city of Ashdod and from among the Ammonites and Moabites with the result that half the offspring of these unions were not even able to speak the language of Judah.

Neh. 13:25.

> So I remonstrated with them
>
> wāʾᵃqallᵊlem,[23]
>
> beating some of them and plucking their hair, and adjured them[24] by God...

If qillel did indeed mean "to curse," Nehemiah would have been guilty of bathos: "cursed... beat... pulled hair." The likelihood is that we have a hendiadys here, the force being: "So I upbraided them roundly (= abusively), beating, etc." That qillel is not used in the sense of imprecation is, furthermore, assured by the climax wāʾašbīʿem, which a prior imprecation would have ruled out.

The theme of Psalm 37 is the sure reward of the righteous and, despite his temporary prosperity, the equally certain punishment of the wicked: The former shall possess the earth through an enduring posterity, the latter's line shall be cut short.

---

[23]Eng. vss. "and cursed them"; SB "(je) les maudis."; ATD "und verfluchte sie"; HAT "und fluchte ihnen" and comment, "Der Fluch war wohl bedingungsweise gesprochen, für den Fall, dass sie dies nich abstellten." LXX καὶ κατηρασάμην αὐτοὺς; Scharbert takes the verb in the sense of "verfluchen"; see above, note. 22.

[24]For the force of wāʾašbīʿem see above, p.48.

Ps. 37:22.

For those blessed by him shall possess the land,

umᵊqullᵊlāw[25]

shall be cut off.

It is not clear who the antecedent of "him" is. JPS, RSV understand God as the antecedent. Yet the verse immediately preceding

> The wicked borrows, and cannot pay back,
> but the righteous spends generously.[26]

leaves open the possibility that the antecedent is not the Deity but the immediately preceding righteous man (ṣaddīq). The latter interpretation would, however, introduce a new and otherwise unattested thought: those blessed by the righteous shall prosper. The traditionally accepted sense (AT's acceptance of LXX version need not detain us here,) is preferable in that it is completely in keeping with the one theme of the psalm. The force then would be: he who is favored by the Deity (i.e., the righteous) will endure while he who is in the Deity's ill graces, mᵊqullᵊlāw (i.e., the wicked) will come to an untimely end. There would thus be no force of "cursed" in mᵊqullᵊlāw, but rather a simple sense antonymous to mᵊḇōrāḵ, "favored" as opposed to "unfavored."

---

[25]AV "they that be cursed of him"; JPS "they that are cursed of Him"; RSV "those cursed by him" specifically referring to "the Lord" who is introduced in the previous clause without any indication that YHWH is not present in the Hebrew. AT "(those who bless...) those who curse him"; SB "ceux qu'il maudit"; ATD "doch wen er verflucht"; LXX οἱ δὲ καταρώμενοι αὐτὸν ; Targ. uḏᵊmiṯlaṭᵊṭīn. Scharbert takes it in the sense of "verfluchen," Biblica 39, 1, p.10, n. 2.

[26]Taking ḥōnen wᵊnōṯen as hendiadys.

It is, indeed, just because *qillel* is an antonym of *bērek* that tradition has assumed that *qillel* means "to curse." But this is the result of ascribing a narrow meaning, involving an utterance, to *bērek*, whereas in fact this latter term has a broad range of meanings in the sense of to treat well -- and "benediction," to speak well of, is only one specialized meaning of the term.

In Psalm 62, the context offers little help in determining the force of *qillel* other than the broad spectrum of meanings inhering in the antonym *bērek*.

Ps. 62:5.

> They only devise plans to thrust him down from his eminence,
> delighting in falsehood,
> they bless with their mouths,
> but inwardly
>
> *yᵊqallᵊlū*.[27]

Although the essence of an imprecation lies largely in "utterance," it would labor the point to deny the possibility of inward cursing. Nevertheless, the minimal meaning of *qillel* supplies adequate sense: The psalmist relies on God alone; men, by contrast, are undependable hypocrites; envying a man's good fortune or high standing, they wish him evil/begrudge him in their hearts, while their lips express the opposite.

Psalm 109 contains a series of imprecations uttered by the psalmist against his adversaries; yet the appearance

---

[27] Eng. vss. "they curse"; SB "ils maudissent"; ATD "fluchen"; LXX κατηρῶντο ; Targ. *yᵊlaṭᵊṭūn*. Scharbert: "verfluchen"; cf. above, n. 22.

of the verb *qillel* in its context provides no evidence that the force of this term is "imprecation."

Ps. 109:28.

yəqalləlū hemmā,[28] but do thou bless!
May my assailants (rd. with LXX, *qāmay*) be put to shame,
but may thy servant (have cause) to rejoice!

This entire Psalm is a protestation of the righteousness of the psalmist, a prayer for vindication and release from his miseries; a condemnation of his accusers and enemies, and invocation of dire misfortunes upon them. Despite these imprecations, there is nothing in the psalm which smacks of the magical in general or incantation in particular. The contention of some commentators that in its original form this psalm was an exorcism directed against a sorcerer is sheer guesswork.

In regard to *qillel* this passage does nothing to strengthen the case for the force of "curse" = "imprecate." Once again the latter sense is derived from its antonymous relationship to *bērek*. But, as the address to the Deity *wəʾattā təḇārek* is not a prayer for a verbal benediction but for material welfare, so the contrasting *yəqalləlū hemmā* is, perhaps, best rendered "despite their abuse/condemnation/evil wishes."

Only a mechanical rendering of the Hebrew tenses

---

[28] AV, JPS, RSV "Let them curse"; AT "They may curse"; SB "Eux maudissent"; ATD "Sie mögen fluchen"; LXX καταράσονται αὐτοὶ ; Targ. *yəlaṭəṭūn*. Scharbert, "verfluchen"; see above, note 22.

(especially in poetry!) could evoke from Oesterley the remark: "That the Psalmist should believe that by appealing to God the curses which he calls down upon the head of his enemy will assume a kind of magical force, reveals an element of religious superstition common enough in those days but far removed from the true religious spirit so predominant in the psalms generally."[29] What indication is there in this verse or in the psalm as a whole that the psalmist's appeal to God to punish his wicked enemies is based on a belief that "his curses...will assume a kind of magical force"?

The following maxim from the Book of Proverbs is understood by Toy as "forbidding meddling in other men's household arrangements... The aggrieved servant will curse his traducer, and the curse will certainly affect the latter."[30]

Prov. 30:10.

> Do not tattle about a servant to his master, lest
>
> <u>yᵊqallɛlᵊḵā</u>[31]
>
> and yourself bear the blame.

Although the terseness of the apothegm precludes a definitive interpretation, this does not warrant the assump-

---

[29] W. O. E. Oesterley, <u>The Psalms</u> (London: SPCK, 1953), p. 460.

[30] Crawford H. Toy, <u>The Book of Proverbs</u>, (<u>ICC</u>, New York: Ch. Scribner's Sons, 1899), p. 525.

[31] AV, JPS (/AT, RSV) "he curse thee (/you)"; SB "qu'il ne te maudisse"; HAT "dir nicht verflucht"; LXX καταράσηται ; Targ. <u>dᵊlāʾ</u> <u>nᵊsaʿarīnāḵ</u>. Scharbert, "ver-

tion that qillel here means "to curse." If talšen and yəqallɛlᵊkā are parallel terms, the argument against "curse" is strong. In any case, "denounce" serves better than "curse" or at least as well; and no eisegis is required in regard to the efficacy of a curse pronounced by an aggrieved servant.

The passage, in which Job expressed the wish that the day on which he had been born had never come to pass, was discussed above, pp. 106 ff. The passage is introduced by

Job 3:1.

After this Job opened his mouth

wayyəqallel[32]

his day.

Although Tur-Sinai draws a distinction of dubious merit between this passage and Jer. 20:14-18, it is difficult to disagree with his conclusion, "Job's words do not represent a curse...Job...does not curse but...expresses wishes, idle wishes, of course: those of a man bemoaning the past."[33]

---

fluchen"; see above, n. 22.

[32]Eng. vss. "and cursed"; SB "et maudit"; HAT "und verfluchte"; LXX κατηράσατο ; Targ. wəlaṭeṭ.

[33]The Book of Job, p. 46 f. His main reason for regarding the passage in Jeremiah as a curse seems to be the use of ʾārūr there in regard to the day and to the man who brought Jeremiah's father the news of his birth. "But the prophet actually curses, in a passionate outburst, the day of his birth, and when he, so to speak, remembers that one cannot curse a day that is gone by, and which anyway is not an animate being that might be affected by a curse, he turns towards a more fitting object; a living person, the man who

Although "curse" conveys the basic idea here to an English reader because it has by metonymy been extended to have a broad range of meanings, the more specific force of qillel here is to rail at/vituperate.

In the following passage from Ecclesiastes, it should be clear that qillel cannot mean "curse" in the sense of "imprecate" unless cursing is regarded as routine activity.

Eccles. 7:21-22.

21) And set no store by all the things that men say,
nor give ear when your servant
məqallᵊlɛkā[34]

22) for you know in your heart that (you), too, (have) many a time
qillaltā[35] others.

This passage is reminiscent of our proverbial: "Sticks and stones will break my bones, but names will never hurt me." "Curse" or "imprecation" as translations of qillel in this text are incongruous. Advice to ignore a curse is almost inconceivable in an age when its power was so feared; nor would the fact (if it were a fact) that cursing was an indulgence common to all be any reason to take it lightly.

---

announced his birth to his father."

[34]AV, JPS "curse thee"; AT, RSV "cursing you"; SB "maudit"; KAT "dir fluchen"; LXX καταρωμένου σε ; Targ. dī yəlōṭ lāḵ.

[35]AV, JPS "thou hast cursed"; AT, RSV "you have cursed"; SB "tu as maudit"; KAT "du...geflucht hast"; LXX σὺ κατηράσω ; Targ. ʾant hᵃwēṯā lāṭē.

The meaning here is that envy and resentment are frequently incurred -- especially at the hands of inferiors and subordinates -- and that derogations, which is what *qillel* means here, from such sources are to be expected; and, furthermore, no more store is to be set by them than by the idle malicious chatter of which all men are sometimes, or often, guilty.

The following passage, its meaning perplexing in general, must be approached with caution in any attempt at exegesis.

Job 24:18.

qal hūʾ ʿal pᵊnē mayīm
tᵊqullal ḥɛlqāṯām bāʾārɛṣ
lōʾ yipnɛ̄ dɛrɛḵ kᵊrāmīm

The difference between the pronoun and the pronominal suffix, the vagueness as to the antecedent(s), together with the ambiguous meaning of the stem *ḥlq* combine to render the text uncertain, if not opaque. RSV renders

> They are swiftly carried away upon the face of the waters;
> their portion is cursed in the land;
> no treader turns toward their vineyards.

Even the term "cursed" in the above context is obviously used in a broad sense, equivalent to "unfavored." Tur-Sinai, taking this verse as applying toone of the titan kings who assisted Leviathan in the mythical conflict against the god of light, renders:

> He was swift upon the face of the water;
> (but) their smoothness was a curse to them upon the land,
> he could not turn into the way of the vineyards.

In this interpretation too curse has the sense of "disadvantage, encumbrance." It is not necessary for the purposes of this study to choose among the many interpretations. Of concern to us is the fact that in this passage, as in the previous ones studied, there is no basis for rendering <u>qillel</u>/<u>qullal</u> by "curse" in the normal sense of that word. Indeed, what this passage once again indicates is that <u>qillel</u> need not even involve an utterance at all.

II. <u>qillel</u> ≠ IMPRECATION. WITH PARENTS AS OBJECT.

Of the several texts which forbid children to treat their parents in the manner represented by the term <u>qillel</u>, the first is the prescription of the death penalty for such behavior in:

Exod. 21:17.

<u>umᵊqallel</u>[36]

his father or his mother shall be put to death.

The instructive similarities (and differences) between the Code of Hammurabi and the Covenant Code (Exod. 20:22-23:33) require no discussion here. One cannot read the verse in question and verse 15 (which immediately precedes MT v. 17 in LXX) without comparing them with their counterparts in the Babylonian Code. The Babylonian parallel to verse 15,

---

[36]AV, JPS "And he that curseth"; AT "Whoever reviles"; RSV "Whoever curses"; SB "Qui traite indignement" and marginal note: "en paroles"; ATD "verflucht"; LXX ὁ κακολογῶν; Targ. <u>wᵊdīlūṭ</u>. Scharbert, "Wenn ein ungeratener Sohn seine Eltern 'schmäht, ihr Ansehen herabsetzt, verächtlich von ihnen redet'..." <u>Biblica</u>, 39, 1, p. 9.

> "Whoever strikes his father or mother shall be put to death,"

is CH § 195, which stipulates that "if a son strikes his father, they shall cut off his hand."[37] Whatever the reason for the severer penalty proscribed for the identical offense in the Bible, the closest analogy to verse 17 is CH § 192:

> If the son of a *girseqû* or the son of a *SAL ZI·IK·RU·UM* states to the father who reared him, or to the mother who reared him, "You are not my father," or, "You are not my mother," they shall cut out his tongue."[38]

The son in this case is clearly an adopted son; the *girseqû*, being a eunuch, and the *SAL ZI·IK·RU·UM*, being a "shut-in" (*sekrum* > *sekertum*) of a special type, are incapable of procreation. The purpose of adoption was almost certainly to provide an heir who would be responsible for the funerary rites for his adopted parent(s).[39]

The difference between Babylonian society, where the family was basically an economic unit, and Israel, where the basic criterion of family was that of blood-kinship, would lead us not to expect identical, or even similar, circumstances. Nevertheless, the analogy between the two pairs of legal provisions strengthens the doubt that *qillel* in verse 17 has the restricted sense of "curse" or "impre-

---

[37] *šumma māru abašu imtaḫaṣ rittašu inakkisū* (DM, Vol. 2, p. 76).

[38] *summa mār girseqī u lū mār SAL ZI·IK·RU·UM ana abim murabbīšu u ummim murabbītišu ul abi atta ul ummi atti iqtabī lišānšu inakkisū*. (DM, VOL. 2, p. 74-76).

[39] For a discussion (and bibliography) of the *girseqû* and *SAL ZI·IK·RU·UM*, (though not necessarily the conclusions) see DM, Vol. 2, pp. 240-41, 245.

cate." The Babylonian law analagous to verse 17, refers to a son's repudiation of his parent(s). The biblical passage seems to bear a similar connotation. Although qillel here need not necessarily have the precise sense of "repudiation," there is every likelihood that it means just that or something very similar. Even "revile" is misleading as a rendering of qillel, for there is no indication that the forbidden action necessarily involves a verbalism. Arnold Ehrlich, whose insight into biblical idiom has been frequently vindicated, states flatly, "qll bedeutet hier nicht fluchen, sondern gröblich verunehren; vgl. Deut. 27, 16, wo es mqlh [maqlē] fur mqll [mᵊqallel] heisst."[40]

What is clearly intended is a serious breach of filial duty, so flagrant as to merit a penalty equal to that prescribed for physical violence. Israelite society defined for itself the kind of behavior subsumed under qillel ʾāḇîw wᵊimmō. That it is not spelled out for us here[41] should occasion no more surprise than in the instance of the injunction of which this one is the antithesis:

---

[40]A. B. Ehrlich, Randglossen, Vol. 1, p. 349.

[41]The case of the faithless and defiant son (ben sōrer umōrɛ̄), Deut. 21:18-21, may well be an expansion on the part of the Deuteronomist(s) of the terse statement of Exod. 21:17. The emphasis appears to be not upon a single, specific act of misconduct on the part of the son, but rather on his persistence in defying the correction of his parents. Cf. v. 18: "If a man have a son, false and defiant/rebellious, who will not obey his father or his mother, and though they chastise him he (still) will not heed them--"

Exod. 20:12.

kabbeḏ ʾeṯ ʾāḇīkā wəʾeṯ ʾimmeḵā...

Normally rendered,

"Honor your father and your mother...,"

an improvement might be "show respect to..." The antonym qillel then might fitly be rendered as "to treat with disrespect."

The counterpart of Exod. 21:17 in the Holiness Code requires no separate discussion.

Lev. 20:9.

For any man who

yəqallel[42]

his father or his mother shall be put to death;

qillel[43]

his father or mother, his blood-guilt is upon himself.

The context of prohibitions in which this verse occurs -- idolatry, witchcraft, adultery, and incest -- would appear to strengthen the case against "curse," and urge a rendering along the lines of "disgrace, dishonor, abuse, treat disrespectfully."

The Book of Proverbs refers twice to the offense of abuse of parents. In keeping with the general view that

---

[42]AV, JPS "(that) curseth"; AT, RSV "curses"; SB "maudira"; HAT "verflucht"; LXX ὃς ἂν κακῶς εἴπῃ; Targ. dīlūṭ.

[43]AV, JPS "he hath cursed"; AT "since he has cursed"; RSV "he has cursed"; SB "il a maudit"; HAT "er hat verflucht"; LXX κακῶς εἶπεν; Targ. lāṭ.

right conduct leads to felicity, and wrong behavior to disaster, the admonition is offered:

Prov. 20:20.

<u>məqallel</u>[44]

his father or his mother, his lamp will be extinguished to utter darkness.

It would be a cause for wonder, indeed, if only the outrage of malediction against parents were picked out from the register of possible unfilial acts. The term "curse" is no more apposite in the above verse than it is in:

Prov. 30:11.

There is the type (<u>dōr</u>) who

<u>yəqallel</u>[45]

his father
and does not bless his mother.

Here, despite the parallel antonym <u>yəbārek</u>, which might lead one to "curse" for <u>qillel</u>, verse 17 provides virtual explication of the offense;

> The eye that mocks his father,
> and scorns obedience to his mother
> Will be picked out by the ravens of the wadi,
> and eaten by the vulture brood.

It may be said in conclusion, in regard to <u>qillel</u>, especially with parents as object, that tradition had a choice to derive its force from either the antonym <u>kibbeḏ</u> or the antonym <u>bēreḵ</u>. Even the latter does not make inevi-

---

[44]AV, JPS "Whoso curseth"; AT "who curses"; RSV "If one curses"; SB "Qui maudit"; HAT "Wer verflucht"; LXX κακολογοῦντος ; Targ. <u>dəlāyeṭ</u>. Ehrlich: <u>mqll</u> heisst wer grobe Geringschätzung bekundet, nicht wer flucht."

[45]AV "(<u>that</u>) curseth"; JPS "that curse"; AT, RSV "who curse"; SB "qui maudit"; HAT "verflucht"; LXX καταρᾶται ; Targ. <u>nəṣaʿār</u>.

tably for qillel = "curse." But be that as it may, tradition, by and large, would seem to have made the wrong choice.

III. qillel ≠ IMPRECATION. WITH KINGS AS OBJECTS.

Although Judges 8:22-23 informs us that Gideon rejected the offer of "the men of Israel" to set up a dynastic rule over them, one of his sons contrives to become king over the city-state of Shechem. Abimelech, son of Gideon by a Shechemite concubine, exploits his kinship with the Shechemites (who are racially distinguished from the Israelites -- cf. Gen. 34 -- and, apparently still constitute the bulk of Shechem's population) to win their support against his full-Israelite brothers, and to become their sovereign. Now Gaal, son of Ebed, a full Shechemite, turns his kinsmen against Abimelech by emphasizing the latter's Israelite blood.

Judges 9:27-28.

> 27) Now having gathered the grapes from their vineyards and having trod them, they held a festival; they entered into the temple of their god, and eating and drinking
>
> wayyᵊqallᵊlū[46]
>
> Abimelech. 28) Gaal ben Ebed declared, "Who is Abimelech, and who (are we of) Shechem that we should serve him? Were not the son of Jerubbaal and his deputy Zebul

---

[46]AV, JPS "and cursed"; AT, RSV "and reviled"; SB "maudirent"; ATD "fluchten auf"; LXX κατηράσατο; Targ. wᵊlāṭū. Scharbert, "Die Sichemiten scherten sich nicht mehr um ihren König Abimelek, sondern sie assen und tranken 'und sprachen von Abimelak geringschätzig.' Den Inhalt des wayyᵊqallᵊlū umschreibt Gaal in V. 28:..." (Biblica 39, 1, p. 9).

> subject to the men of Hamor, ancestor of Shechem?[47]
> Why should we now be subject to him?

It should thus be clear that <u>qillel</u> here means neither to curse nor to revile. The words of Gaal indicate that "disparaged" is the most likely force of the verb here, the general sense being that the Shechemites "renounced or repudiated" Abimelech as their king.

Equally explicit as to the content of the verb <u>qillel</u> is the text in II Samuel, where the target of the verb is King David.

II Sam. 16:5-11.

> 5) When King David had come as far as Bahurim, there came out a man of the kindred of the line of Saul, Shimei ben Gera by name
>
> <u>umᵊqallel</u>[48]
>
> as he came. 6) He hurled stones at David, all the courtiers of David the King, the entire force and all the paladins who were on his right and his left. 7) And this is what Shimei said
>
> <u>bᵊqallᵊlô</u>[49]
>
> "Run, run, you bloodguilty scoundrel. 8) YHWH has requited upon you the shed blood of the line of Saul, in whose place you have reigned. Yes, YHWH has put the kingship into the hand of your son Absalom. Your plight

---

[47] Lit., <u>the father of Shechem</u>. Although the terms "father (<u>ʾāḇ</u>) and "son (<u>ben</u>)" stand, respectively, for lord and vassal, the term <u>ʾaḇî</u> here has the force of the eponymous ancestor of the Shechemites, analagous to the patriarchs of Israel. Cf. Gen. 33:19, 24:2-26; Josh. 24:32.

[48] AV, RSV "cursed"; JPS "and kept on cursing"; AT "uttering a stream of curses"; SB "en proférant des malédictions"; ATD "unter fortwährendom Fluchen"; LXX καὶ καταρώμενος; Targ. <u>umᵊlāṭēṭ</u>.

[49] AV, JPS (/RSV) "when (/as) he cursed"; SB "en le maudissant"; ATD "als er fluchte"; LXX ἐν τῷ καταρᾶσθαι; Targ. <u>bᵊlāṭaṭûṯēh</u>.

is due to your wickedness, for you are guilty of bloodshed." 9) Then Abishai ben Zeruiah said to the king, "Why (should) this dead dog

y^əqallel[50]

my lord, the king! Let me cross over and take off his head." 10) But the king said, "What have I in common with you, you sons of Zeruiah?

ki yəqallel;[51]

YHWH has told him

qallel[52]

David, so who can say to him, 'How dare you do this?' 11) Now," continued David to Abishai and to all his subjects, "here my own son, sprung from my loins, seeks my life. How much the more now may this Benjaminite! Let him alone

wī(y)qallel;[53]

YHWH has indeed bidden him.

This narrative, with its fullness of detail, could hardly have been better designed to inform us what qillel means, and what it does not mean. It must be remembered that the Books of Samuel are by an author who is partisan to David. Thus in Chapter 4 of II Samuel, David orders the death of the assassins of Ishbosheth, son of Saul, to show that the removal of the one obstacle to his assumption of rule over a united Israel was not of his doing. In Chapter 21 of II Samuel we are told of the execution of two sons

---

[50]Eng. vss. "curse"; SB "maudisse"; ATD "...zu fluchen"; LXX καταρᾶται ; Targ. yəlāṭeṭ.

[51]AV, JPS "let him curse"; AT, (/RSV) "If he curses (/is cursing)"; SB "S'il maudit"; AT "wenn er flucht"; LXX καὶ οὕτως καταράσθω; Targ. kədēn yalṭēṭ.

[52]Eng. vss. "Curse"; SB "Maudis"; ATD "Fluche"; LXX καταρᾶσθαι ; Targ. laṭēṭ.

[53]Eng. vss. "and let him curse"; SB "Laissez-le maudire"; ATD "Lasst ihn fluchen"; LXX ἄφετε αὐτὸν καταρᾶσθαι ; Targ. wī(y)laṭēṭ.

and five grandsons of Saul. These deaths, which are to be placed chronologically prior to the revolt of Absalom, are attributed to the will of God. But would a kinsman of Saul have been convinced of David's innocence? It is clear that Shimei was not. He charges David with responsibility for the death of members of the late king's family. And David's present misfortune, he announces, is heaven-sent retribution for his crimes.

David's refusal to have Shimei punished, or at least arrested, would be strange indeed if Shimei was engaged in imprecation. Furthermore, why should YHWH who is already punishing David, require Shimei to curse the king? David's statement that Shimei's conduct is due to a command from YHWH is not to be taken literally. In keeping with the psychology of the time, David understands his plight (as, indeed, any misfortune) as traceable to the will of God.[54] The fact that he has been so reduced is warrant enough for Shimei's conduct. The pious man confesses his wrongs (although here David does not necessarily plead guilty to the specific accusation of Shimei's), bears his punishment with resignation, and prays that at the expiration of his sentence, God will restore him to favor.[55]

---

[54]For an exact parallel to v. 11 <u>kī ʾāmar lō YHWH</u> cf., Isa. 36:10 (II Kings 18:25) where YHWH <u>ʾāmar ʾēlay</u> does not mean that YHWH has literally revealed his will to the king of Assyria, but rather that YHWH's support of Assyria is implicit to Hezekiah's breach of the covenant with the former, sworn to by YHWH. Cf. above, p. 38, n. 34.

[55]Cf. v. 12 in this account and Pss. 6, 9, 10, 13, 17, 22, 25, and many others.

Shimei's words do not constitute imprecation or malediction; they do constitute a vituperative denunciation. And the proper translation of qillel in this context is "rail at/vituperate/denounce."[56]

In Isaiah 8:21, two terms, mɛlɛk (king) and ʾᵉlōhīm (normally, 'God' or 'gods') appear as the objects of the verb qillel. The problem is somewhat complicated by the fact that these two nouns are not governed directly by the verb but by the verb together with the preposition bᵊ-. The following translation by H. L. Ginsberg,[57] makes sound sense:

Isa. 8:16-21.

> 16) Bind up message, seal up the oracle in the children... 19) And should anybody say to you, "Consult the ghosts and the familiar spirits, that chirp and mutter; for a people can consult its numina -- the dead on behalf of the living -- 20) for oracle and message," surely he shall speak thus for whom there is no dawn.

---

[56] An instance of how far one may be led astray by the traditional rendering of qillel as curse is the interpretation of Sheldon Blank (HUCA, Vol. 23, Part 1, 1950-51), pp. 86 ff. "A curse in the imperative-vocative form of a spell occurs in 2 Sam. 16:7: ṣēʾ ṣēʾ... 'Begone, begone...,' a repeated imperative followed by a double vocative. For the relation between the spell and the curse it is highly significant that although this utterance has the precise form of a spell, it is referred to in the context as a 'curse.'" To this writer's mind, there is no occurrence here of either spell or curse. Incidentally, the words ṣēʾ ṣēʾ (some have suggested reading ṣīʾ "excreta") have no special significance. Hebrew normally employs specific terms according to the direction of motion (Cf. II Kings 2:23-24, where the taunt ʿᵃlē...ʿᵃle uses the verb for going up only because Elisha is literally going up to Bethel.) The rendering "Run, run" aims to convey the jeer of Shimei. David is not merely going out; he is withdrawing in a humiliating retreat from the capital city. The occurrence of qillel in the derivative account in I Kings 2:8 requires no separate discussion.

[57] H. L. Ginsberg, "An Unrecognized Allusion to Kings Pekah and Hoshea of Israel," Eretz-Israel (Jerusalem: Israel Exploration Society, 1958), pp. 61 ff.

21) Upon him shall come hardship (?) so that he shall suffer hunger; and when he is hungry, he shall become enraged

<u>wᵊqillel</u> <u>bᵊmalkō</u> <u>ub̲ēʾlōhāw</u>[58]

(H.L.G. "and revolt against his king(s?) and his numina...")

Cursing in the sense of imprecation is palpably unsatisfactory in this context. The ancient versions for all their departure from MT have the verb governing a direct object; and to take <u>bᵊ</u>- as "by" is to leave the verb without any object at all -- whom or what would he "curse"? On the other hand, if <u>malkō</u> and <u>ʾᵉlōhāw</u> are the direct objects of the verb, what good would it do to imprecate against king and "gods," assuming the latter were subject to imprecations. The passage yields satisfactory sense only if <u>qillel</u> is rendered, in keeping with the force thus far attested for it, by "spurn, repudiate." The thought would then be entirely consistent with Isaiah's oft-repeated theme that the reliance of Judah must be upon YHWH and no other -- in the realm of the natural or supernatural.

The following passage also fails to bear out so specific or strong a force for <u>qillel</u> as "curse."

Eccles. 10:20.

Even in your thought[59]

---

[58]AV, AT, RSV "and curse their king and their God"; JPS "and curse by their king and their God"; SB "blasphémant son roi et son Dieu"; ATD "und er flucht seinem König und seinem Gott"; LXX καὶ κακῶς ἐρεῖτε τὸν ἄρχοντα καὶ τὰ παταχρα (πατρια?); Targ. <u>wᵊyilūṭ</u> <u>wᵊyib̲zē</u> <u>šūm</u> <u>pᵊṭak̲rēh</u> <u>wᵊṭaʿawāṯēh</u>.

[59]Or, if, with Ehrlich, one accepts the emendation suggested by Perles to read <u>bᵊmaṣaʿk̲ā</u> (‖ <u>miškāb̲ᵊk̲ā</u>) in

ʾal tᵊqallel[60] a king
and in the privacy of your bedchamber
ʾal tᵊqallel the rich ;

for a sky-borne bird will convey your voice
or a winged creature report the matter.

The meaning of the dictum is transparent: politic advice to be prudent in one's relations with men of power. Even in one's bedchamber it is not safe to speak in derogation or disrespect (qillel) of king or magnate, for "the walls have ears" -- or, "a little bird will tell" them.

IV. qillel ≠ IMPRECATION.
WITH DEITY AS OBJECT.

The perplexities in the following passage are due to a number of features: 1) the paradigmatic coalescence in the imperfect of nqb "to prick, specify," and qbb "to curse"; 2) the occurrence of qillel both with and without an object; 3) the question as to the meaning of qillel. The problem in regard to the first of the above-mentioned features will be solved here by the simple expedient of taking wayyiqqob in verse 11, as do Targum and Rashi, as the imperfect of nqb.

Lev. 24:10-16, 23.

10) Now a certain man, son of an Israelite mother and of an Egyptian father, went out among the Israelites; and a struggle ensued in the camp between

---

place of bᵊmaḏāʿᵃkā, "Even on your couch." Ehrlich, on the verb here writes, "tqll ist im Sinne von 'schmähen' zu verstehen." (Randglossen, Vol. 7), p. 101.

60AV, JPS "curse not"; RSV "do not curse"; AT "do not defame"; SB "Ne maudis pas"; HAT "fluche nicht"; LXX μὴ καταράσῃ ; Targ. lāʾ tᵊlūṭ.

the half-Israelite, and a full-Israelite. 11) And the half-Israelite, specifying/enunciating the Name[61]

wayyᵊqallel;[62]

so they brought him to Moses... 12) They placed him under guard, waiting upon a decree of YHWH's. 13) And YHWH spoke to Moses: 14) "Bring

ʾeṯ hammᵊqallel[63]

outside the camp, let all who heard him lay their hands upon his head, then let the entire congregation stone him. 15) And to the Israelites you are to declare as follows, 'Any man that

yᵊqallel ʾᵉlōhāw[64]

shall bear his punishment;[65] 16) but he who enunciates (*nōqeḇ*) the name YHWH[66] shall be put to death -- all the congregation shall stone him -- be he alien or native, for enunciating (*bᵊnoqᵊḇō*) the Name,[67] he shall die...
. . . ."

---

[61]Eng. vss. "blasphemed the Name"; SB "blasphéma le Nom"; HAT "lästerte...den (göttlichen) Namen"; LXX καὶ ἐπονομάσας... τὸ ὄνομα; Targ. *upārēš...yāṯ šᵊmā*.

[62]Eng. vss. "and cursed"; SB "et le maudit"; HAT "und verfluchte ihn"; LXX κατηράσατο; Targ. *wᵊʾargēz*. Ehrlich, "er sprech aus." (*Randglossen*, Vol. 2, p. 87.)

[63]AV, JPS "him that hath cursed"; AT (/RSV) "the one (/him) who has cursed"; SB "qui a prononcé la malédiction"; HAT "den Lästerer"; LXX καταρασάμενον; Targ. *yaṯ dᵊʾargēz*. Scharbert (Biblica 39, 1, p. 9); "Der Mischling, den Moses wegen Gotteslästerung hinrichten lässt, hat wahrscheinlich 'Jahwes Namen kleingemacht, als unbedeutend abgetan,' indem er ihn mit den mächtigen Göttern Ägyptens verglichen hat."

[64]AV, JPS "curseth his God"; AT, RSV "curses his God"; SB "(qui) maudit son Dieu"; HAT "(der) seinem Gotte flucht"; LXX ὃς ἐὰν καταράσηται θεόν; Targ. *ʾarē yargēz qᵊḏām ʾᵉlāhēh*.

[65]Lit., "his sin/offense" but it must mean the penalty for it.

[66]The various renderings are along the same lines as those cited in n. 61.

[67]Renderings along lines cited in n. 61.

23) So Moses addressed the Israelites, whereupon they brought

ʾɛt hammᵊqallel[68]

outside the camp and stoned him...

The renderings of this passage in English, French, and German are as misleading as they are demonstrably wrong. They assume that wayyiqqoḇ in verse 11 derives from the root qbb "to curse," render it by "blaspheme" or an equivalent term, and then take the following wayyᵊqallel as a separate action, but one not differentiated in meaning from the preceding verb. One is hard put to discover just what is meant by "blasphemed the Name and cursed." The confusion is further compounded in verse 16 where nqb, occurring twice -- and informing on the root of wayyiqqoḇ in verse 11 -- is translated by "blaspheme" on the conjecture, no doubt, that nqb is a secondary formation from qbb. It is, indeed, this very passage which has led lexicographers astray,[69] for nowhere else is the denotation or the connotation of nqb in question. Nor should it be here. In both verse 11 and verse 16 the verb nqb has the well attested meaning "prick off, designate, specify." Assuming for the moment that qillel means "to curse," verse 11 clearly reads, "And the half-Israelite, specifying (or, specifically employing) the Name, cursed." Verses 15 and 16 (where the unambiguity of the verb nqb should have supplied the clue to both root and meaning of verse 11) differentiate, then, between one who "curses" in general, and one who does so

---

[68]Renderings as in n. 63.

[69]Cf., e.g. BDB, p. 666b II. nāqaḇ.

specifying YHWH by name.[70]

Two questions remain to be settled. Who is the object of wayy$^{\partial}$qallel in verse 11? What is the meaning of y$^{\partial}$qallel ʾᵉlōhāw in verse 15?

In answer to the first I would suggest, first, that qillel does not stand in immediate need of an object. As in II Sam. 16:5, 10, 11 (see above, p.138 f.) the verb means "to hurl abuse" (cf., also, Targ. in notes 62, 63, 64). I would further suggest that the target of the abuse, here, is not the Deity but the full-Israelite antagonist. The nexus of the entire passage is, after all, the quarrel between the two men. This suggestion is supported by verses 17-22. Imbedded in the heart of the incident, part of YHWH's oracular response in regard to the way a m$^{\partial}$qallel is to be treated, they are hardly likely to be an accidental and irrelevant intrusion.[71] Yet these verses deal with offenses against one's fellow man and his property -- and not at all with offenses against the Deity -- i.e., homicide, mayhem, destruction of property. It would appear then that certain acts represented by qillel with man or men as the object might ipso facto be acts of qillel against God. Such acts (v. 15: ʾīš ʾīš kī y$^{\partial}$qallel ʾᵉlōhāw) would have had their prescribed penalties (v. 15: w$^{\partial}$nāśā ḥeṭʾō); but when the abusive act involved a disposition of the name

---

[70]Since YHWH, rendered "the Lord," is a proper name, the translation "name of the Lord" is unacceptable.

[71]It is noteworthy that this is the fourth time that the verb hikkā (v. 18 ʾīš ʾīš kī yakkē...) occurs in close association with qillel. The other three passages, previously discussed, are Gen. 8:21, Exod. 21:15, 17, and Neh. 13:25. Cf. above, respectively pp. 119 f., 132 f., 124.

YHWH (v. 16: *wənōqeḇ šēm YHWH* -- certainly not the mere mention of the name in an innocuous context) then that additional feature would call for the death penalty, be the culprit alien or Israelite (v. 16: *kagger kāʾεzrāḥ bənoqəḇō šēm yūmāṯ*).

Further exploration of this interpretation of *qillel ʾelōhīm* must be deferred until the discussion of Exodus 22:27 (*ʾelōhīm lōʾ təqallel wənāśīʾ bəʿamməḵā lōʾ ṯāʾor*). For the present, the following considerations may be urged against taking *qillel* with *ʾelōhīm* as object to mean "curse God": 1) thus far, not a single occurrence of *qillel* has proven to mean "curse"; 2) in an age in which, to the best of our knowledge, there were few atheists or none, in which *numina* of all kinds were dreaded, a moral prescription not to curse God would be meaningless. Self-interest alone would be enough to keep people from such suicidal behavior;[72] 3) despite analogies drawn from Arab practice, the Bible does not supply a single instance in which God (or any deity) is the object of an imprecation; 4) the common expression for "blasphemy" -- or verbal abuse of deity -- usually confined to tests of power between hostile parties and the gods invoked by each side, is *ḥērep*, *giddep*, or a combination of the two. These expressions, too, reflect cutting taunts but not imprecation.

---

[72]Even when Job's wife counsels Job to undertake such a suicidal course, the verb *qillel* need not mean "imprecate." See below, p. 171 f.

The following passage is discussed here on the strong presumption that the word lāhɛm in MT should read ʾelōhīm.

I Sam. 3:11-14.

> 11) YHWH said to Samuel, "I am about to do something in Israel, of such a nature that both ears of anyone who hears about it will be set a-ringing. 12) At that time I will fulfill from first to last against Eli every word which I have spoken concerning his line. 13) I am telling him that I am passing sentence upon his dynasty for all time on account of the crime, that knowing that his sons (were)
>
> mᵊqallᵊlīm lāhɛm (rd. ʾelōhīm),[73]
>
> he did not check them. 14) Therefore have I sworn concerning Eli's dynasty that never will the crime of his house be expiated through sacrifice or offering.

In addition to LXX, Rashi and Kimchi also understand ʾlhm as the object of the verb; the latter explicitly numbering this passage as one of the eighteen tiqqūnē sōpᵊrīm (i.e., scribal emendations of euphemistic purpose). S. R. Driver accepts the LXX version, pointing out that the verb qillel "does not mean to bring a curse upon anyone, and is followed not by a dative but by an accusative."[74]

Neither the Greek κακολογέω (lit., "to speak evil of, rail at") nor "curse" in any sense of the word is acceptable, however. For we know what constituted the offense of Eli's sons -- and it is clear that it involved no

---

[73]AV "made themselves vile"; JPS "did bring a curse upon themselves"; AT, RSV "were blaspheming God" and marg. note, "Gk: Heb. for themselves"; SB "maudissaient Dieu"; ATD "(dass sie) Gott missachteten"; LXX ὅτι κακολογοῦντες θεὸν; Targ. margᵊzīn lᵊhōn bᵊnōhī.

[74]S. R. Driver, Notes on the Hebrew Text of the Books of Samuel (Oxford: Clarendon Press, 1913), p. 43 f.

utterance whatsoever.[75] Indeed, we have two separate accounts, giving two different versions of the offense. In I Sam. 2:22-25, the offense is that the sons are having relations with women who gather at the entrance to the "tent of meeting." Eli's words to his sons (v. 25: wᵊʾim lᵊ-YHWH yɛḥᵉṭāʾ ʾîš) make it explicit that this is an offense against YHWH. The other version of the offense is detailed in 2:12-17. As against the normal procedure (mišpāṭ) of taking pot-luck, the sons of Eli insisted on taking their portion in raw meat, even before the fat was burned on the altar. Verse 17: "The offense (haṭṭaʾt) of the men was thus deemed highly serious by YHWH for the men were treating with contempt the offering belonging to YHWH."

To which of these two offenses does the mᵊqallᵊlîm *ʾᵉlōhîm of 3:13 refer? At first glance it might appear to refer to the latter offense as constituting a more direct case of disrespect to the Deity's cult. Just as there are two versions of the offense, however, there are two versions of the rejection by God of the Eliad priestly dynasty. The other account of the rejection (2:27-36) has an anonymous "man of God" mediating the word of YHWH to Eli. And this account specifically refers to the offense of priestly self-aggrandizement at the expense of reverence for offerings brought to YHWH. Verse 29: "...and you have honored your sons at my expense (wattᵊkabbeḏ...mimmɛnnî)

---

[75]Cf. Scharbert (Biblica, 39, 1) p. 8, 9: "Gegen Gott gerichtet kann es qillel...nur heissen: '..., das Ansehen herabsetzen'; das letztere trifft besonders fur 1 Sam. 3, 13 zu: Helis Sohne haben durch ihr schändliches Benehm beim Kult Gottes Ansehen herabgesetzt und in Misskredit gebracht."

fattening them[76] on the first cuts of all the offerings brought by my people Israel."[77] It follows, therefore, that the m^əqall^əlīm *ʾᵉlōhīm "(the act of) disrespect to God," of 3:13 refers to the offense of cohabitation in 2:22. Thus, we have here, not only confirmation that qillel as applied to God has nothing to do with curse or utterance, but dramatic support for the suggestion made in the discussion of Lev. 24:10-22 that a specific mode of immoral behavior towards mortals may be and is regarded as an act of qillel ʾᵉlōhīm.

A discussion of Exod. 22:27, had, perforce, to wait upon a comprehensive discussion of the uses of the two verbs ʾārar and qillel.

Exod. 22:27.

ʾᵉlōhīm lōʾ tᵊqallel wᵊnāśīʾ bᵊʿammᵊkā lōʾ tāʾor[78]

---

[76]Rd. lᵊhabrīʾām. MT's lᵊhabrīʾᵃkεm is impossible Hebrew, aside from the fact that the preceding banēkā is the antecedent.

[77]This offense, too, unquestionably constituted an act of qillel against God. In the light of this the occurrence of the antonym kibbed in v. 30 should not go unremarked kī mᵊkabbᵊday ʾᵃkabbed ubōzay yēqāllu "for those who honor me will I honor, and those who despise me shall be demeaned." Cf., also the remark of Rashi on 3:13: "wᵊken kol qᵊlālā lāšōn qālūt ubizzāyōn hūʾ -- and every case of qᵊlālā is an expression of irreverance and opprobrium."

[78]AV "Thou shalt not revile the gods, nor curse the ruler of thy people." JPS "Thou shalt not revile God (marg.: "That is, the judges"), nor curse a ruler of thy people." AT "You must not revile God, nor curse a ruler of your people." SB "Tu ne blasphèmeras pas Dieu (marg.: ou "les dieux," peut-être les juges, ici et 22:7, 8: cf. Ps. 82:1), ni tu ne maudiras un chef de ton peuple." ATD "Gott sollst du nicht verfluchen, und einen nāśīʾ in deinem Volk sollst du nicht verwünschen." LXX θεοὺς οὐ κακολογήσεις καὶ ἄρχοντα(s) τοῦ λαοῦ σου οὐ κακῶς ἐρεῖς ; Targ. dayānā lāʾ taqīl wᵊrabā bᵊʿammāk lāʾ tᵊlūt.

The traditional renderings of this verse lead to the bland interpretation that the object of the command is "reverence to be shown to God, and to those in authority."[79] The verse, however, is an interdiction, not a positive exhortation, and requires an exploration of the prohibited actions inhering in the two verbs. It has already been seen that the verb qillel need not and, indeed, more often does not involve a spoken content; while the verb ʾārar has a range of meanings far more specialized and significant than the general and ambiguous "curse." Is it possible to recover the force of this pregnant verse? Some of the possibilities for the content of qillel ʾelōhīm have been seen in the discussion of Lev. 24:10 ff. and I Sam. 3:11 ff. What does it mean to "ʾārar" a nāśīʾ; and what is the significance of the juxtaposition of these two offenses?

The recovery of so much of the culture and institutions of the near-Eastern world of biblical times may here supply, once again, a helpful analogue. Noting that "it is clear, at all events, that the mechanical translations 'curse' and 'revile' are altogether out of place in that passage [Exod. 22:27]," Speiser suggests "Cf. provisionally G. Boyer, ARM VIII 174 n. 1."[80] I reproduce here, in abridged form, the content of Boyer's discussion in the

---

[79]S. R. Driver, The Book of Exodus (Cambridge, 1953), p. 233 n. For the exclusions of "the judges" for ʾelōhīm see Driver's discussion, and Anne E. Draffkorn, "ILANI/ELOHIM," JBL 76, 3 (Sept. 1957), pp. 216-24.

[80]E. A. Speiser, "An Angelic 'Curse'," JAOS, 80, 3 (July-Sept., 1960), p. 199.

"Commentaire Juridique."[81]

The expression _asakka(m)_ _akālu(m)_ "to eat the _asakku_" (of king or god), occurs in a number of the Mari texts as a metaphor by which is expressed the sense that he who disobeys a royal order or decree is considered as being guilty of a serious offense against the king or a divinity. In other texts, this metaphor is applied to the violation of an oath taken by the life of the king; while in one text, the expression _asak_ DN...DN..._u_ PN _Ikul_ "he will have eaten the _asakku_ of the named gods and of Yasmah-Addu (son of the king, Samsi-Addu)," occupies the place which in the normal formula is occupied by an oath. In one juridical text[82] the parties to a compact, instead of swearing by the life (_MU_ = _nīšum_) of the king, swear by his _asakku_ -- thus indicating that these two expressions, "the life of the king" and "the _asakku_ of the king," while not synonymous, are closely related in meaning.

The basis of this "close relationship" can be discerned in one text where the _asakku_ of the formula is replaced, or displaced, by the Sumerian ideogram _ŠAR_^{mes}, _i.e._, "the herbs of the king"; whence it becomes evident that the _asakku_ has a concrete meaning over against the abstract

---

[81] _Archives Royales de Mari_ (Paris: Imprimerie Nationale, 1958), pp. 116 ff.

[82] ARM VIII 1. In this text the sanction of the "oath" is apparently applied not to either of the contracting parties, but to a third party who might seek to violate or abrogate the terms agreed to by the contracting parties. Hence the force here is to invoke for the agreement the same immunity to breach as is possessed by a royal decree... It would appear, however, that what is involved is nothing more or less than a kind of _māmītu_, equal to Heb. _ʾālā_. Cf. above the discussion of both these terms.

sense of "proscription" or "tabu" which is normally assigned to it; (the) asakku designates a material object capable of being eaten. In view of the established connection between the life of the king and his asakku, the conclusion is inescapable that the asakku, at least in its primitive sense, might consist of a certain plant or plants whose existence bore a mystic or magical tie to the life of the king.

Now an oath is an asseveration or promise supported normally by the invocation of a non-human agency (magical or divine) to provide the penalty or sanction against the party making a false assertion or failing to keep his word. The formula "by the life of the king" represents an invocation of the royal authority, which has the power to enforce respect for agreements; hence its substitution for the ritualistic invocation of the supernatural.[83] The only possible assumption underlying an oath "by the life of the king" is that the oath puts the life of the king at stake. Just like the Roman who swore by the well-being of the Emperor, or like people today, who swear on the head of one dear to them, the citizen of Mari who swore by the life of the king thereby determined that the king would be placed in danger if the condition which was the object of the oath was not respected. Hence the interchangeability in oaths

---

[83]Boyer points out that in Mari, as in contemporary Sippar and Nippur, the essential element of the oath lies in the invocation of the king, by title or by proper name. Invocation of divinity plays a secondary role or is entirely missing. Nor can this be attributed to the divine power of the kings, for oaths by the life of the king are the rule at places and times in which no claim of divinity is made by royalty.

and adjurations of the life of the king and the _asakku_ on which his life was dependent.

To the argument that it is hardly likely that a mortal's imprecation could be regarded as capable of imperiling the life of a deity, the answer is that in the course of centuries the sense or the force of the oath by the life of the king was modified. The force of the imprecation was so weakened that violation of the terms of the oath was construed only as a grave offense against the crown, or, in the case of oath by a deity, as sacrilege. In any event, the fact that a violator of an oath imperiled the king's life had the effect of changing the breach of a contract from a simple violation of individual rights to the crime of _lèse-majesté_. Even if the threat to the king's life were a fiction, this would be something which the king could not tolerate.

Such, in brief, is George Boyer's argument.

Boyer's explanation of the meaning of an oath by the life of the king is in itself altogether reasonable and persuasive. The evidence of the _asakku_ texts fortifies the explanation almost to the point of conviction. And the answer which Boyer gives to the question of the likelihood of a god's life being imperiled, _i.e._, that the oath by the life of the deity may be a secondary development on the analogy of the oath by the king's life, may be correct. This last conjecture however, need not be necessary. The gods of Mesopotamia are born or created, live and die.[84]

---

[84]Cf. the fate of Apsu, Tiamat, and Kingu in the _Creation Epic_; cf., also, _Nergal and Ereshkigal_ in ANET,

Their powers are limited and enhanced by powers beyond themselves;[85] it is, therefore, far from inconceivable that acts of men might shake the foundations of heaven as well as those of earth. As for the life-giving potency of magical plants, Marduk facing Tiamat in battle holds in his hand a plant to put out poison,[86] Etana ascends to heaven to attain the plant of birth,[87] and Gilgamesh dives into the deep for the plant of rejuvenation.[88]

What are the features common to the biblical matter under study and Boyer's discussion of the Mari texts? For one thing, oaths by the life of deity or king are common to both.[89] At least in the early strata of the Bible, as in Mesopotamia, there are indications of belief in the operation of certain forces independent of the ethical workings of sin and retribution, guilt and punishment.[90] And despite

---

p. 66, ll. 26-7.

[85]Cf. the role of the Tablets of Destinies in the Myth of Zu. ANET, p. 111 ff.

[86]Creation Epic, Tablet IV l. 62 (ANET p. 66).

[87]Cf. ANET pp. 114 ff.

[88]Cf. Tablet XI, 258-289. (ANET p. 96).

[89]Cf. Moshe Greenberg, "The Hebrew Oath Particle HAY/HE," JBL 76, 1 (March 1957), p.34 ff. Prof. John J. Tepfer has pointed out to me, in connection with the question of the (to us, bizarre) concept of the life of the deity being put in jeopardy, that this is just the manner in which the rabbis understood blasphemy. Blasphemy was regarded as an imprecation upon the deity. Since there was only one God, the expression in the Mishnah, Sanhedrin 7:5, "May Jose smite Jose" is one in which Jose represents a euphemism for the name of God. (Cf. The Mishnah, transl.by Herbert Danby, London: Oxford University Press, 1950, p. 392.)

[90]Cf. above, p. 80, the hapless plight of Jonathan and Saul; the death of Uzzah (II Sam. 6:10), just one of the manifestations of the Ark's dread mana; the efficacy of

the biblical deemphasizing and downgrading of mythology, magic, and what we are pleased to call superstition, there can be no question that substantial traces of older layers of belief are everywhere to be found. Even where the magical or idolatrous substratum has yielded almost completely to the newer concepts of Israelite theology, vestiges of the presence and force of older and discredited institutions appear in contexts where their force is no longer to be taken literally.[91] Something of the original magical force has been seen still to inhere in the root ʾrr. And something like the force of the danger of the "eating of the asakku" of king or god may lie behind or still inhere in the prohibition of Exodus 22:27, where we have the conjunction of god and mortal leader together with two terms which, at their weakest, stand for some kind of malignant action.

We have, however, more than this to go on. Until an alternative explanation is offered to Boyer's interpretation of "by the life of" king or deity, it would appear inescapable that, whether the concept of that "life" being made the stake ("enjeu") and therefore the warrant for the inviolability of the asseveration was understood literally or as a fiction, any false oath taken "by the life of God" would constitute an act of qillel against him. That the

---

human sacrifice (II Kings 3:26-28). An instructive discussion of the nature of Israelite superstitions is Ch.III of Yehezkel Kaufmann's The Religion of Israel, transl. and abrdgd. by Moshe Greenberg, University of Chicago Press, 1960.

[91] Cf. Anne Draffkorn, "ILANI/ELOHIM," JBL 76, 3, pp. 216 ff.

expression qillel ʾᵉlōhīm does not appear in connection with false oaths may be an accident of preservation or non-preservation of a not uncommon idiom; in all, the expression appears (ruling out Isa. 8:21) only three times. As it is, however, the interpretations offered here of I Sam. 3:13 and Lev. 24:10-23, would indicate that qillel ʾᵉlōhīm was an expression that probably covered a whole range of offenses against man and God. As for the difference in the verbs governing these two objects, it is clear (as has, indeed, been pointed out by almost everyone who has had occasion to comment on these verbs) that ʾrr is by far the stronger of the two, hence inconceivable as employed against the Deity.[92]

It seems likely that the traditional interpretation of this verse[93] has been due largely to its being part of the "Covenant Code." Now a code inevitably involves laws -- but is Exodus 22:27 a "law" at all? Law is that part of human morality which has been concretized by societal ac-

---

[92]Cf., e.g. Scharbert (Biblica 39, 1), p. 9, "In Ex. 22, 27 sind...qll Pi und ʾrr keineswegs Synonyma, die man einfach vertauschen könnte. Mit Bedacht steht hier in Verbindung mit dem König, den man sehr wohl verfluchen kann, ʾrr, in Verbindung mit Gott, den man nur 'herabsetzen, lästern', aber nicht ausschalten kann, qll Pi." Gen. 12:3, YHWH's promise to Abraham wāʾᵃḇārᵊḵā mᵊḇārᵊḵeḵā umᵊqallᵊleḵā ʾāʾor may now be rendered to bring out the distinction between the two terms: "I shall treat with favor those who so treat you, but those who abuse you will I ban utterly."

[93]Indeed, the renderings of LXX for both qillel and ʾārar indicate that the specific force of these terms was already lost to Bible scholars of the third pre-Christian century.

ceptance and provided with human sanctions.[94] (It is certainly clear in Lev. 24:10-23 that God's oracle had to be sought because the offense was undefined and, till that moment, not provided with a stipulated penalty.) Since "revile" and "curse" are hardly meaningful in the context of this verse, it is probable that what we have before us in this verse is not a specific law -- but, rather, a general and summarizing precept: Do not do anything which is an assault on the moral standards of heaven and earth. I suggest as a translation, "Do not act in disrespect of God nor bring under a ban an elected chieftain of your people."

That a leader should be brought into the Deity's disfavor by the actions of his people, might at first blush seem a strange thought.[95] Yet this exactly is what Moses describes as his condition in Chapter 1 of Deuteronomy. The generation of the wilderness was barred from entry into the promised land for its lack of faith in God who had already demonstrated his Providence. But not they alone were barred -- for their lack of faith Moses, too, is banned from the land of his heart's desire.

---

[94]It should be obvious that verses 20-26 (with the possible exception of v. 24) are not laws but precepts. That they have no man-enforced sanctions is indicated in vv. 23 and 26, where it is made explicit that God will not be indifferent to violations of these precepts. The probabilities are, furthermore, that vv. 28-30 and most, if not all, of the imperatives in Ch. 23 are precepts -- going beyong enforceable law. Thus 22:27 would be just one general precept among a number.

[95]In addition to the illustration which follows, other instances of "vicarious penalization" have been met previously in this study. Cf. Gen. 3:17, "<u>ʾᵃrūrā</u> is the earth on your account (<u>baʿᵃbūrɛkā</u>)"; Gen. 8:21, "I will not again (<u>lᵊ)qallel</u> the earth on account of (<u>baʿᵃbūr</u>) the man..." See above, pp. 86, and 119 respectively.

Deut. 1:34-37.

> 34) When YHWH heard the tenor of your words, he became angry and swore (wayyiššāba^c),[96] "35) Not one of these men -- of this wicked generation -- shall see the good land which I swore to give to your fathers..." 37) With me also did YHWH become angry -- on your account (biglal^ekɛm) -- saying, "You also shall not enter therein!"

The understanding of Exod. 22:27 as a general precept comprehending a range of crimes, rather than as a prohibition of lèse majesté and blasphemy, leads to a better understanding of the events narrated in I Kings 21. (And the latter, in turn, brings confirmatory support to this interpretation of Exod. 22:27.)

King Ahab of Israel has gone into a sulk because Naboth the Jezreelite has refused to sell or barter to him a piece of ancestral property. The difference between an Israelite king and a Phoenician autocrat is dramatically underscored in Jezebel's sneering reference to her husband's scruples and by her ruthless action in gratifying his desire.

I Kings 21:7-13.

> 7) Then his wife Jezebel said to him, "Do you really, now, exercise kingship over Israel! Get up, eat and cheer up. I will get you the vineyard of Naboth the Jezreelite." 8) Forthwith she wrote messages (s^əpārīm = "commissions") in Ahab's name, sealed them with his seal and sent the messages to the elders and burghers of his city (^ʾašɛr b^əʿīrō) who sat in council (hayyōš^əbīm) with Naboth. 9) Now in these messages she wrote to this effect, "Proclaim a fast, and seat Naboth as president of the council (hāʿām); 10) and seat against him two unprincipled men to charge/accuse him as follows

---

[96]Considering the frequency with which a form of šbʿ is followed by the term ʾārūr, and the penalty here of the "ban" on entry into the land, one is almost tempted to supply the "missing" word. Serious critics have made suggestions more bold.

'bērakṯā ᵓᵉlōhīm wāmɛlɛḵ'

Then take him outside (the city) and stone him to death."
11) So the leading men (ᵓanšē) of his city, the elders and the burghers, who were the councilors (hayyōšᵊḇīm) in his city did as Jezebel commissioned them in the messages she had sent to them: 12) They proclaimed a fast, seated Naboth as president of the council, 13) and the two unprincipled men came, seated themselves over against him and raised in council (nɛgɛḏ hāᶜām) the charge

"bērek nāḇōṯ ᵓᵉlōhīm wāmɛlɛḵ,"

whereupon they took him outside the city and stoned him to death.

Virtually every translation consulted on the above passage (the most recent being SB, 1956), has missed the fine details which, if correctly understood make for an entirely intelligible narrative. The confusion is as old as LXX which, in v. 8 renders hayyōšᵊḇīm by τοὺς κατοικοῦντας and omits ᵓᵃšɛr bᵊᶜīrō. Ehrlich would expunge ᵓɛṯ nāḇōṯ and reverse the order of bᵊᶜīrō hayyōšᵊḇīm to make the phrase identical to that in verse 11.[97] He refers to I Kings 12:8 as does Montgomery[98] for the identical syntax of relative particle followed by the definite article ᵓɛṯ hayyᵊlāḏīm...ᵓᵃšɛr hāᶜōmᵊḏīm lᵊpānāw[99] "the young men who were his courtiers" (Cf. RSV "who stood before him"); though neither spells out that the meaning of hayyōšᵊḇīm in verse 8 and 11 is "those who sit in the seat of authority," whether as councilmen or magistrates.[100]

---

[97]Randglossen, Vol. 7, p. 273.

[98]J. A. Montgomery, The Book of Kings, ICC (New York: Ch. Scribner's Sons, 1951), pp. 258 and 334.

[99]Cf. the Akkadian equivalent manzaz pān šarri(m).

[100]For this technical use of the verb "to sit," cf. CH § 5 (DM, Vol. 2, p. 14-15) where a judge (dayānum) is

In any case, no emendation of MT is required or advisable. It is of significance that verse 8 as it stands states explicitly that Naboth was an important personage in his city who sat regularly at council sessions. On this particular occasion he was to be made the presiding officer.[101]

How are we to understand the background of the _ṣōm_, the fast which the queen orders proclaimed? Montgomery notes, "'the proclamation of a fast' was to be based upon some alleged and accordingly fearful offense against Deity."[102] The precedent of a fast proclaimed as the recognition of offense against the deity is plain in I Sam. 7:6, but how was the existence of such an offense recognized by

---

removed from his judicial seat (_kussū dayānūtišu_), never to sit again as a judge (_ina dīnim ul ušš(!)ab_); and JEN 332 _ša ina qaqqari ša dīni ašbū_ "who sit on the (judiciary) bench." That the translations are still suffering a "cultural lag" is indicated by the fact that C. F. Burney (_Notes on Heb. Text of the Books of Kings_, Oxford, 1903) p. 244 quotes Thenius (1873) and Klostermann (1887) as rendering _hayyōšᵊḇîm_ by "Beisitzer." Cf. also _hayyōšᵊḇîm_ ‖ _ziqnē ʿammî_ in Ruth 4:4.

[101]V. 9 _hōšîḇū ʾet nāḇōt bᵊrōʾš hāʿām_. Naboth was made a _nāšîʾ_. Cf. Speiser's translation of the term (_JAOS_, 80, 3) p. 199 n. 8: "elected chieftain." If etymology does not suffice (nor the revelatory _nᵊśîʾē ʿēdā qᵊrîʾē mōʿed_ in Num. 16:2) to wean translators from the conceptually misleading "prince," there is the witness of Bab. Tal. _Pesaḥim_ 66a, telling of the election of Hillel _miyyad hōšîḇūhū bᵊrōʾš uminnūhū nāśîʾ ʿalēhem_ "forthwith they seated him at the head and appointed him chief over them(selves)." In view of the attested use of Semitic _w/yšb_ in connection with the "session" of a council, legislative or juridical, is it not likely that the term _yᵊšîḇā_ is an original Hebrew term translated into Greek by συνέδριον rather than being derived from the Greek? In any case, the equation _hayyōšeḇ ʾet_ = σύνεδρος = councilor is clear. See _now_ E. A. Speiser, "Background and Function of the Biblical _NĀŚÎʾ_," _CBQ_ XXV 1 (Jan. 1963), 111-117.

[102]_The Book of Kings_, p. 332.

the community? The answer can be adduced from other sources. The displeasure of the deity is revealed at times by his refusal to render an oracle,[103] or by a visitation -- in the form of defeat by an enemy, drought and famine, or pestilence.[104] In older times, resort would be had to the Urim and Thummim to ascertain in whom and in what action lay the cause of the Deity's displeasure. The use of these appears no more in narratives dealing with post-Davidic times; the North, in any case, is not known to have possessed this means of ascertaining the Deity's will. It is highly probable that some such disaster was being visited upon Israel,[105] and that the purpose of the fast and the sitting of the council was the attempt to ascertain via judicial inquiry the identity of the culpable party. (In this particular case it was, literally, a "witch-hunt.") It is noteworthy that the subornation in this case is not merely of witnesses but of the magistrates themselves. How else could a verdict of guilty have been reached against so respected a person as Naboth? And the crime? Surely not slander of the king and blasphemy! It is almost impossible to imagine how convincing evidence could have been fabricated if the charge consisted of an utterance, as gratuitous

---

[103]*E.g.*, I Sam. 14:36-37; 28:6; Isa. 8:16-21.

[104]Cf. Josh. 7:1-11; II Sam. 21:1-6.

[105]Perhaps the drought for whose existence Ahab and Elijah charge each other with responsibility. That the Naboth incident is told after the duel on Carmel and the coming of the rains does not militate against this possibility. Cf. the rabbinic dictum *ʾen muqdam umᵊʾuḥar battōrā* -- the order of biblical narrative is not necessarily chronological.

as it would have been dangerous, laid to Naboth. No, the specific accusation is not given in this sketchy narrative. But the specific charge was that Naboth had committed an offense of such gravity as to come under the category of the prohibition of Exod. 22:27.[106] Only such a crime could result in a community-wide disaster and the institution of a public fast and judicial inquiry.

That the execution of Naboth on the charge of b̄ērek (= qillel) ʾᵉlōhīm[107] was followed by the king's confiscation of the property of the putative offender has been the occasion of much speculation by commentators since medieval times. Montgomery observes that, "it was against such arbitrary power that the constitutional limitation of the rights of kings was written into the Deuteronomic code (Deut. 17:14 ff.)"[108] An examination of the Deuteronomic

---

[106]Montgomery (The Book of Kings, p. 331), like all commentators, connects the charge against Naboth with Exod. 22:27, but sees in the charge only the crimes of cursing and blasphemy: "The actual indictment of Naboth was, 'Thou didst curse God and King'... Such a curse of 'God' or 'prince of the people' was forbidden by the ancient code (Ex. 22:27) and blasphemy of YHWH's name was punishable by death with stoning, according to illustrative precedent (Lev. 24:10 ff.)."

Incidentally the use of only one verb here is another indication that Exod. 22:27 refers to one offense and not to two separate ones.

[107]The assumption that the verb qillel rather than ʾārar is the original for which the euphemism bērek is substituted is based on the first clause of Exod. 22:7, on the negative evidence that ʾārar is never applied to ʾᵉlōhīm, and that the strong force of ʾārar renders it highly unlikely that this verb was ever applied to the Deity as object. See above, p. 157, note 92.

[108]The Book of Kings, p. 332.

passage does not reveal any limitations on the king's power to confiscate. Ahab's sullenness after Naboth's refusal to sell him his patrimonial inheritance, as well as Jezebel's resort to a "frame-up" is strong indication of the rights of a citizen of Israel even in pre-Deuteronomic times. On the other hand, II Sam. 16:1-4 and 19:25-31 leave no room for doubt that the king had confiscatory powers, at least when the offense was treason or disloyalty to the crown.

If, then, qillel ʾᵉlōhīm never means "to curse God," we should have to explain the total absence of blasphemy in the Bible. Sheldon Blank, in keeping with his basic theme, writes:

> The fear of the effective power of the spoken word best explains the total absence of blasphemy in the Bible. Although there are numerous examples of the formula for blessing with God as the object of the blessing, the Bible nowhere contains the curse formula directed against God, i.e. blasphemy. This is all the more remarkable because the Bible is by no means lacking in passages referring to the possibility of a curse directed against God.[109]

I would suggest that blasphemy as an imprecation against the Deity would indeed be a phenomenon calling for an explanation if it were found in the Bible. In a system which knows or acknowledges one supreme Deity, how could imprecation against Him even be conceived? (Cf. above, note

[109] HUCA, Vol. 23, Part I (1950-51), p. 83. Prof. Blank then goes on to discuss the various passages where bērek occurs as a euphemism with ʾᵉlōhīm as the object. Incidentally, I am unable to resolve the apparent contradiction between the statement, "Job 2:9, where Job's wife urges him to curse God and die. The substitution of brk ("bless") for ʾrr in this passage is itself significant, suggesting that even the use of the verb ʾrr with God as its object could not be tolerated and a euphemism had to be employed," and the footnote on the same page, "Note that although the verb ʾrr is used when the object is nsyʾ it is avoided in the parallel where the object is ʾlhym."

89 for the odd formula invented by the rabbis to give content to a phenomenon which never existed, and never would have been thought to exist but for the misunderstanding of the meaning of the term qillel and the phrase qillel ʾᵉlōhīm in particular.) And even if it could be conceived, why the need to outlaw an action which, as was suggested above in the discussion of Lev. 24:10-23, would have been tantamount to suicide?

V. AN ANTONYM TO qillel -- WITH GOD AS OBJECT.

It would be idle to wish for more occurrences of qillel with ʾᵉlohim as object against which to test the interpretation of the phrase as a breach of morality. The case for this interpretation would, however, be strengthened immeasurably if we could find an antonym for qillel which, with ʾᵉlōhīm as object, could be shown to mean moral rectitude (as, to be sure, the case for the interpretation would have to be regarded as weakened by the failure to find such an antonymous idiom). In I Sam. 2:30, where God speaks to Eli concerning the abuse of his offerings, the expression kī mᵊkabbᵊday ʾᵃkabbed ubōzay yēqāllū "for those who treat me with respect will I treat with respect, but those who are contemptuous of me will be demeaned," suggests the kind of expression to be sought. But neither kibbed nor bērek, the two common antonyms for qillel, satisfies our requirements -- either in the number of their occurrences with the Deity as object, or in the contexts of these occurrences.

There is a term, nevertheless, which can serve as a synonym for bēreḵ and kibbeḏ and as an antonym for qillel. That term is yārēʾ. There is no question but that the basic sense of the term is "to fear, be afraid of." But that its meaning extends to "be in awe of, show reverence or respect for" can be demonstrated easily enough.[110] In Deut. 28:58 it appears in complementary synonymity with kbd, ləyirʾā ʾɛṯ haššēm hannikbāḏ wəhannōrāʾ hazzɛ̄ "to reverence this awesomely honored name." Again in conjunction with kbd,

Mal. 1:6

A son respects (yəḵabbeḏ) his father,
    and a servant his master.
If I am a father,
    where is the respect due me (kəḇōḏī)?
If I am a master,
    where is the reverence of me (mōrāʾī)?[111]

In Lev. 19:31, "Observe my sabbaths and my sanctuary tīrāʾū," the latter term can be rendered by "show respect for" but hardly by "fear." Additional examples could be adduced,[112] but one more will suffice. Joshua's stature is

---

[110]The third meaning of yārēʾ is "to worship, be a servant of (a deity)." This sense is clearly the meaning of the term in Jonah 1:9 where the reluctant prophet identifies himself as a worshipper of YHWH, God of Heaven, who created land and sea; in 2 Kings 17:7-39 where yārēʾ appears in synonymous association with ʿbd. Cf. also Judg. 6:10; I Sam. 2:14; and the numerous occurrences in Psalms of the yirʾē YHWH. All three meanings of yārēʾ are paralleled in Akkad. palāḫu, which meaning basically "to fear" is used of parents and the gods in the sense "show reverence for, do right by" etc.

[111]For other occurrences of yārēʾ with kbd and brk cf. e.g. Ps. 15:4; 115:11; 128:4; 135:20. Surely in Mal. 3:16, yirʾē YHWH hōšəḇē šəmō should be rendered, "those who reverence YHWH, who reckon (respectfully) with his name."

[112]Cf. Exod. 1:24; Ps. 130:4; Neh. 7:2, to mention a few.

enhanced when YHWH grants him the magnificent victory over Jericho.

Josh. 4:14.

> At that time YHWH raised Joshua in the esteem of all Israel so that they revered (wayyirᵓᵓū) him as they had reered (yārᵊᵓū) Moses all the days of his life.

One cannot but be struck by the fact that all fourteen occurrences of the term yārēᵓ with ᵓᵉlōhīm as object, have reference to morality, i.e. relations between man and man. Not one refers to cult, ritual, ceremony or other aspects of man's relation to the Deity.[113]

When Abimelech asks Abraham why he had lied to him in declaring Sarah his sister the latter answers that he did not have confidence in the moral standards of his host's city.

Gen. 20:11.

> Abraham said, "It was because I thought there is surely no yirᵓat ᵓᵉlōhīm in this place -- and they will kill me over my wife."

Joseph, having accused his brothers of being hostile spies scouting out the weakness of Egypt, shows his sense of justice by proposing a way in which his prisoners can prove their innocence. His expression for his sense of justice -- the still common expression: "I am a God-fearing man."

Gen. 42:18-19.

> On the third day Joseph said to them, "Do this and stay alive -- ᵓɛt hāᵓᵉlōhīm ᵓᵃnī yārēᵓ -- 19) if you are honest..."

---

[113]Right and wrong in regard to the latter category employ the terms qdš and ḥll.

Jethro, advising Moses to share with others his judicial burdens, characterizes the men to be chosen for the "district courts."

Exod. 18:21.

> And for your part, seek out from all the people, substantial men (*ʾanšē ḥayil*), *yirʾē ʾᵉlōhīm*, true men (*ʾanšē ʾᵉmeṯ*), who spurn ill-gotten gains (*śonʾē bāṣāʿ*)..."

In the Holiness Code the verse forbidding abuse of the handicapped (cf. above, p. 120 ff.) ties the prohibition in with the injunction "to fear God."

Lev. 19:14.

> You shall not abuse (*lōʾ tᵊqallel*) the deaf, nor place a stumbling-block before the blind -- *wᵊyārēʾtā mēʾᵉlōhẹ̄kā*...

This last injunction appears in Leviticus four more times: 19:32, in connection with respect due to the aged; 25:17, in connection with a prohibition against oppression of a fellow Israelite; 25:36, in conjunction with the prohibition against taking interest from an Israelite;[114] and, 25:43, in conjunction with the prohibition of harsh treatment of an Israelite who has entered another Israelite's household as an indentured servant.[115]

---

[114]For the actual context here, cf. E. A. Speiser, "Leviticus and the Critics," *Yehezkel Kaufmann Jubilee Volume*, ed. by M. Haran (Jerusalem: Magnes Press, 1960) pp. 39 ff.

[115]Is it accidental that Exod. 22:27 immediately follows the prohibition of interest (v. 24), and keeping a pledge overnight vv. 25-26? The end of v. 26, "and if he cries out to me I will hear for I am gracious," is another way of saying: *wᵊyārēʾtā mēʾᵉlōhẹ̄kā*. It would appear that the equation is complete: Exodus 22:27 is not a law but a precept warning against immoral conduct.

The heinousness of Amalek's attack on Israel's rear, during the escape from Egypt is glossed, Deut. 25:18, *wᵊlōʾ yārēʾ ʾᵉlōhīm*. Job is described in the first verse of that book as a man of integrity (*tām*), upright (*yāšār*), *wī(y)rēʾ ʾᵉlōhīm*, who turns away from any wrongdoing (*wᵊsār mērāʿ*). Nehemiah refers to *yirʾaṯ ʾᵉlōhīm* in Neh. 5:9 as the consideration which should keep Judeans from loading their brothers with interest which results in their reduction to slavery; and in 5:15 as the consideration which kept him from levying onerous taxes or otherwise lording it over his Judean compatriots. Finally, there is the lament of the psalmist in Psalm 55 over his fellow Israelite(s) who, in violation of the *bᵊrīṯ* to which both owe allegience, and which determines proper and improper conduct, deals treacherously with him; in v. 21 we find *wᵊlōʾ yārᵊʾū ʾᵉlōhīm* followed by v. 26, "he attacked his confederates (*šālaḥ yāḏāw bišlōmāw*), violating his covenant (*ḥillel bᵊrīṯō*)."

There is no necessity to discuss every instance in detail.[116] It will come as no surprise to anyone reared in the Western world, sharing an ethic so largely shaped by Hebrew tradition and so frequently expressed in biblical idiom, that fear/awe/reverence of God is virtually synonymous with moral conduct. What is of concern to the present study is that the biblical expression antonymous to fear/

---

[116]The remaining instance is II Sam. 23:3, "...a ruler of men must be righteous, a ruler must (have) *yirʾaṯ ʾᵉlōhīm*." Not included in this discussion are the numerous occurrences of *yārēʾ* with YHWH as object, nor such passages where, though *ʾᵉlōhīm* is the object, the passage provides no clue as to whether the context is ethical, pietistic, or possibly both. Cf. *e.g.* Eccles. 3:14, 5:6, 7:18, 8:12, 13.

reverence of God = moral behavior is *qillel ʾᵉlōhîm* = immoral conduct. The failure of tradition, for more than two millenia, to grasp the basic content of the latter idiom was due to the fact that only a few instances of the expression were preserved, and to the general misunderstanding of the equation *qillel* ≠ *bērek*/*kibbed*/*yārēʾ*. The converse of Sheldon Blank's suggestion is true. The manifestations of *qillel* in the Bible are not an indication of the significance which biblical psychology vested in "the word" *per se*. To the biblical mind both *qillel* and *bērek* represented material, concrete acts (in which utterance might or might not be represented). It was later tradition which understood *bērek* primarily as an oral phenomenon (*benedico*) and interpreted the antonym *qillel* as a corresponding oral phenomenon (*maledico*). This gave rise to the concept of imprecation against deity = blasphemy, a concept unattested for, and almost certainly alien to, biblical thought.

VI. THE TERM *bērek* AS EUPHEMISM FOR *qillel*.

As was previously indicated there is little reason to question that when *bērek* occurs as a euphemism, with the Deity as object, it is filling the place of *qillel*. In addition to I Kings 21:13 the euphemism occurs again only three times, all in the Book of Job.[117]

---

[117]The instance in Ps. 10:3 is not a euphemism: *ubōṣēaʿ bērek niʾeṣ YHWH* should be rendered "when the rapacious blesses (= thinks that all is well, congratulates) he is holding YHWH in contempt." See v. 4 for the explicating thought: there will be no calling to account, hence, this is practical atheism (*ʾen ʾᵉlōhīm kol mᵊzimmōtāw*).

Job 1:5.

> And when the days of the feast had run their course, Job would commission their purification, and punctually in the morning would offer up holocausts in the number of his sons, Job's thought being: on the chance that my children have sinned in giving offense (ubērᵊkū) to God by some inner thought (bilᵊbābām).

If this passage were to be studied for its theological implication it would take us far afield. What is the meaning of bilᵊbābām? To what extent did the author of Job believe that mental lapses were punishable by God? What was the act of cleansing from sin (wayyᵊqaddᵊšem)?[118] But though these problems remain unresolved, the basic intent of the passage is clear: to establish the fact that Job went to every extreme to avoid trespass against the Deity either by himself, or even on the part of his children. "Curse in their hearts" yields no sense whatsoever.

In the following two passages there seems no reason to depart from the sense "repudiate, renounce, spurn."

Job 1:9-11.

> And Satan (lit., the adversary) answered YHWH, "Is it for nothing that Job is a God-fearing man? 10) Have you not protected him, his household and all his possessions everywhere, prospering (bērak̲tā) the work of his hands so that his property spreads through the land? But just reach out your hand and touch anything of his, and see if he does not renounce you (yᵊbārᵊk̲ek̲ā) to your face!"

Of interest in the above passage is the juxtaposition of the expressions yārēʾ ʾᵉlōhīm, bērek̲ and bērek̲ = qillel.

Job 2:9.

So his wife said to him, "Do you still hold fast

---

[118]For the force of the verb cf., e.g., Lev. 16:19 wᵊṭihᵃrō wᵊqiddᵊšō miṭṭumʾōt...

to your integrity? Repudiate (bārek) God and die."

VII. qillel WITH THE FORCE OF MALEDICTION.

In all the passages which have been analyzed, qillel has been seen to possess a force ranging from verbal abuse to action or conduct of an injurious nature. The majority of the cases fall into the latter category, in which verbalization is totally absent or, at a minimum, extrinsic. These results, despite their variance from the force given to the verb in traditional translations, should not, in view of the known meaning of the qal stem and that of its antonym kibbed, occasion surprise. How then is one to account for the traditional translations and interpretations? The answer is not far to seek. It lies in part with the cognate noun qᵊlālā (discussed in the following chapter), from which the verb is not sufficiently differentiated; in larger measure, as has been suggested, with its other antonym bērek whose semantic range extends from the actual endowing of someone with the goods of life to salutations of greeting and farewell and wishes for good fortune, and its cognate noun bᵊrākā ("prosperity, good fortune, salutation, gift," etc.); and, lastly, with the relatively few passages where the verb qillel seems to have the unambiguous force of imprecation, or, at least, malediction.

Actually, this unambiguous force of qillel is confined to four passages, two of which (I Sam. 17:43 and II Kings 2:24) supplement the verb with "by deity" or "by the name YHWH," and the other two (Deut. 23:5 and Josh. 24:9) are secondary to and derivative from an original account which does not employ the verb qillel.

I Sam. 17:43.

> The Philistine said to David, "Am I a dog that you should come to me with sticks?"
>
> wayyᵊqallel bēʾlōhāw[119]
>
> the Philistine David.

The force of an imprecation is lent to the verb qillel in this passage only by the word bēʾlōhāw. The commentators, medieval and modern, are almost without exception silent or reticent on this expression; and perhaps there is no alternative to the explanation offered by the Mᵊṣūdat Dāwīd,[120] to the effect, "may the gods of the Philistines slay you or the like." Yet consideration must be given to Scharbert's explanation, which even in this passage would deny to qillel the sense of imprecation.

> Jedoch auch die alte Goliat-Erzählung versteht... unter qillel zunächst das Beschimpfen und Herabsetzen des Gegners, wie die Worte des Philisters eindeutig zeigen. Allerdings haben solche Schimpfreden, die wir vor dem Kampf auch bei anderen Völkern des Altertums finden, einen sehr realen Sinn. Man glaubt nämlich, dadurch den Gegner wirklich 'kleinmachen,' d.h. seine Kraft lähmen zu können, zumal dann, wenn man sich dabei auf die eigenen Gottheit beruft. So ist das bēʾlōhāw hier gemeint: Goliat beschimpft David 'unter Hinweis auf (die Macht) seiner Götter.' Jetzt verstehen wir, wie qll Pi die Bedeutung 'verfluchen, verwünschen' bekommen kann.[121]

---

[119]AV, AT, RSV (/JPS) "cursed...by his gods (/god)"; SB "maudit par ses dieux"; ATD "verfluchte bei seinen Göttern"; LXX καὶ κατηράσατο ... ἐν τοῖς θεοῖς αὐτοῦ ; Targ. wᵊlāṭēṭ...bᵊṭāʿūṭēh.

[120]Commentary by Yehiel Hillel ben David Altschul, Galician rabbi of the 18th century.

[121]Biblica, 39, 1, p. 10.

The words of the Philistine to which Scharbert refers, in the immediately following verse do not, indeed, constitute an imprecation. "Come over to me, and I will give your flesh to the birds of heaven and the beasts of earth." Nor do David's words supply a counter-imprecation; his retort is that whereas his opponent comes armed with sword, spear, and javelin, he, David, comes in the name of his God -- YHWH-Hosts -- God of the army of Israel which Goliath has taunted/abused (<u>ʾaʿšer ḥēraptā</u>). If <u>ḥērep</u> here is a synonym for <u>qillel</u>, there was no imprecation at all. "Malediction," however, might still be appropriate for <u>qillel</u>.[122]

Elisha, on the way up from Jericho to Bethel is accosted by a throng of children who, possibly referring to a distinctive tonsure or cutting on the scalp,[123] jeer him on his way -- addressing him as "Baldy."

II Kings 2:24.

He turned around to see them

<u>wayyᵊqallᵊlem</u>[124]

---

[122]It should be kept in mind that imprecation is resorted to out of a sense of helplessness. When all other resources fail -- that is when the gods are called upon to take a hand. Goliath's disdain for his youthful opponent would not lead us to expect an imprecation from him.

[123]Cf. the narrative in I Kings 20:35-43, where the head-bandage may have been necessary to conceal such a prophetic mark. Cf. also the prohibition addressed to the priest in Lev. 21:5 <u>lōʾ yiqrᵊḥū qorḥā bᵊrōʾšām</u> "they shall make no bald spots upon their scalps."

[124]Eng. vss. "cursed them"; SB "les maudit"; HAT "fluchte ihnen"; LXX κατηράσατο ; Targ. <u>wᵊlaṭīnūn</u>. Scharbert (<u>Biblica</u> 39, 1) p. 10, "Einderartiges Verfluchen 'mit dem Nahmen Yahwes'..."

> by the name YHWH, whereupon two she-bears came out of the woods and rent forty-two of the boys.

Montgomery notes that "the story reads like a *Bubenmärchen* to frighten the young into respect for their revered elders."[125] Although the object is to inculcate respect for prophets rather than "revered elders" in general, the *Bubenmärchen* character of the story, the last in a series celebrating the wonder-working powers of the prophet, is hardly to be questioned. Here again the force of "imprecation" is given to the verb *qillel* only by the addition of *bᵊšēm YHWH* "by YHWH." Since this is the only instance in which the expression appears, the possibility must be left open that originally *bᵊšēm YHWH* did not appear in the account and were added later to spell out the cause and effect relationship between Elisha's act of *qillel* and the disaster which befell the youngsters.

The remaining occurrences of the verb *qillel* are in the following passages:

Deut. 23:4-5. (quoted in Neh. 13:1-2).

> 4) No Ammonite or Moabite shall enter the assembly of YHWH (= people of Israel)... 5) because they did not meet you with food and water on your way out of Egypt, but rather engaged Balaam ben Beor from Pethor of Mesopotamia against you
>
> *lᵊqallᵊlɛkā*...[126]

Josh. 24:9-10.

> 9) Then Balak ben Zippor, king of Moab, bestirring himself to battle against Israel, sent a summons to Balaam ben Beor

---

[125]*The Book of Kings*, p. 355.

[126]Eng. vss. "to curse"; SB "maudire"; HAT "zu ver-

you, 10) but I would not listen to Balaam; so that, indeed he blessed you...

In these reminiscences of the events narrated in Num. 22-24, the verb qillel is employed to describe the purpose for which Balaam was fetched from his homeland. Yet it is noteworthy that in the account in Numbers the verb qillel is not employed. Clearly the verb qillel does duty for the terms which appear there: ʾārar, qāḇaḇ and zāʿam. Equally clearly, it is substitute duty which qillel performs. Why a substitute term is used at all cannot be determined with confidence. Perhaps the presence in both passages of the antonym bērek is the determining factor.

VIII. SUMMARY

The verb qillel has a wide range of meanings, ranging from verbal abuse to material injury. In every instance its force must be determined on the basis of its context. As an antonym for kibbeḏ and bēreḵ it means to treat with disrespect, abuse, derogate, denigrate, repudiate. As a coordinate of hikkā, it involves material injury. In the passive, it has the sense of to be unfavored, unfortunate, afflicted. With parents as object it means "to show disrespect for." With kings as object its basic meaning seems to be "to repudiate." With God as object it

---

fluchen"; LXX καταράσασθαι ; Targ. lᵊlāṭāṭūṭāḵ.

[127]Eng. vss. "to curse"; SB "maudire"; ATD "verfluchen"; LXX ἀράσασθαι ; Targ. limlāṭ.

denotes the lack of fear or respect for the ethical standards which the Deity expects of man. The antonymous expression, occuring virtually always in contexts of ethical conduct, is *yārēʾ ʾᵉlōhīm*. A consequence of this meaning of *qillel* with *ʾᵉlōhīm* as object is that blasphemy, understood as imprecation against the Deity, is a concept unknown and alien to biblical psychology. Only in a very few instances, and these of dubious significance, does *qillel* have the force of imprecation. The interpretation of *qillel* as "to curse," as old as the Septuagint translation, is the result of understanding *qillel* as primarily the antonym of *bērek*, the latter term understood in the sense of an utterance expressing a favorable wish. The limitation of either of these terms to a spoken phenomenon is as misleading as it is without foundation.

IX. AKKADIAN *qullulu*, *qillatu*, *qullultu*.

As was indicated in the preliminary discussion,[128] CAD, in a departure from hitherto standard practice, renders the first consonant of the above terms as *g* rather than *q*. Although we must assume that the reasons dictating the change are both good and sufficient, it is not unlikely that the phenomenon represents a specialized formation, and it need not deter us from regarding these terms, as they have always been considered, as cognate with Hebrew *qillel*.

What is immediately striking about the Akkadian verb

---

[128]Above, p. 19.

is that though it is a D-stem (corresponding to Hebrew *piᶜᶜel*), it appears by and large to be intransitive. Translated by CAD as "to commit a sin," it normally governs an object not directly but through the preposition *ana*, often preceded by the relative particle.[129] Since "sin" is a term which has theological overtones, it is perhaps advisable to use the term "crime" or "offense" in rendering the Akkadian terms. Thus the Akkadian verb would share with the Hebrew *qillel* the intransitive feature,[130] but would be differentiated from it in the way it governs its object.

The latter distinction, however, may not be of significant import in the matter of meaning. The frequent occurrence of *ana ilim/ilī qullulum* "to commit an offense against his god/the gods" presents an intriguing analogue to the biblical *qillel ʾelōhīm* as herein interpreted. As Speiser has emphasized,[131] the expression has particular reference to the violation of oaths taken in the name of deity and the breaking of international agreements. In ARM I 3, Yasmah-Addu's letter to his god, ll. 5-6 *ištu ṣītiya mamman [š]a ana* (!) *ilim uqal[l]ilū ul ibašši* "there is no one of my line who has committed an offense against the

---

[129] *E. g.*, *qullul[ti* x x x *sa ana* ᵈ]*Šamši-*[ᵈ*Ad*]*du* [*u*]*qallilū* in ARM I 3, Rev. ll. 15-16; *arni ša uqallilū* Craig ABRT 1 14 r. 2.; *uqallil-mi qilla[ta(?)]* PBS 1/1 2 ii 40.

[130] For this aspect of *qillel* "to behave in an abusive manner," cf. II Sam. 16:5, 10, 11 (above, p.138f), Lev. 24:11, 14, 23 (p. 143 ff).

[131] "Ancient Mesopotamia" in *The Idea of History in the Ancient Near East*, ed. Robert C. Dentan (*AOS* 38, New Haven: Yale University Press, 1955). Cf. particularly pp. 56-60.

god," is followed by the pregnant l. 7 <u>kalušunu</u> <u>mē</u> <u>ša</u> <u>ilimma</u> <u>ukal</u> "they have all kept the 'divine norms.'"[132] In the case of a society like that of Mesopotamia, where macrocosm and microcosm, heaven and earth, were inextricably intertwined, and, as Speiser (in this essay and elsewhere) has emphasized, history itself was seen as "theocratic history," it is idle to question whether such offenses were primarily against god(s) or against men. The answer is -- both. And if the Akkadian analogue does not offer conclusive proof for the interpretation of <u>qillel</u> <u>ᵓᵉlōhīm</u> which has been advanced here, it does provide in depth the historic background for a concept of morality which, refined and mediated by the Bible, has become the heritage of the Western world.

---

[132]Cf. <u>idem</u>, p. 37, the discussion of <u>mē</u> and bibliography.

CHAPTER V

THE NOUN *qəlālā*

Nouns in Hebrew (as elsewhere) have a way of assuming specialized functions, with the result that one cannot rely for their meaning on the force of the verbs from which they may derive. It has been shown that despite the common assumption that the verb *qillel* means "to curse," the sense of "imprecation" for this verb is borne out in only a fraction of its occurrences. One basis for the mistaken assumption was seen in the verb's being an antonym to *bērek* "to treat with favor, to shower blessings upon, to invoke blessing" -- with an emphasis placed on the last sense of this verb. It was also suggested, tentatively, that another basis for the assumption might well be the force of the cognate noun *qəlālā*. In the examination of this noun, the careful use of the examiner's language assumes major importance, since the terms of his own language may be equivocal. Thus, for example, in English the word "curse" can mean an invocation of harm or evil, the evil that comes as if in response to the invocation, or, in its broadest sense, any harm or misfortune. The danger of translating a term which in one language may have a range of meanings by an equally equivocal term in another language is obvious: a blurring of semantic boundaries and, consequently, misapprehension of the intent and content of the text in question.

The assumption that *qəlālā* means "curse" in the

sense of "imprecation" is even more widespread than the corresponding assumption for the verb qillel. Even Scharbert, who is careful to distinguish many of the non-imprecatory meanings of the verb, makes this assumption for the noun:

> Das Substantivum qᵊlālā hat nur noch die Bedeutung "Fluch"; doch spürt man den Sinn von 'Beschimpfung' vielleicht noch aus 3 Kg 2, 8 heraus. Hier wird das niederträchtige Benehmen Shimeis als eine qᵊlālā nimreṣeṯ bezeichnet, eine 'gefährliche Beschimpfung' deshalb, weil eben in Glauben des alten Orients eine Beschimpfung die Macht haben kann, nicht nur das Ansehen, sondern wirklich das Glück des Betreffenden zu mindern. Sonst bezeichnet das Nomen das mündlich ausgesprochene oder schriftlich niedergelegte Fluchwort, die durch das Fluchwort ausgelöste unheilschwangere Potenz, die den Frevler oder Gesetzübertreter bedroht, und schliesslich das bereits aktualisierte, an dem Getroffenen sich auswirkende Unheil.[1]

It was suggested in the preliminary discussion[2] that since the noun qᵊlālā is derived from the ground stem of the verb, it would seem probable that the noun derives most of its crystalized meaning -- not from either the qal or piʿel stem of the verb -- but rather by virtue of being the antonym of bᵊrāḵā. Should this be so, the assumption that qᵊlālā means, primarily, imprecation or malediction would be based on the assumption that bᵊrāḵā, for its part, has the primary meaning of benediction. Yet there is nothing in the root brk to suggest that the basic action inhering in it is an oral one; nor is there any indication that the noun bᵊrāḵā involves, primarily, an utterance. It seems far more likely that the sense of bᵊrāḵā is, first, "good

---

[1]Biblica 39, 1, p. 11.

[2]Chapter I, p. 18.

fortune, freedom from harm, felicity," and that the sense of "benediction" is derived from the material meaning by metonymy of effect for cause. If this is so, then qᵊlālā would, correspondingly, have a basic material meaning "harm, misfortune, disaster," and the sense of "malediction" would be a derivation from this meaning by the same process of metonymy. All this is by way of suggestion only. What should be clear at this juncture is that any prejudice as to what the term means is likely to be dangerously misleading. The contexts alone, together with what has already been learned about the other Hebrew terms for "curse," will have to determine just what qᵊlālā means.[3]

In what follows, the texts are treated in the following order: 1) those in which the sense of "imprecation" for qᵊlālā is not clearly demonstrable; 2) those in which qᵊlālā appears to be "imprecation" or, at least "malediction"; 3) those passages in which the sense of the noun is ambiguous.

I. qᵊlālā NOT IN THE SENSE OF "IMPRECATION."

In Deuteronomy (and in a pertinent passage from Joshua), the theme of reward for obedience to God's commandments and punishment for disobedience occurs frequently. The general term for reward -- good fortune -- is bᵊrāḵā

---

[3]In view of the virtually universal assumption that qᵊlālā means "imprecation," and in order to avoid needless repetition, the translations of the term will be given only when they depart from the following: English, "curse"; French, "malédiction"; German, "Fluch"; Greek, κατάρα; Aramaic, lᵊwāṭā/lîṭān/lᵊlōṭā/lᵊwāṭāṭā/lāṭāṭûṯ.

"blessing." The general term for punishment -- misfortune, disaster -- is q^əlālā. If q^əlālā is to be translated by "curse," it should be understood that this latter term is used in its broadest sense, semantically equivalent to "harm, calamity," etc., and that there is not present even a trace of utterance. All the passages are cited here for the sake of completeness.

Deut. 11:26-29.

> 26) See now, I set before you today the (alternatives of) good fortune (b^ərāḵā) and misfortune (q^əlālā) -- 27) good fortune if you hearken to the commands of your God YHWH... 28) and misfortune (q^əlālā) if you do not obey... 29) and when your God YHWH brings you to the land...then shall you set the blessing (b^ərāḵā) upon Mount Gerizim and the curse (q^əlālā) on Mount Ebal.

In verse 29, where the antonyms may stand for the expression of good fortune or bad, whether as invocation or prediction, the English terms "blessing" and "curse," which possess the same equivocal meanings as the Hebrew terms, are admirably suited to the context.

The meaning of the "setting" of the b^ərāḵā and q^əlālā on the two mountains is, apparently, their reduction to or reproduction in a "written" record, for it is just this which is done when the Israelites have crossed the Jordon and conquered Jericho and Ai.

Joshua 8:32-34.

> 32) And there he recorded upon the stones a copy of the teaching (tōrā) which Moses had written in the presence of the Israelites, 33) and all Israel... was stationed on either side of the ark...half facing Mount Gerizim and half facing Mount Ebal according to the prior instruction of Moses, servant of YHWH, to bless the people Israel. 34) After this he read out all the words of the teaching (hattōrā) - (concerning) the good fortune and the misfortune (habb^ərāḵā w^əhaqq^əlālā) exactly as it was written in the record of

the teaching (b^{ə}seper hattōrā).

In the above passage (as more often than not elsewhere), "law" as a translation of tōrā is altogether unacceptable. Verse 34 specifically gives, in apposition, the contents of the tōrā: habb^{ə}rākā w^{ə}haqq^{ə}lālā. Now it is clear that blessing and curse, good fortune and misfortune, do not constitute "law." The word tōrā here is the "instruction, teaching," which Moses, as the oracular spokesman of the Deity, imparted to the Israelites.

The clause in verse 33, "according to the prior instruction of Moses...to bless...Israel," indicates that the ceremony, narrated in Joshua 8, is related to the more detailed account in Deuteronomy 27.

Deut. 27:12-13.

> 12) These shall stand upon Mount Gerizim to bless (l^{ə}bārek) the people... 13) and these shall stand upon Mount Ebal ʿal haqq^{ə}lālā.

S. R. Driver, in his commentary on this passage, writes,

> ...the nature of the ceremony intended is: six of the tribes are to stand upon one of the two mountains named, invoking a blessing upon the people, in the event of their obedience, and six upon the other, invoking similarly a curse in the event of their disobedience.[4]

The fact that in verse 14 it is the Levites -- and not the tribes -- who pronounce the "curses" does not trouble Driver, for he regards verses 14-26 as being in such indifferent agreement with what precedes "that it is hardly possible for them to have been the original sequel of verses 11-13, or even to have formed part of the origi-

---

[4]S. R. Driver, Deuteronomy (ICC, 3rd ed.; Edinburgh: T & T Clark, 1902), p. 298.

nal Deuteronomy." Even if Driver's view is accepted, there is still the intriguing question of why the antithetic parallel to the verb l^{ə}bārek of verse 12 is not l^{ə}qallel but ʿal haqq^{ə}lālā. Since the infinitive would be a more natural antithesis it is unlikely that the preference for the noun is merely a stylistic accident. Is it possible that the "curses" were never to be pronounced? This, I think can be ruled out. Even if verses 14-26 are not original here, certainly the admonitions of Chapter 28, detailing the blessings attending obedience and the calamities (q^{ə}lālōt) resulting from disobedience, would have been read -- as, indeed, Joshua 8:34 says they were. Admonitions, however, are not imprecations -- even contingent imprecations (ʾālōt). Another possibility is that ʿal haqq^{ə}lālā represents a kind of watering-down, a euphemistic circumlocution for "to curse." Finally, there is the possibility -- here regarded as the most likely -- that the verb was not used simply because, as demonstrated in the preceding chapter, l^{ə}qallel did not have the force of "to imprecate."[5]

The possibilities are arguable. As far as our immediate interest is concerned, however, it is safe to make

---

[5]Ehrlich (Randglossen, Vol. 2, p. 328), while he does not solve the problem, has the following interesting comments on verse 11: "Das Subjekt zu lbrk sind nicht die im Folgenden genannten sechs Stämme, sondern dasselbe ist vorläufig unbestimmt und wird erst V. 14 genannt"; and on v. 13, "ʿl hqllh ist = gegen den Fluch, d.i., gegen die den Fluch aussprechen gewendet. Die den Segen und den Fluch sprechenden hat man sich zwischen beiden Bergen stehend zu denken. Beim Segen wandten sich die Sprechenden gegen den einen, beim Fluch gegen den andern Berg."

the negative judgment that *qəlālā* in this passage cannot be demonstrated to have the force of "imprecation."

In the following four passages from Deuteronomy there is no warrant for translating *qəlālā* by any term which possesses more than the general force of misfortune, harm, disaster.

Deut. 28:15.

> But it will come about -- if you do not obey the bidding (*qōl*) of your God YHWH, to fulfill punctiliously[6] all his commandments... -- that all these *qəlālōt* will overtake and overcome you.

This verse is followed by three verses using the *ʾārūr* formula, in prediction and not imprecation (cf. above, p. 79), and then by the enumeration of such disasters as pestilence, disease, blight, drought, defeat in war, violation of wife and daughters, etc. This melancholy catalogue is then summed up in verse 45.

> All these *qəlālōt* shall come against you, pursuing and overtaking you until you are destroyed, because you did not obey the summons of your God YHWH to observe the commandments and statutes with which he charged you.

The next passage appears in the context of the warning that no tribe will be safe from the *ʾālōt*, the imprecations, sanctions of the covenant (cf. above, pp. 28 ff.). When YHWH will have ravaged the land of a covenant-breaking tribe, people will attribute the disaster to Him and trace the doom to the calamities threated in the Deuteronomic record. They will say, further...

---

[6]Taking *lišmor laʿaśot* as hendiadys.

Deut. 29:16.

"therefore was the anger of YHWH kindled against that land, bringing upon it all the q^ə^lālā written in this record."[7]

Deut. 30:1.

And when all these things have come upon you, the good fortune (habb^ə^rāḵā) and the misfortune (haqq^ə^lālā), which I have set out before you...

Utterance is ruled out for each of the antonymous pairs in the following verse, where the two terms receive prior explication as life and death.

Deut. 30:19.

I now call heaven and earth to witness against you: life and death have I set before you -- felicity (b^ə^rāḵā) and disaster (q^ə^lālā).

If further indication is needed of what these antonymous terms have for content, there is the witness of the parallel verse.

Deut. 30:15.

See, I have set before you today life and all things good (w^ə^ʾεṯ haṭṭōḇ) and death and all things evil (w^ə^ʾεṯ hāraʿ).

It was seen above (cf. p. 138 ff.) that Shimei ben Gera's address to David on the occasion of the latter's abandoning Jerusalem to his rebel son, did not constitute an imprecation. It would follow necessarily that the noun corresponding to the verbal action in this case would have the same semantic force. Thus, in the following two passages, q^ə^lālā would connote "abuse, denunciation, vilifica-

---

[7]Verse 21 of this chapter provides as synonyms for q^ə^lālā: makkōṯ and taḥ^a^lūʾīm (RSV "afflictions and sickness.").

tion."[8]

II Sam. 16:12.

> Perhaps YHWH will look upon my affliction (reading bəʿonyī) and requite me with good in place of his abuse (qiləlātō) of today.

I Kings 2:8.

> Now you have with you Shimei ben Gera...who vilified me most cruelly (qilləlanī qəlālā nimreṣeṭ) at the time that I was on the way to Mahanaim.

The majority of the instances in which the specific force of qəlālā is difficult to determine are predictions of disaster by Jeremiah. Terms for imprecation, malediction appear in a series with terms for calamity and doom so that it is difficult to decide to which of these categories qəlālā belongs. In the following passage, however, there should be no doubt.

Jer. 24:9.

> I will make them (an example of) frightful evil (ləzawaʿā lərāʿā) to all the kingdoms of the earth,
>
> ləḥerpā uləmāšāl lišnīnā wəliqlālā
>
> in all the places where I drive them.

The translation by AT, RSV (which is typical), "a reproach, a byword, a taunt and a curse," implies that these four terms are independent members of a series. But this cannot be so. The parallel terms are ḥerpā ‖ qəlālā

---

[8]Scharbert is so convinced that the noun qəlālā means "curse" that he permits this conviction to blunt his awareness that qillel does not mean "curse." This might indeed be characterized as "taking the wrong exit out of a traffic circle." Biblica 39, 1, p. 9: "Auch die Behandlung Davids durch Shimei wird als qallel bezeichnet, das zunächst ein Höhnen, Schmähen ist, allerdings auch in ein Fluchen übergeht."

and _š^{ə}nīnā_ ‖ _māšāl_ in the order a-b-b-a. A recognition of the hendiadys will yield the following translation, "a by-word for scorn (/humiliation), a proverb for misfortune (_q^{ə}lālā_)."

Proverbs 26:1 provides an interesting example of how one may be skeptical of an interpretation held in common by LXX, Rashi, Kimchi, Ibn Ezra, Scharbert and all modern translators.

RSV Like a sparrow in its flitting,
like a swallow in its flying,

so _qil^{ə}lat ḥinnām_[9]

does not alight.

A different purport is seen in the verse if it is recognized as the complement of verse 1 and considered in its context.

RSV Like snow in summer
or rain in harvest

so honor (_kāḇōḏ_)

is not fitting for a fool.

The parallelism of the two verses is assured by the simile at the beginning of each verse. From the point of view of content, however, the parallelism is antithetic. The antithetic parallel to _q^{ə}lālā_ in verse 2 is _kāḇōḏ_ in verse 1, leading to the conclusion that these terms are antonyms. Since the force of _kāḇōḏ_ is clear, the equation yields for _q^{ə}lālā_ the force of "disgrace."[10] According to

---

[9]AV "the curse causeless"; JPS (/RSV) "the (/a) curse that is causeless"; AT "The curse that is groundless"; SB "la malédiction gratuite"; HAT "der unberechtigte Fluch"; LXX ἀρὰ ματαία ; Targ. _l^{ə}wat^{ə}tā d^{ə}maggān_.

[10]Cf. the related noun _qālōn_ "dishonor, ignominy"

this analysis, then, the first verse says that honor is not the portion of the kəsīl, the "fool" in moral matters, while the second states as a converse that disgrace does not befall a person undeservedly. In this passage, qəlālā is not "curse" in any sense of the word -- and nothing is said about the effectiveness of an imprecation, deserved or gratuitous.

Despite the perplexities which commentators find in the following verse,[11] it would seem that its sense is or should be transparent.

Prov. 27:14.

mәbārek rēᶜēhū bәqōl gādōl
babboqɛr haškem
qәlālā[12] tēḥāšeb lō

RSV He who blesses his neighbor with a loud voice,
rising early in the morning,
will be counted as cursing.

The meaning of mәbārek here, as often (cf. e.g., Gen. 47:7, 10), means "greet, salute" (upon meeting or parting), and the infinitive absolute haškem as adverb with the

---

(Prov. 11:2; Hos. 4:7; Isaiah 22:18); the remark of Rashi's (quoted below, p. 190) that qəlālā in general is a term for disesteem, humiliation; and the stem qlh similar in its Hiphᶜil use to qillel: Exod. 21:17, məqallel ‖ Deut. 27:16, maqlɛ.

[11] Cf. e.g., A. Ehrlich, Randglossen, Vol. 6, p. 156: "Der Ausdruck bbqr hskym, der nur wörtlich und nicht bildlich verstanden werden könnte, ist wahrscheinlich nicht ursprünglich. Andere streichen die Worte bqwl gdwl bbqr, allein dann ist hskym syntaktisch falsch. Aber wie man hier tut, der Sinn des Ganzen bleibt immer unklar."

[12] AV, JPS, AT "a curse"; SB "une malédiction"; HAT "Als Fluch"; LXX καταρωμένου ; Targ. ləwāṭāṭā.

force of "early" is well attested.[13] One does not "bless" one's neighbor (except in the original sense of "hail," "salute") as a matter of normal social procedure, morning or evening, early or late -- but one does greet him. To do so in a loud voice at an unearthly hour would be regarded as abuse (<u>qəlālā</u>) rather than as a compliment. The verse should be translated along the following lines, "He who greets/hails his neighbor early in the morning is charged with abuse/abusive conduct." The translation fails, to be sure, to convey the play on the Hebrew words <u>bērek</u> and <u>qəlālā</u>. In English the force can be achieved only via circumlocution, if at all: Anyone who favors his fellow early in the morning with a shouted salutation will find himself charged with boorish/churlish conduct.

The most perplexing text centering around the noun <u>qəlālā</u> is:

Deut. 21:22-23.

> 21) If a man, charged with a capital crime is put to death, and you then hang him on a tree, 23) his corpse shall not remain on the tree through the night. On the selfsame day shall you give him burial for a hanged man is
>
> <u>qiləlat</u> <u>ʾᵉlōhīm</u>;[14]
>
> so shall you not defile the land which your God YHWH is giving to you as your possession.

---

[13]Other meanings, "persistently, diligently, expeditiously"; Cf. I Sam. 17:16; Jer. 7:13; 11:7; 25:3, 4; 26:5; 29:19; 35:14; 44:4.

[14]AV "accursed of God"; JPS "a reproach unto God"; AT "a terrible disgrace"; RSV "cursed by God"; SB "une malédiction de Dieu"; HAT "ein Fluch Gottes" (and comment, "vom Fluch Gottes Betroffener"; LXX ὅτι κακατηραμένος ὑπὸ θεοῦ.

The problem inheres first in the question as to whether qilᵊlat̲ ʾᵉlōhīm is a subjective or objective genitive. The Greek versions and most modern commentators and translations favor the subjective genitive. S. R. Driver would understand the sense of the passage as follows:

> ...probably the exposure of a malefactor's corpse by hanging was resorted to only in the case of heinous offenses: it could be taken therefore as significant of the curse of God (Gen. 4:11, Deut. 27:24) resting specially upon the offender; and as murder, like other abominable crimes, was held to render the land in which it was perpetrated unclean (Num. 35:33 f.; Lev. 18:24 f.), so the unburied corpse, suspended aloft, with the crime as it were clinging to it, and God's curse resting visibly upon it, had a similar effect. Hence, as soon as the requisite publicity has been attained, the spectacle is to end: the corpse, at sunset, is to be taken down, and committed to the earth, as a token that justice has completed its work, and that the land has been cleansed from the defilement infecting it..."[15]

The very tortuousness of Driver's explanation is enough to raise doubts as to the plausibility of a subjective genitive here. Just what is meant by "the curse of God"? Hardly "imprecation"! And if His displeasure or anger is intended, what punishment is greater than execution? If the answer to this last question is the act of hanging, or if the crime clinging to the suspended corpse as "God's curse resting visibly upon it" had the effect of rendering the land unclean, why hang at all? Ehrlich rightly remarks, "Andere Erklärer verstehen die Vereinigung des Landes von dem längern Lassen des Gehangten am Holz, doch ist diese Fassung durchaus unlogisch, weil für die Verunreinigung auch ein einziger Augenblick genügt."[16]

---

[15]S. R. Driver, Deuteronomy, ICC, p. 248.

[16]A. Ehrlich, Randglossen, Vol. 2, p. 313-14.

As Driver notes, "there was, however, a current Jewish interpretation which treated ᵓᵉlōhīm as objective genitive." Targum Onqelos understands the subject of the qᵊlālā-action as the hanged malefactor and the kī-clause (misplaced, to be sure) as the reason behind the hanging: ᵓᵃrē ᶜal dᵊḥāḇ qāḏām YHWH ᵓiṣṭᵊlaḇ "because he has offended against YHWH is he hanged."

A more persuasive rendering of the objective genitive is that of Pseudo-Jonathan and Rashi, who see in the ignominy of the hanged victim a slight to God in whose image he is made. Pseudo-Jonathan uses the cognate qīlūṯā for the disgrace, while Rashi terms it zilzūl šɛl mɛlɛḵ "disrespect to the King" equal to lèse majesté against God, and, aware that in rabbinic tradition qᵊlālā had become the general term for "curse," takes the trouble to add that kol qᵊlālā šɛbammiqrā lᵊšōn hāqel wᵊzilzūl "every qᵊlālā in Scripture is an expression for slight and disrespect," referring the reader to I Kings 2:8 (Cf. above, p. 188).

The wide range of conjecture on this passage is the result of two factors: 1) the uniqueness of the expression qilᵊlaṯ ᵓᵉlōhīm, and 2) the ambiguity of the word qᵊlālā itself. In regard to the latter, the study of the noun at this stage of the present investigation would go far to support Rashi's conclusion that we are confronted here not by a "curse" but by an act of disrespect. In regard to the former, the conclusions reached herein concerning qillel ᵓᵉlōhīm and the antonymous yārēᵓ ᵓᵉlōhīm may serve to remove the expression from the limbo of isolation. Despite the conclusion that qᵊlālā, a noun based on the ground-stem rather than on the pi^cel, receives most of its crystallized meaning by virtue of being an antonym to bᵊrāḵā, II Sam. 16:12 and I Kings 2:8 (Cf. above, p. 188) reveal that the noun also corresponds to the verb qillel. It follows, therefore, that just as yirʾat ʾᵉlōhīm is the nominal correspondent to yārēʾ ʾᵉlōhīm, so the nominal correspondent to qillel ʾᵉlōhīm could certainly be qilᵊlat ʾᵉlōhīm; and the meaning would be identical: a mode of behavior in regard to a fellow human being which constitutes an offense in the eyes of (hence, against) the Deity.

How then would we understand the entire passage? The offense cannot lie in the act of hanging (or impalement), for if it did, that act itself would have been prohibited. So, despite the term tālūy (which, by metonymy, refers to the "hanging" rather than the "hanged one"),[17] the offense is the prolonged exposure of a corpse, as is made explicit by the antithesis kī qāḇōr tiqbᵊrennū bayyōm hahūʾ "to the contrary, on the selfsame day shall you inter him." The reason for the narrowing of this prohibition to the case of a hanged man is due, undoubtedly, to the fact that this case constituted the only instance in which, as a matter of normal procedure, a cadaver was deliberately exposed. A pre-Deuteronomic instance of such an execution and exposure is narrated in II Sam. 21:8-14.[18]

---

[17]Cf. Ehrlich, ibid., "qᵊlālā heisst nicht Fluch, sondern Entehrung... Wir würden sagen "das Hängen 'statt' der Gehängte," doch ist diese Ausdrucksweise echt hebräisch; vgl. Gen. 46, 34 twʿbt mṣrym kl rʿh ṣʾn..."

[18]It is possible that hanging after execution was particularly practiced in the case of an offense that involved a breach of a solemn compact. Thus, for example,

At all events the expression qilᵉlat ʾᵉlōhīm means neither a "curse sent by God," nor a "curse directed against God."

II. qᵊlālā IN THE SENSE OF IMPRECATION.

In Deut. 23:4-6, a reminiscence of Moab's summons to Balaam to curse the Israelite invaders, the verb qillel as has been seen (cf. above, p. 175) takes the place occupied by other terms in the original account in Numbers. The noun corresponding to the verb occurs in

Deut. 23:6

> But your God YHWH would not listen to Balaam and turned the qᵊlālā into a blessing (bᵊrākā).

In Judges 9:7-20 the imprecation uttered by Jotham, following upon a parable, is clearly -- although it is not so identified -- an ʾālā, not only because it is an impre-

---

Saul and his sons, who were originally subjects of the Philistines are hanged or impaled (both terms are used I Sam. 31:10 tāqᵊʿū; II Sam. 21:12 tᵊlāʾūm; 21:13 hammūqāʿīm); Adonizedek and the four allied kings, who are so treated by Joshua, had made war against Gibeon, a city with which they seem to have had an alliance, cf. Josh. 10:2, 4, 26-27; The two officers of Mephibosheth who assassinate their sovereign are hanged, after execution, by David. Cf. II Sam. 4. Saul's sons and grandsons are executed and hanged for his breach of the covenant with the Gibeonites (Cf. II Sam. 21); Sennacherib suspends on stakes the warriors of Hirimme, whose rebel status is certified by the following notice that that province was reorganized after the crushing of the rebellion. (Cf. Col. I, ll. 57-61 of the prism of Sennacherib), and the rebel leaders of Ekron ša ḫiṭṭu ušabšū "who had caused offense to take place," while pardoning those who were not guilty of ḫiṭītu u gullulti (Col. III ll. 7-14). (The page numbers in D. D. Luckenbill, The Annals of Sennacherib, University of Chicago Press, 1924, are respectively 26 and 32.) In view of the treaty-breaking contexts of ana ili gullulu (cf. above, p. 178), these exposures may assume heightened significance.

cation, but intriguingly enough, a contingent imprecation. Nevertheless it is termed a <u>q^ə^lālā</u> in

Judg. 9:56-57.

> 56) Thus God requited the wickedness of Abimelech... 57) and all the wickedness of the men of Shechem did God requite upon their heads. Thus, there came upon them (<u>qil^ə^laṯ yōṯām</u>...) the <u>q^ə^lālā</u> of Jotham son of Yerubbaal.

The following passage is virtually a demonstration that the sense of imprecation which comes to be owned by <u>q^ə^lālā</u> derives from the use in an imprecation of a particular <u>q^ə^lālā</u> "disastrous fate." Predicting the doom of the false prophets, Ahab ben Kolaiah and Zedekiah ben Maaseiah, at the hands of Nebuchadrezzar, king of Babylon, YHWH says that their fate will become proverbial among the Judeans in exile.

Jer. 29:22.

> And from them (<u>i.e</u>. their fate) a <u>q^ə^lālā</u> will be taken up by all the exiles from Judah, who are in Babylon, to wit: "May YHWH make (/treat) you like Zedekiah and Ahab, whom the king of Babylon roasted in fire!"

Genesis 48:20 provides an explicit example for <u>b^ə^rāḵā</u> corresponding to that which Jer. 29:22 provides for <u>q^ə^lālā</u>, "By you (as example) shall Israel offer benediction, to wit, 'God make you like Ephraim and Menassah.'"

Both expressions appear in:

Zech. 8:13.

> And as you have been a <u>q^ə^lālā</u> among the nations (<u>i.e</u>., an example to be used in invocations of disaster), O house of Judah...so will I deliver you that you may be a <u>b^ə^rāḵā</u> (<u>i.e</u>., an example to be used in invocations of good fortune)...

III. *qᵊlālā* IN AN AMBIGUOUS SENSE.

It has been seen that where the force of *qᵊlālā* can be determined with the help of the context, the majority of instances (by a ratio greater than three to one) bear out the force of material misfortune rather than the invocation of it. Nevertheless, once the operation of metonymy is admitted one must be prepared for cases where it is either impossible -- or idle -- to attempt to differentiate the original or derivative force.

Thus, in Jacob's reply to his mother's proposal that he deceive his father in order to win a benediction reserved for his older twin, and in his mother's retort:

Gen. 27:12-13.

> 12) "But perhaps my father will touch me -- then I shall appear as a trickster and bring upon myself *qᵊlālā* and not *bᵊrākā*"; 13) whereupon his mother said to him, "Upon me be your *qᵊlālā*, my son..."

Blessing and its invocation, misfortune and its invocation -- both are so intertwined in the context as to defy semantic unraveling, and to suggest the likelihood that there was no distinction in the mind of the narrator himself.

In II Kings 22:19,

> ...when you heard what I had promised concerning this place...that it would be(come)
>
> *lᵊšammā wᵊliqlālā*

it is difficult to decide whether to translate these two terms by "a calamitous waste," or by "a waste proverbial for curse(s)."

In Jeremiah, 25:18...*lāṯeṯ ʾōṯām lᵊḥorbā lᵊšammā*

lišrēqā wəliqlālā might very well be "to make them a desolate waste, a hissed-at calamity" or "a ruinous waste, object of hissing and byword for curse." In Jer. 26:6, "I shall make this city into a qəlālā, the noun may stand for "(an example of) calamity," or a "(proverb for) disaster/ malediction." In Jer. 42:18 (and the same series in 44:12) the prophecy that the Judeans would be(come) lə'ālā uləšammā wəliqlālā uləḥɛrpā, it is impossible to determine whether the term parallel to 'ālā "imprecation," is qəlālā or ḥɛrpā. If it is ḥɛrpā, then in the pattern a-b-b-a, the translation would be "an imprecation of ruin, a taunt pointing to disaster"; if the parallel to 'ālā is qəlālā, then in the pattern a-b-a-b, the force would be "an imprecation of devastation, a curse of (i.e. invoking) humiliation." Jer. 44:8, "that you may be(come) liqlālā uləḥɛrpā among all the nations of the earth" the Hebrew could be "a curse and a taunt," "a humiliating disaster," or "a disastrous humiliation." The problem is similar for 44:22...ləḥorbā ləšammā wəliqlālā, perhaps "a wasteful disastrous ruin"; 49:13... ləšammā ləḥɛrpā ləḥorɛḇ wəliqlālā, possibly "a shameful waste, a disastrous ruin."

In Psalm 109, the occurrence of the verb qillel in verse 28 was discussed above. In verses 17 and 18, the noun occurs.

> 17) He preferred qəlālā, so let it come upon him!
> He rejected bərāḵā, so may it be far from him!
> 18) He clothed himself with qəlālā like a garment,
> may it soak into his body like water,
> like oil into his bones.

Here again, qəlālā as antonym to bərāḵā could as well be "abuse" in contrast to "graciousness" as "malediction" in contrast to "benediction."

SUMMARY

There is nothing in the etymology of either brk or qll to indicate that the terms necessarily involve utterance. There is no indication in the usage of the nouns bᵊrāḵā and qᵊlālā that they represent, respectively, wishes for good and evil rather than material good fortune and misfortune. On the contrary, in the case of qᵊlālā at least, in the majority of its occurrences it has the sense of material misfortune or abusive treatment. In the latter sense, it is the noun corresponding to the action involved in qillel. As applied to ʾᵉlōhīm in a single occurrence, it very likely is the antonymous expression to yirʾaṯ ʾᵉlōhīm and represents conduct frowned upon by the Deity. By the operation of metonymy, qᵊlālā qua misfortune can be used of the person or place suffering misfortune; and as an example or precedent of disaster in a malediction, qᵊlālā in a few instances comes to stand for the malediction itself. The same considerations which prompted tradition to understand qillel as "to imprecate" operated even more strongly in fostering the notion that every qᵊlālā is a "malediction/curse." This mistaken assumption is responsible for introducing confusion in regard to a number of passages whose meaning becomes transparent when the term is understood in its basic force.

CHAPTER VI

MISCELLANEOUS TERMS

I. THE VERB qbb

J. Scharbert begins his discussion of nqb/qbb as follows:

> Wegen des seltenen Vorkommens lässt sich qbb bzw. nqb weniger genau bestimmen. Die beiden Formen gehen kaum auf verschiedene Stämme zurück sondern die zweite dürfte eine Nebenform der ersten sein. Ein etymologischer Zusammenhang mit nqb = "durchbohren" besteht kaum. Dagegen liegt wohl Verwandtschaft mit Tigre qb = "schmähen, entwürdigen" [and note referring to E. Littmann, Das Verbum der Tigre-Sprache, II, in ZA 14 (1899), 28.] und arab. qabiba = "dünn sein" vor. Wir werden also eine ähnliche Bedeutungsentwicklung wie bei qll vorauszusetzen haben. Beide Abwandlungen der Wurzel qb kommen nur im Qal vor.

Scharbert then goes on to the occurrence of qbb/nqb in Lev. 24:11, 16. As was indicated in the discussion of that text (cf. pp. 143 ff.), nowhere else in the Bible does the root nqb appear in a sense synonymous with qll or ʾrr; and the only basis for a conjectural byform nqb is a misunderstanding of that entire passage.

But as Scharbert correctly points out, the paucity of occurrences of the verb makes it virtually impossible to determine its basic denotation. Indeed, the basis for the assumption that it means "to curse" is its repeated occurrence in the Balak-Balaam narrative in Numbers, its occurrence once in Job in close association with ʾrr and in Proverbs as an antonym to bᵊrāḵā. But to say this is virtually to exhaust its occurrences.

Num. 22:11, 17.

> 11) Come qobā it (the people of Israel) so that I may be able to war against them and expell them... 17) ...come now qobā for me this people.

Num. 23:8, 11, 13, 14, 27.

> 8) How (can I) ʾɛqqob (whom) God has not qabbō (and goes on to speak glowingly of Israel's destiny, whereupon) 11) Balak said, "What are you doing to me? I fetched you lāqob this people and here you have blessed them!"

Balak appears to think that it is the sight of Israel's huge encampment which prevents Balaam from performing the desired action, so he takes him to a spot from which only a small portion of the Israelite host is visible.

> 13) ...and qobnō for me from that place. (This expedient fails and Balak cries in frustration:) 25) ..."gam qōb lōʾ tiqqᵊbɛnnū and do not bless them either." (But Balak decides to try once more) 27) ..."Let me take you to another spot; perhaps it will suit God wᵊqabbōtō for me from there.

The absence from this portion of the narrative of any of the principal terms for imprecation makes it possible for all the English translations to render the verb by "curse"; other translations are, French: maudire; German: verfluchen; Greek: ἀράομαι / καταράομαι; Aramaic: lūṭ.

Job 3:8 (discussed above, p. 106 ff)

> ...yiqqᵊbūhū the spell-binders of day

Prov. 11:36.

> The people yiqqᵊbūhū (him) who holds back grain but a blessing is (put) upon him who provides it.

Prov. 24:24-25.

> 24) He who says to the wicked, "You are right/

righteous, peoples yiqq^{ə}ḇūhū, nations yizᶜāmūhū
25) but those who reprove the wicked will be favored and a birkaṯ ṭōḇ will accrue to them.

In all three of the passages above the rendering of qbb follow those in the Numbers narrative. The last passage from Proverbs, however, betrays something more of the force of the verb. Since a "blessing" is virtually synonymous with "good," the expression birkaṯ ṭōḇ indicates a "favorable, friendly greeting." The antonym would, accordingly be a spoken expression of antithetical force.

In Job 5:3, "I have seen the fool (in a moral sense) take root but suddenly wāʾɛqqoḇ his dwelling," wʾqb is probably, with BH, Ehrlich, ATD and many others, to be emended to wayirqaḇ or, better w^{ə}rāqaḇ "and it rotted, decayed," both on the strength of LXX, Syriac and, above all, the context of the verse.

II. THE VERB zᶜm

The evidence for the meaning of zᶜm is purely contextual.

In Numbers 23:8 it occurs as a parallel to qbb

mā ʾɛqqoḇ lōʾ qabbō ʾel
umā ʾɛzᶜom lōʾ zāᶜam YHWH

as in Prov. 24:24

yiqq^{ə}ḇūhū ᶜammim yizᶜāmūhū l^{ə}ʾummīm

while in Numbers 23:7 its parallel term is ʾrr

l^{ə}ḵā ʾorā lī yaᶜ^{a}qoḇ
ul^{ə}ḵā zoᶜ^{a}mā yiśrāʾel

Variously rendered in a variety of contexts by "execrate, treat with anger, abominate, be angry with, loathe" and the like, it is clear that the content of the verb is "hostility" and that it is not limited to an utterance.

Thus it occurs with YHWH as its subject with the following as object:

his enemies (Isa. 66:14)

Jerusalem and Judah (Zech. 1:12)

the people Edom (Malachi 1:4)

All of these occurrences of the verb are in the qal perfect, as is the instance in Dan. 11:30 where a future king is the subject and a holy covenant is the object. In Ps. 7:12, the qal active participle occurs with God as subject and a missing object. The qal passive participle occurs twice: in Prov. 22:14, he who is zāʿūm to/by YHWH falls into the pit which is how the mouth of "loose women" is characterized; and in Micah 6:10 a short measure (ephah) is zəʿūmā. In Proverbs 25:23 the niphʿal participle is applied to a face, visage.

III. THE NOUN ḥrm

The term ḥrm would not appear in this study at all but for the fact that AV renders the noun ḥerɛm by "a curse," "an accursed thing." The meaning of the verb in the hiphʿil is clear: to set a thing or person apart (its associated term is qdš) as reserved to/for a deity and tabu to all others. Hence, such renderings as German "Bann" and French "l'anathème" for the noun. That which is subject of the verb -- the noun ḥerɛm -- was sometimes devoted to the cult, sometimes utterly destroyed. Hence the translations, "destruction, immolation; doomed, devoted."

CHAPTER VII

CONCLUSIONS OF PREVIOUS STUDIES AND SUMMARY

Our attention may now be directed to an examination and evaluation of those conclusions of previous studies which have hitherto not come under direct focus in this investigation.

How well do Hempel's conclusions about the magical concepts discernible behind biblical manifestations of blessing and curse stand up? In the summation of his ideas in Chapter 1 his observation was noted that the magical origins, or the roots in magic of biblical blessing and curse, may be seen in their pronouncements, which are characterized by the features of incantation (Zauberspruche), to wit: schematic and rhythmic organization, frequent antithetical parallelism, and repetition to strengthen the force of the utterance. As reasonable as this statement may seem at the first meeting, it must be rejected; for according to this logic virtually all biblical poetry would have to be rooted in magical incantation. Although innumerable examples could be adduced, a few typical ones will suffice. All these characteristics appear in war poems (Exod. 15:1-18); poetic taunts (Gen. 4:23-24); love lyrics (Canticles); nature poetry (Ps. 104); elegies (2 Sam. 1:19-27); homilies (Prov. 30:24-31); epithalamia (Ps. 45).

The stretching out of the javelin in the direction of the enemy by Joshua (Josh. 8:18) is interpreted by Hempel as the utilization of a magical device. But even a cursory reading of the incident discloses no evidence of magic whatsoever. Joshua employs what even then may have been a time-worn device. After a frontal attack on the defenders of Ai, the Israelites fall away in a simulated rout, drawing their pursuers far afield. With the city empty of defenders, YHWH commands Joshua to point his javelin toward Ai. That this is only a signal for the launching of the attack is made explicit by the next verse: those Israelites who have been lying in ambush "arose quickly out of their places, running at the stretching of his hand (kinᵊṭoṯ yāḏō)" and stormed the city.

Another magical device is seen by Hempel in the mention in Isa. 58:9 of the pointing of the finger. Here too a study of the context will reveal the incongruity of this interpretation. The entire chapter, including this passage, is a promise of God's favor if only social wrongs are set to rights. Verse 9 b continues: "if you remove the yoke (of oppression) from your midst, the putting forth of the finger and speaking wickedness." It can scarcely be doubted that the last phrase (wᵊdabber ʾāwɛn) is virtually a definition of the preceding one (šᵊlaḥ ʾɛṣbaᶜ). The pointing or stretching out of a finger is an idiom for accusation in CH § 127 šumma awīlum ubānam ušatriṣ "If a man causes a finger to be pointed" and cannot prove (the charge) ...and CH § 132 šumma aššat awīlim ubānum eliša ittariṣ, "If a finger is pointed (lit. outstretched) against a married woman," is paralleled in CH § 131 by šumma aššat awīlim mussa ubbiršī "If a woman's husband accuses her" (of adultery).[1] The verse in Isaiah can be understood only as an appeal for the cessation of slanderous accusations. Of magical practice there is no trace.

In Deut. 25:9 where a childless widow loosens the shoe and spits in the face of her husband's brother who has declined to perform the levirate obligation, Hempel discerns a magical act in the spitting. But the ritual is one in which a shirker is humiliated. There is no hint of a curse -- and to this day spitting is a form of expressing contempt.

All these devices are seen by Hempel as means to effect a kind of contact between subject and object, i.e. the imprecator and his victim. Yet no imprecation is present in any of these instances, and where imprecation is explicit none of these methods of "contact" is mentioned.

The use of the right hand in blessing as in Gen. 48:13, argues Hempel, is rooted in magic. Now it is true that atavistic superstitions die hard, but the rites accompanying them do not necessarily involve a consciousness of magical potency. Dexterity is still today preferred over left-handedness -- irrationally, to be sure -- but in the passage to which Hempel refers the position of the right hand is only an indication of preferment, for Manasseh, too, is blessed with Jacob's left hand resting on his head.

Perhaps a more weighty point is the one that Hempel makes in regard to (2 Kings 22:19-20) Josiah's penitence upon hearing the reading of the threats of disaster prom-

---

[1] Cf. DM, Vol. 2, p. 50-53.

ised in the newly-found tōrā-document: that repentance can postpone, but not avert, the disaster invoked by a curse. But here, despite the apparent truth of the generalization, the question is whether the phenomenon is a matter of superstition or religion, and whether it is limited to imprecation or is expressive of a general concept of reward and punishment. The deferment of retribution to a later time figures also in 2 Kings 20:16-19, where Hezekiah is quite content that disaster strike his dynasty as long as it does not come in his own lifetime. Exodus 34:6-7 indicates that nāśā᾽ ʿāwōn means not forgiveness of sin -- but, rather, temporary forbearance[2] -- for it is immediately followed by wᵊnaqqē lōʾ yᵊnaqqɛ i.e., the slate is not wiped clean. Retribution for past crimes may be suffered three or four generations later. This concept is made explicit in Exod. 32:34 where YHWH, yielding to the entreaties of Moses not to exterminate the Israelites for the sin of the golden calf, adds ominously ubᵊyōm poqᵊdī upāqádtī ʿᵃlēhɛm haṭṭāʾtām "but when I do call to account, I will count against them these sins of theirs." It would seem that what we have here is a concept of punishment -- deferable but inexorable -- which, repugnant as it may be to modern sensibilities, may not be labeled "magical."

If the foregoing is correct, then the importance of preventing the expression of an imprecation by Balaam would

---

[2]For this understanding of the phrase and of the entire passage, which, to the best of my knowledge, has not appeared in print, I am indebted to a friend and colleague, Rabbi Jochanan Muffs of the Jewish Theological Seminary of America.

not be explainable in terms of the magical effects of a curse once uttered. And, indeed, one may wonder: if Balaam had disobeyed YHWH's instructions, would Hempel argue that the curse would nonetheless have been efficacious?

Along similar lines one may doubt the conjecture about the adhesive power of blessings and curses. Gen. 12:1-3, which Hempel cites as an example of this principle has been given an altogether different interpretation here (cf. above, p.197 n.92.). In regard to the notion that a cursed person is a danger to the whole land, the biblical concept of collective responsibility is well enough known to militate against the limitation of this thinking to the magical substratum underlying blessing and curse. A rotten apple affects the whole bushel, but is there any magical significance to the phenomenon?

In any case, the examples which Hempel adduces for the "adhesive" quality of curse must all be rejected here. To use Cain's fate as an illustration of this principle ("wer ihn findet, erschlägt ihn") is to overlook the fact that the "mark of Cain" is put upon him for his protection. The interpretation of Deut. 21:22-23 offered here (cf. p. 191 ff.) rules out the infectiousness of curse attaching to a hanged man. And as for Moses' warning to the Israelites to separate themselves from the rebel Korah, it is prudent to stay away from the vicinity of someone who is about to be swallowed up in an earthquake -- but it is God who chooses this way of vindicating Moses and condemning his opponents, and there is nothing magical about it.

The difference between the interpretations offered

here of Lev. 19:18; Isa. 8:21; Jer. 15:10; Prov. 30:10 and the significance of these verses as seen by Hempel, may easily be noted by a comparison of the discussions ad loc. and Chapter I, page 5f. In regard, however, to Hempel's notions about the "mechanical spreading" of the curse (cf. above, p. 6), it must be emphasized that the biblical text nowhere bears out the identification of every misfortune as an independent, automatic Ding-an-sich instrumentality, executing a putative imprecation on the part of the Deity. That evidence of the original magical force of the stem ᵓrr is not lacking, that vestiges of magical or superstitious beliefs lie behind such institutions as the scapegoat -- and animal sacrifice, in general -- are points which few will contest. This does not, however, justify a syllogism with an undistributed middle. Traces of magical thought in the Bible are one thing, the assumption that the operation of curses is magical and independent of the Deity is quite another.

One more assumption of Hempel's requires close attention: that the efficacy of an imprecation is strengthened by every repetition, and that it is the fear of the consequence of the utterance which accounts for the abbreviation of the oath-formula to kō yaᶜaśɛ YHWH lī wᵊkō yōsīp ᵓim... "May YHWH do so to me and more if...," which is to say, to the utter exclusion of the sanction. This suggestion, taken up and expanded by Sheldon Blank, is as gratuitous as it is self-contradictory. It is all the more surprising in view of Hempel's own citation of the following passage from Hirzel's Der Eid,

> Der Fluch erscheint als das Wesentliche im Eide, und Verwünschungseide, weil in ihnen dieses Wesen des Eides am reinsten und stärksten hervortritt, gelten eben deshalb als die kräftigsten. Er gehört zum Eide, wie zum Gesetz die Androhung der Strafe.

Now if the sanction of the oath is not expressed lest it befall the oath-violator, there is no oath at all. The significance attached to the "abridged" oath-formula by Hempel and Blank can be based only on a misunderstanding of the "abridgment"; for, if we are not given the content of the kō yaᶜaśɛ "So may He do" because there was none, then the addition of wᵊkō yōsīp = "and more of the same" would represent a compounding of the initial nonsense.

In view of the above, then, and in the light of the many examples which Blank himself cites of biblical oaths in which the sanctions are fully -- and even harrowingly -- expressed, the kō yaᶜaśɛ formula can be understood only as a kind of short-hand or ellipsis on the part of the biblical narrator or speaker when he does not know, or is not interested in detailing, the specific content of the sanction clause of the oath. The only meaningful translation of the phrase is: "May YHWH do such-and-such to me and more, if..."[3]

The passive construction of the biblical curse formula "ʾārūr (be)..." is interpreted by Blank (cf. above, p. 9 ff.) as revealing the underlying notion that the curse is automatic and self-fulfilling, the power residing in the

---

[3]It is noteworthy that the kō yaᶜaśɛ formula is not limited to the oath. In I Sam. 3:17 it is employed by Eli in an adjuration addressed to Samuel. If, according to the Hempel-Blank theory, self-interest accounts for the "omission" of the curse in the oath-formula, what would account for its omission in an adjuration?

spoken word itself. Gevirtz, comparing this passive construction to the active invocation of deities in Mesopotamian curses, accepts Blank's interpretation of the former and concludes that the Western Semites relied upon the power of the spoken word, the Eastern Semites upon divine agency, to effectuate a curse. Gevirtz closes with the statement,

> A discussion of the religious import attaching to each of the two kinds of formulation individually, or to the differences in religious attitude between "East" and "West" expressed by these generally, properly in the domain of history or philosophy of religion, lies beyond the scope of the present study.

Now it is just the domain at whose boundaries Gevirtz pulls up short -- the history of religion -- which suggests a skeptical approach to the Blank-Gevirtz hypothesis. Mesopotamia is steeped in magic; ancient Israel is unrelenting in its campaign against it. In Mesopotamia the gods themselves are subject to and dependent upon forces of magic external to their own being; in the religion of Israel, at whatever stage -- be it monolatrous, henotheistic, or monotheistic -- the Deity is supremely independent of outside power, Himself the source of all power. Mesopotamia is polytheistic; Israel is the battleground from which monotheism emerges triumphant.[4] How anomalous is a hypothesis according to which the leaders of Israel's battle for monotheism and the Deity himself rely upon the automatic and magical power of words, while in the land of magic, magic is eschewed and reliance placed in deities who are them-

---

[4]Cf. Yehezkel Kaufmann: The Religion of Israel, tr. by Moshe Greenberg, Chs. 2 and 3.

selves subject to magic! Even without a study of the *ʾārūr* rubric, one might counter Gevirtz's explanation of the contrasting phenomena as follows: Is it not likely that in a land where deities (of both sexes and multitudinous functions) proliferate it would be necessary to specify the agents who are to effectuate the sanction(s)? By contrast a society which recognized but a single source of power could use passival constructions in its imprecations (and prayers), without there being any question as to the agent who rewards and punishes, vindicates and condemns.[5]

We are not, however, without evidence that a passive construction may be merely a stylistic accident rather than an indication of the absence of an agent. A striking case in point is I Sam. 11:7, a verse whose content is generally misunderstood by both translators and commentators. When Saul, returning with his "cattle from the field," learns of the Ammonite threat to Jabesh-Gilead and of the agreement of the citizens of that town to surrender to the enemy if within a week they cannot summon help from their confederate tribes, he dismembers a brace of oxen. He sends the joints through all the territory of Israel with the proclamation *kō yēʿāśē* to the cattle of any Israelite who does

---

[5]Thus, for example, Martin Noth is not disturbed by the passive construction of the formula in Deut. 27. There is no question in his mind that it is the Deity himself who executes the curse. ("Die Mit des Gezetzes Werken Umgehen, Die Sind unter dem Fluch," in *Gesammelte Studien zum A. T.*, Munich: Kaiser, 1957), p. 167-68: "Ein Übertreten des Gesetzes...bedeutet Verlassen des Bundestreue, damit Bundesbruch und Abfall; und für diesen Fall ist das Wirksamwerden des dem Gesetz beigefügten Fluches vorgesehen, den Jahwe selbst vollstrecken wird."

not respond to the summons to battle. All the translations take the verb as a simple future -- a threat by Saul. But it must be remembered that Chapter 11 follows immediately the narrative of 9:1-10:16 inclusive (10:17-27 belongs to the second and later account of Saul's assumption of kingship). Saul is not king but an obscure farmer (or herdsman), young enough to be part of his father's household. Who would be intimidated by a threat from such a person? What is involved here is not a threat, but an imprecation (an ʾālā, without question),[6] and kō yēʿāśɛ́ is to be translated as a jussive, "May it be done so..." Yet the immediately following clause wayyippol paḥad YHWH ʿal hāʿām wayyēṣʾʾū kʾʾîš ʾɛḥād "There fell upon the people the terror of YHWH with the result that they came forth as one man," demonstrates conclusively that despite the passive voice in the imprecation there was no question that the agent invoked was YHWH.

If further argument be needed against the thesis that the passive voice as used in imprecation is an indication of the automatic, self-fulfilling, power of the word, it may be provided by the study here of the verb ʾrr. An examination of the table in the Appendix will show that ac-

---

[6]The full force of the ʾālā can be understood only in the light of the fact that the Israelites and the residents of Jabesh-Gilead are baʿalē bərît, joined in a covenant which doubtless provides for mutual assistance in such an eventuality. The original imprecation, we may be confident, was not on the cattle of the Israelites but upon themselves. Cf. the bərît bēn habbətārîm in Gen. 15 and the treaty between Bir-Gaʾyah and Matiel in J. A. Fitzmyer, "The Aramaic Inscriptions of Sefire I and II," JAOS, LXXXI 3 (Sept. 1961), 178-222, with special attention to the translation and commentary of FACE A, ll. 36-40.

cording to the interpretations of the texts offered herein, of twenty occurrences of the passive participle ʾārūr,[7] ten at the most, and possibly only one, constitute clear, unambiguous instances of imprecation.

Even the magical sense of "spell" underlying the term ʾrr is no indication of anything automatic, self-fulfilling in the curse, for it is the Deity who wields the power of the spell.

In brief, it is the conclusion here that the evidence for magical concepts underlying the biblical phenomena of curse (and of blessing) has been grossly overvalued.

SUMMARY

The specific biblical term for "curse" in the sense of "imprecation" is ʾālā. The function of imprecation is reflected in the fact that virtually every instance of imprecation (whether ʾālā appears as noun or verb) is one in which the imprecation is contingent or conditional. Thus in the oath (šᵊbūʿā) the sanction clause or curse (ʾālā) is conditioned by the truth of the asseveration or the fulfillment of the promise. The sanction(s) ʾālā/ʾālōṯ of a solemn compact (which intrinsically involves an oath or oaths) are contingent upon the violation of the agreement. The ʾālā as imprecation to produce or preclude a given action, to produce witnesses to a crime or a confession of guilt is contingent upon the future action or inaction of

---

[7]Each passage is counted as a single occurrence, regardless of the number of times that the term ʾārūr appears in it.

the object of the imprecation, or upon the fact of guilt or innocence of a named party, or upon the anonymity of the perpetrator of a known offense. In short, imprecation is resorted to only when a failure of human resources is acknowledged or anticipated. By metonymy, a person or place afflicted by the consequences of an imprecation may be termed an ʾālā, the sense being that that person or place is an example of the efficacy of an ʾālā and/or an example or illustration to be referred to in future imprecations. It is regarded as likely that the third statement of the decalogue is a prohibition of the use of the name YHWH in unjustifiable imprecations. The Akkadian word corresponding to Hebrew ʾālā and, like it, subject to extension to mean "oath" by synecdoche of the part for the whole, or to the extension to cover the victim or consequence of the imprecation by metonymy of cause for effect, is māmītu. Whereas the etymology of Hebrew *ʾlw is obscure, that of māmītu, deriving from the verb amû "to speak," reflects the basic force of the noun, "a solemn pronouncement." By a reverse process of metonymy the term for oath occasionally stands for "curse" and the hiphʿil of šbʿ, normally "to cause someone to take an oath," is extended to be equal to hiphʿil of *ʾlw "to place (someone) under a contingent imprecation."

Distinct from the sense of "pronouncement" in ʾālā is the force of the verb ʾrr and its corresponding noun məʾērā. The force underlying this stem is the curse from the operational point of view. Whether by means of an incantation or other procedure this stem has the sense of to impose a ban or barrier, a paralysis on movement or other capabilities. Corresponding to Akkadian <u>arāru</u>, an action invoked (in imprecations) of the gods, the subject of the active verb in the Bible is always the Deity, an unusually potent person who derives his powers from the Deity, or a leader of the people who acts on their behalf. The passive participle <u>ʾārūr</u> thus becomes the rubric for imprecations; it does not, however, by its mere occurrence testify to the presence of an imprecation, for it may also be the rubric of a decree, of a prediction of doom, of a statement acknowledging the existence of a hitherto unrecognized operation of the active verb. Thus, although closely associated with <u>ʾālā</u>, "curse" in the sense of imprecation, it is also independent of it.

Of the three stems, <u>*ʾlw</u>, <u>ʾrr</u>, <u>qll</u>, the last possesses the broadest and most general semantic range. The verb in the <u>piʿel</u> stands for a wide range of abuse, from spoken insult to inflicted destruction. As an antonym of <u>bērek</u> and <u>kibbed</u> it means to treat in a disrespectful manner. With parents or kings as object, it may have the sense of "repudiate." With the Deity as object, it represents a lack of respect for the moral standards sanctioned by the Deity and is the expression antonymous to <u>yārēʾ</u>(/<u>yirʾat</u>) <u>ʾĕlōhîm</u> "to show respect for (the moral standards ordained by) God"; thus, it never refers to imprecation against the Deity, a concept alien to the biblical mind. In only a few passages does the possibility exist that <u>qillel</u> means to pronounce an imprecation -- passages which are derivative, or in which the verb is supplemented by "God" or the like.

The expression *qillel ʾĕlōhīm* seems somewhat analogous to Akkadian *ana ili qullulu* "to commit offense against (a) god(s)," an expression which occurs particularly in the context of violation of international agreements. In contrast with the Akkadian nouns *g/qillatu*, *g/qullultu* which appear to be limited to the sense of crime, offense, guilt, sin, the Hebrew noun *qəlālā* may denote not only abusive conduct, but the result of the latter, namely, misfortune, disaster. The tradition that both *qillel* and *qəlālā* have the primary meaning of to speak ill of, or against (*i.e.* malediction and imprecation) is traceable tothe assumption by tradition that these terms are antonyms of *bērek* and *bərākā* ("to bless" and "blessing") in the narrow sense of these terms as utterances (*benedico*), rather than in their broad material connotations "to treat favorably, cause to prosper."

In the Bible, good fortune and misfortune (*bərākā* and *qəlālā* respectively) are traceable to God, and prayers or imprecations invoking these are, even when not made explicit in the text, addressed to the Deity.

APPENDIX

TABLE I

The Distribution of the Passive Participle *ʾārūr*

Texts[1]	In Impre-cation	In Decree by Man	In Decree by Deity	In Predic-tion	In Statement of Fact
Gen. 27:29	X				
Num. 24:9	X		X	X	
Deut. 27:15-26	X		X	X	
Deut. 28:16-29	X		X	X	
Josh. 6:26	X		X		
I Sam. 14:24	X	X			
Jer. 11:3			X		
Jer. 20:14-18	X?				
Jer. 48:10	X		X		
Mal. 1:14			X		
Gen. 3:14			X		
Gen. 4:11			X		
Gen. 3:17-18			X		
Gen. 9:25	X	X?			
Gen. 49:7			X		
Josh. 9:23		X			
Judg. 21:18	X	X			
I Sam. 26:19			X		X
Jer. 17:5			X		
Ps. 119:21					X

[1] In the order in which they appear in Chapter III.

TABLE II

The Distribution of the Verb qillel

	No utterance involved	Utterance -- not impreca-tion	Imprecation--Malediction
Gen. 8:21	X		
Lev. 19:14		X	
Isa. 65:20	X		
Jer. 15:10	X	?	
Neh. 13:25	X	?	
Ps. 37:22	X	?	
Ps. 62:5		X	?
Ps. 109:28		X	?
Prov. 30:10	?	X	?
Job 3:1		X	
Eccles. 7:21-22		X	?
Job 24:18	X		
Exod. 21:17	X	?	?
Lev. 20:9	X	?	?
Prov. 20:20	X	?	?
Prov. 30:11	X	?	?
Judges 9:27-28		X	
II Sam. 16:5-11	X	X	
Isa. 8:21	X	?	
Eccles. 10:20	?	?	
Lev. 24:10-23	?	?	
I Sam. 3:13	X		
Exod. 22:27	X		
(I Kings 21:7-13)	X		
(Job 1:5)	X	?	
(Job 1:10)	X	?	
(Job 2:9)	X		
I Sam. 17:43		X	?
II Kings 2:24		X	?
Deut. 23:4-5		X	X
Josh. 24:9		X	X

TABLE III

The Distribution of the Noun qəlālā

	Material Misfortune Abusive Behavior	Imprecation/ Malediction	Ambiguous
Deut. 11:26-29	X		
Josh. 8:32-34	X		
Deut. 27:12-13	X		
Deut. 28:15	X		
Deut. 29:26	X		
Deut. 30:19	X		
II Sam. 16:12	X		
Jer. 24:9	X		
Prov. 26:2	X		
Prov. 27:14	X		
Deut. 21:23	X		
Deut. 23:6	?	X	
Judg. 9:57		X	
Jer. 29:22	?	X	
Zech. 8:13	?	X	
Gen. 27:12-13	?	?	X
II Kings 22:19	?	?	X
Jer. 25:18	?	?	X
Jer. 26:6	?	?	X
Jer. 42:18	?	?	X
Jer. 44:8	?	?	X
Jer. 44:22	?	?	X
Jer. 49:13	?	?	X
Ps. 109:17-18	?	?	X

SELECTED BIBLIOGRAPHY

Baentsch, Bruno. Exodus-Leviticus-Numeri, HAT, Göttingen: Vandenhoeck & Ruprecht, 1903.

Baer, S. Libri Regum. Leipzig: Tauchnitz, 1895.

Bauer, Hans. "Ein aramäischer Staatsvertrag aus dem 8. Jahrhundert v. Chr. Die Inschrift der Stele von Sudschīn," AfO, Band VIII 1/2, 1932.

Bergsträsser, G. Hebräische Grammatik. II Teil. Leipzig: Hinrichs, 1929.

Bertholet, Alfred. Leviticus, KHAT. Tübingen: J. C. B. Mohr, 1901.

Blank, Sheldon H. "The Curse, Blasphemy, the Spell, and the Oath," HUCA, XXIII 1. (1950-51), 73-95.

Borger, R. "Zu den Asarhaddon-Verträgen aus Nimrud," ZA 54, 1961.

Boyer, George. Archives Royales de Mari, VIII. Paris: Imprimerie Nationale, 1958.

Burney, G. F. Notes on the Hebrew Text of the Books of Kings. Oxford: Clarendon Press, 1903.

Canaan, T. "The Curse in Palestinian Folklore, JPOS XV, 1935.

Chapman, A. T., and Streane, A. W. The Book of Leviticus. Cambridge: Cambridge Press, 1914.

Cheyne, T. K. Hosea. Cambridge: University Press, 1889.

_______, The Book of Psalms. 2 vols. London: Paul, Trench, Trubner, 1904.

Chiera, Edward. Excavations at Nuzi: Texts of Varied Contents. Volume V of Harvard Semitic Series. Cambridge: Harvard University Press, 1929.

Delitzsch, Franz. The Psalms. 2 vols. transl. by F. Bolton. Edinburgh: T & T Clark, 1871.

Draffkorn, Anne E. "ILANI/ELOHIM," JBL LXXVI 3 (Sept. 1957), 216-24.

Driver, G. R. and J. C. Miles. The Babylonian Laws. 2 vols. Oxford: Clarendon Press, 1956.

Driver, S. R. Deuteronomy, ICC, 3rd ed. Edinburgh: T & T Clark, 1902.

Driver, S. R. Notes on the Hebrew Text of the Books of Samuel. Ocford: Clarendon Press, 1913.

______, The Book of Exodus. Cambridge: University Press, 1911.

Ebeling, Erich. Die Akkadische Gebetsserie "Handerhebung." Berlin: (Deutsche) Akademie-Verlag, 1953.

Ehrlich, Arnold B. Randglossen zur Hebräischen Bibel. 7 vol. Leipzig: Hinrichs, 1908.

______, Die Psalmen. Berlin: Poppelauer, 1936.

Ewald, G. H. A. Commentary on the Psalms. 2 vols. transl. by E. Johnson. London: Williams & Norgate, 1880.

Fitzmyer, J. A. "The Aramaic Inscriptions of Sefire I and II," JAOS, LXXXI 3 (August-September, 1961). 178-222.

Fohrer, Georg. Ezechiel, HbAT. Tübingen: J.C.B. Mohr, 1955.

Frankenberg, W. Die Spruche, HAT. Göttingen: Vandenhoeck & Ruprecht, 1898.

Galling, Kurt. Die Bücher der Chronik, Esra, Nehemia, ATD. Göttingen: Bandenhoeck & Ruprecht, 1954.

Gevirtz, Stanley. "Curse Motifs in the Old Testament and in the Ancient Near East." (unpublished Doctor's thesis, Graduate Library School: University of Chicago, 1959).

Giesebrecht, F. Das Buch Jeremia, HAT. Göttingen: Vandenhoeck & Ruprecht, 1907.

Ginsberg, H. L. "An Unrecognized Allusion to Kings Pekah and Hoshea of Israel," Eretz-Israel. Jerusalem: Israel Exploration Society, 1958.

______, Koheleth. Tel Aviv: M. Newman, 1961, (Hebrew).

Gordis, Robert. Koheleth -- The Man and his World. 2nd aug. ed., New York: Bloch, 1955.

Gray, G. B. Numbers, ICC. New York: Ch. Scribner's Sons, 1903.

Greenberg, Moshe. "The Hebrew Oath Particle HAY/HE," JBL, LXXVI, 1 (March 1957).

Hempel, Johannes. "Die israelitischen Anschauungen von Segen und Fluch im Lichte altorientalischen Parallelen," ZDMG Neue Folge, Band 4 (1915), 20-110.

Hertzberg, Hans Wilhelm. Die Bücher Josua, Richter, Ruth,

ATD, Göttingen: Vandenhoeck & Ruprecht, 1953.

Hertzberg, Hans Wilhelm. Die Samuelbücher, ATD. Göttingen: V & R, 1960.

______, Die Prediger, KAT. Leipzig: Deichert, 1932.

Hoffmann, D. Das Buch Leviticus. 2 vols. Berlin: Poppelauer, 1906.

Hölscher, Gustav. Das Buch Hiob, HbAT. Tübingen: J.C.B. Mohr, 1952.

Holzinger, H. Numeri, KHAT. Tübingen: J.C.B. Mohr, 1903.

Kaiser, Otto. Der Prophet Jesaia, ATD. Göttingen: Vandenhoeck & Ruprecht, 1960.

Kaufmann, Yehezkel. The Religion of Israel. transl. and abrdgd. by Moshe Greenberg. Chicago: University of Chicago Press, 1960.

Kautzsch, E. und Socin, A. Die Genesis. Freiburg I.B.: J.C.B. Mohr, 1891.

Kennedy, A. R. S. Leviticus & Numbers. Century Bible. Edinburg: Jack

King, L. W. Babylonian Magic and Sorcery. London, 1896.

Kissane, Edward J. The Book of Psalms. 2 vols. Dublin: Browne & Nolan, 1954.

Kittel, Rudolf. Die Bücher der Könige, HAT. Gottingen: Vandenhoeck & Ruprecht, 1900.

______, Die Bücher der Chronik und Esra, Nehemia. HAT. Göttingen: Vandenhoeck & Ruprecht, 1902.

Knudtzon, J. A. Die El-Amarna-Tafeln. 2 vols. Leipzig: Hinrichs, 1915.

Kraetzschmar, Richard. Das Buch Daniel, HAT. Göttingen: Vandenhoeck & Ruprecht, 1894.

Luckenbill, D. D. The Annals of Sennacherib. Chicago: University of Chicago Press, 1914.

Marti, Karl. Das Buch Jesaja, KHAT. Tübingen: J.C.B. Mohr, 1900.

Meier, Gerhard. Die assyrische Beschwörungssamlung Maqlû. AfO. Beiheft 2, 1937.

Melamed, E. Z. "Two Which Are One (EN ΔIA ΔYOIN) in the Bible" (Hebrew). Tarbiz 16, 1945.

Mendenhall, G. E. "Covenant Forms in Israelite Tradition," BA, XVII.

Mercer, S. A. B. The Oath in Babylonian and Assyrian Literature. Munich: C. Wolf and Son, 1911.

_______, "The Malediction in Cuneiform Inscriptions," JAOS 34, 1915.

Mitchell, H. G. Haggai and Zechariah, ICC. New York: Ch. Scribner's Sons, 1912.

Montgomery, James A. The Book of Kings, ICC. New York: Ch. Scribner's Sons, 1951.

Mowinckel, Sigmund. Segen und Fluch in Israels Kult und Psalmendichtung. Kristiana: Videnskapsselskapets Skrifter II, Hist.-Filos. (Klasse 1923) 3.

Noth, Martin. "'Die mit des Gesetzes Werken umgehen, die sins unter dem Fluch'," Gesammelte Studien zum Alten Testament. Munich: Chr. Kaiser, 1957. Pp. 155-71.

_______, Das zweite Buch Mose: Exodus. ATD. Göttingen: Vandenhoeck & Ruprecht. 1961.

Nowack, D. W. Die kleinen Propheten, HAT. Göttingen: Vandenhoeck & Ruprecht, 1897.

Oesterley, W. O. E. The Psalms. London: S.P.C.K., 1953.

_______, The Book of Proverbs. London: Methuen, 1929.

Pedersen, Johs. Der Eid bei den Semiten. Strassburg: Trübner, 1914.

________, Israel -- Its Life and Culture. 2 vols. London: Oxford University Press, 1926.

Plassman, Thomas. The Signification of Bᵊrāḵā. Paris: Imprimerie Nationale, 1913.

Pritchard, James B. (ed.) Ancient Near Eastern Texts. Princeton University Press, 1955.

Reiner, Erica. Šurpu, AfO. Beiheft 11 (1958).

Rudolph, Wilhelm. Ezra und Nehemia, HbAT. Tübingen: J.C.B. Mohr, 1949.

Scharbert, Josef. "'Fluchen' und 'Segen' im Alten Testament," Biblica, XXIX (1958), 1-26.

_______, Solidarität in Segen und Fluch im Alten Testament und in seiner Umwelt. Bonn: Peter Hanstein, 1958.

Siegfried, D. C. Prediger und Hoheslied, HAT. Göttingen: Vandenhoeck & Ruprecht, 1898.

Skinner, John. Genesis, ICC. New York: Ch. Scribner's Sons, 1910.

______, Isaiah. 2 vols. Cambridge: University Press, 1915.

Smith, Henry Preserved. The Books of Samuel, ICC. Edinburgh: T & T Clark, 1899.

Smith, J. M. Powis. The Book of Malachi, ICC. New York: Ch. Scribner's Sons, 1912.

Speiser, E. A. "Nuzi Marginalia," Orientalia, 25, 1 (1956).

______, "'Coming' and 'Going' at the 'City' Gate," BASOR, (Dec. 1956).

______, "An Angelic 'Curse': Exodus 14:20," JAOS, 80, 3 (July-Sept. 1960).

______, "Leviticus and the Critics," Yehezkel Kaufmann Jubilee Volume. ed. by M. Haran. Jerusalem: Magnes Press, 1960.

______, "Ancient Mesopotamia," The Idea of History in the Ancient Near East. ed. by Robert C. Dentan. AOS 38. New Haven: Yale University Press, 1955.

______, "Background and Function of the Biblical NĀŚĪʾ," CBQ XXV 1 (Jan. 1963).

Sperber, Alexander. The Bible in Aramaic. (Vol. 1. The Pentateuch acc. to Targum Onkelos. Vol. 2. The Former Prophets acc. to Targum Jonathan). Leiden: Brill, 1959.

Spiro, Abram. "A Law on the Sharing of Information," AAJRP, XXVIII, 1959.

Steuernagel, Carl. Deuteronomium und Josua, HAT. Göttingen: Vandenhoeck & Ruprecht, 1900.

Strack, Hermann L. Die Genesis. München: Beck, 1905.

Toy, Crawford H. The Book of Proverbs, ICC. New York: Ch. Scribner, 1899.

Tsevat, Matitiahu. "The Neo-Assyrian and Neo-Babylonian Vassal Oaths and the Prophet Ezekiel," JBL, LXXVIII, 3 (Sept. 1959).

Tur-Sinai, N. H. The Book of Job, Jerusalem: Kiryath Sepher, 1957.

Van Selms, Adrianus. De Babylonische Termini Voor Zonde. Wageningen: H. Veenman & Zonen, 1933.

Von Rad, Gerhard. Genesis, ATD. Göttingen: Vandenhoeck & Ruprecht, 1961.

Weiser, Artur. Das Buch Hiob, ATD. Göttingen: Vandenhoeck & Ruprecht, 1951.

______, Die Psalmen, ATD. Göttingen: Vandenhoeck & Ruprecht, 1950.

______, Das Buch der zwölf kleinen Propheten, ATD. Gottingen: Vandenhoeck & Ruprecht, 1949.

Wiseman, D. J. The Vassal Treaties of Esarhaddon. London: British School of Archaeology in Iraq, 1958.

BIBLES, GRAMMARS & LEXICONS

Massoretic Bible: Miqrā'ōt Gedōlōt, New York: Pardes, 1951.

Biblica Hebraica, ed. Rud. Kittel. Stuttgart: Württ, Bibelanstalt, 1937.

Septuaginta. ed. Alfred Rahlfs. Stuttgart: Württembergische Bibelanstalt, 1949.

Gesenius' Hebrew Grammar. ed. by E. Kautzsch and A. E. Cowley. Oxford: Clarendon Press, 1951.

Grammatik des Biblisch-Aramäischen. von Hans Bauer und Pontus Leander. Halle: Max Niemeyer, 1927.

A Hebrew and English Lexicon of the Old Testament. by Francis Brown, S. R. Driver and Charles A. Briggs. Oxford: Clarendon Press, 1952.

Akkadisches Handwörterbuch von Wolfram Von Soden. Wiesbaden: Otto Harrassowitz.

Aramäisch-Neuhebräisches Handwörterbuch von Gustaf H. Dalman. Frankfurt a. Main: J. Kauffmann, 1922.

The Assyrian Dictionary of the Oriental Institute of the University of Chicago.

Assyrisches Handwörterbuch von Friedrich Delitzsch. Leipzig: J. C. Hinrichs, 1896.

Webster's Third New International Dictionary. Springfield, Mass.: G. & C. Merriam Co., 1961.

The Oxford English Dictionary. Oxford: Clarendon Press, 1933.

INDEX TO PASSAGES CITED -- HEBREW SCRIPTURES

(The letter n after a page number refers to a footnote)

Genesis

1:14....................99n
3:14....................83
3:17............86,109,158n
3:17-18...........86ff.,103
4:2....................110n
4:11...........84f.,86,192
4:12...................5,85
4:14......................5
4:15....................37n
4:23-24.................205
4:26...................110n
5:29....................109
8:21........119f.,146n,158n
9:21-22.................110
9:25-26..............87,90n
12:1-3...............5,209
12:3...................157n
12:6....................49n
14:12-14..................5
16:4....................19n
20:11...................167
21:10...................19n
24:2-26................138n
24:40-41...........22,25f.
24:41...................26n
26:28-31...........22,27f.
27:12-13................196
27:29....................77
27:35.....................5
33:19..................138n
34......................137
42:18-19................167
46:34..................194n
47:7-10.................190
48:13................5,207
48:20...................195
49:6-7.................108f.
49:7.....................87

Exodus

1:24..................166 n
12:32....................10
14:20........96ff.,106,109
15:1-18.................205
18:21...................168
18:22..................119n
20:7............59ff.,150n
20:12...................135
20:16....................61
20:22-23:33.............132
21:15...................132
21:15,17...............146n
21:17..........132,135,190n
22:20-30.........158n,168n
22:27...7,9,147,150ff.,156,
157ff.,163,168n.
23:30..................105n
32:34...................208
34:6-7..................208

Leviticus

5:1........22,42n,43,44n,55
5:21-24.................58f.
7:24...................105n
16:19..................171n
17:15..................105n
18:24f..................192
19:12................60,62n
19:14...............120,168
19:18................6,210
19:31...................166
19:32...................168
20:9....................135
21:5...................174n
22:28..................105n
24:10-23......9,143ff.,151,
157,158,163n,
165,178n,
200
25:17...................168
25:36...................168
25:43...................168

Numbers

5........................23
5:11ff...........50ff.,111
5:18ff............49ff.,53
5:19,21..................48
14:37...................79n
16:2...................161n
16:25.....................5
21:17....................10
22........................5
22:6-12.................99f.
22:11,17................201

22-24....................176
23:7....................202
23:8....................201
23:8-27............100n,202
24:9....................77
32:20f..................79n
35:33f..................192

Deuteronomy

1:34-37...............158f.
5:11..................59ff.
5:18....................61
11:26-29...............183
11:30...................49n
13:6.....................5
14:21..................105n
17:14ff................163
21:18-21...............134n
21:22-23.......5,191ff.,209
23:4-6......172f.,175,195f.
23:6...................102
24:10...................53
25:9..................6,207
25:18..................169
27:11-14..........184,185n
27:15-26.........78,184,185
27:16..................190n
27:24..................192
28:15..................186
28:16-20...............79f.
28:20..............95n,112
28:45..................186
28:58..................166
29:9-20...............28ff.
29:11...................76
29:11,13,18,19..........22
29:16..................187
29:20...................76
29:21..................187n
29:16..................187
30......................31
30:1...................187
30:7....................32
30:15..................187
30:19..................187

Joshua

4:14...................167
6:26..................48,79
7........................5
7:1-11.................162n
8:18.................5,205
8:32-34...............183f.
8:33...................184
9:14....................88n
9:22-23..............89,90n
9:23...................101
10:2,4.................195n
10:12...................10
10:26-27...............195n
24:7....................97
24:9.............123n,172f.
24:9-10................175
24:32..................138n

Judges

5:23..................101f.
5:13...................101n
6:10...................166n
8:22-23................137
9:7-20.................195
9:27-28................137
9:56-57................195
17:2.....10,16n,22,29n,44f.
21:18...............90,101

I Samuel

2:12-17...............149f.
2:14...................166n
2:22-25................150
2:27-36...............149f.
2:30...................165
3:11ff.................151
3:11-14..............148ff.
3:13............9,149n,157
3:29...................149
6:5....................119n
7:6....................161
9:1-10:16..............214
11:7...................213
14.......................5
14:24..........22,45ff.,80
14:27-28................48
14:35..................110n
14:36-37...............162n
14:39...................80
17:12..................101n
17:16..................191n
17:43.................172f.
17:44..................174
17:44-46................93
18:23..................118n
21:12ff................121n
22:15..................110n
24:28...................22
25:21...................61n
26:19..................91f.
26:21..................91 n
28:6...................162n
31:10..................195n

II Samuel

1:19-27..................205
1:23...................118n
4.................139,195n
6:10...................155n
6:22...................118n
16:1-4.................164
16:5...................178n
16:7...................141n
16:5-11.........138ff.,146
16:9....................10
16:10..................178n
16:11..................178n
16:12.........140n,188,194
16:17...................10
19:25-31...............164
19:44..................119n
21................139,195n
21:1-6.................162n
21:1-13.............10,89n
21:8-14................194
21:12-13...............195n
23:3...................169n

I Kings

2:8........141n,181,193,194
2:42-43.................48
2:45....................10
8:31............15n,54n,66
8:31-32........45,52ff.,67
12:4-9f...............119n
12:8...................160
16:34..................79n
20:35-43..............174n
21:7-13.............159ff.
21:13................9,170
21:23...................92
22:16...................48

II Kings

2:23-24...............141n
2:24...............172,174
3:18..................118n
3:26-28...............156n
9:34....................92
17:7-39...............166n
18:25.................140n
20:10.................118n
20:16-19...............208
22:11...................10
22:19-20.........5,196,207

Isaiah

8:16-21...........141,162n
8:21...........6,9,157,210
8:23..................119n
10:13.................108n
14:9..................108n
19:13...................69
22:15-18................93
22:18.................190n
23:9..................119n
24:4-6...............35ff.
24:6....................23
30:16.................118n
36:10.................140n
49:6..................118n
51:9-10...............108n
58:9.................5,206
58:11..................29n
65:20..................122
66:14..................203

Jeremiah

2:30....................61
4:13..................118n
4:24..................119n
6:14..................118n
7:9.....................61
7:13..................191n
8:1-3...................93
8:11..................118n
11:3....................81
11:7..................191n
11:9...................123
15:10............6,123,210
17:5-7................93f.
20:14..................106
20:14-16................81
20:14-18...............129
23:10...................23
23:10-11.............34ff.
24:9...................188
25:3-4................191n
25:18..................196
26:5..................191n
26:6...................197
29:19.................191n
29:22..................195
29:26.................121n
35:14.................191n
36:23...................10
42:18..................197
44:4..................191n

44:8....................197
44:12...................197
44:22...................197
48:10....................82
49:13...................197

Ezekiel

4:14...................105n
8:17...................118n
16:59..................36ff.
17:11-19...............36ff.
17:13,16,18..............27n
19:13....................29n
21:26...................119n
22:7....................119n
44:31...................105n

Hosea

4:1-2...............56f.,63
4:7.....................190n
9:7.....................121n
10:4.....................39f.

Amos

2:16....................101n
6:8.......................65

Jonah

1:5.....................119n
1:9.....................166n

Micah

6:10.....................203

Habakkuk

1:8.....................118n

Zechariah

1:12.....................203
3:2......................95n
5:1-4.....................68
5:3.......................23
7:2.......................68
8:13.....................195

Malachi

1:4......................203
1:6......................166
1:14..................82,105
2:2.............102,105,113
2:3................95n,103
3:9......................113
3:9-11..............103ff.
3:16....................166n

Psalms

6.......................140n
7:12.....................203
9.......................140n
10......................140n
10:3-4..................170n
10:7..............57n,59,63
13......................140n
15:4....................166n
17......................140n
22......................140n
24........................64
25......................140n
25:1......................64
37:22..................9,125
45.......................205
55:25-26.................169
59:13..................57n,63
62:5...............123n,126
74:13-14................108n
82:1....................150n
104......................205
109:17-18................197
109:28..........123n,127,197
111:5...................105n
115:11..................166n
119:21...................94f.
128:4...................166n
130:4...................166n
135:20..................166n

Proverbs

3:3......................114
11:2....................190n
11:25......................6
11:36....................201
14:6....................118n
20:20....................136
22:14....................203
24:24-25.................202
25:23....................203
26:1-2...................189
27:14....................190
28:27....................114
29:24...............43f.,55
30:10.........6,123n,128,210
30:11....................136
30:17....................136
30:24-31.................205
31:15...................105n

Job

1:1....................169
1:5....................171
1:9-11.................171
2:9.............9,164n,171
3:1....................129
3:8...............115n,201
3:1-9...............106ff.
5:3....................202
7:6....................118n
7:12...................108n
9:13...................108n
9:25...................118n
15:24..................108n
24:13f.................108n
24:18..................131
26:12-13...............108n
31:29-30...............55f.

Ruth

4:4....................161

Canticles

2:7....................48
3:5....................48
5:8,9..................48

Lamentations

3:5....................69
3:65...................69

Ecclesiastes

3:14...................169n
5:6....................169n
7:18...................169n
7:21-22................130
8:12-13................169n
10:10..............119n,142
10:20..................142f.

Esther

8:13...................108n

Daniel

9:11...................32
9:29...................33n
11:30..................203

Nehemiah

5:9....................169
5:15...................169
7:2....................166n
10:29-30...............33f.
13:1-2............123n,175
13:25.....48,123n,124,146n

I Chronicles

12:1...................101n

II Chronicles

6:22...................15n
6:22-23................52ff.
10:4,9f................119n
18:15..................48
34:24..................32

www.ingramcontent.com/pod-product-compliance
Lightning Source LLC
Chambersburg PA
CBHW031311150426
43191CB00005B/181
* 9 7 8 1 5 8 9 8 3 2 3 3 6 *